M000022212

AMERICA *in the* BIBLE

STEVEN GRANT

Unless otherwise noted, Scriptures are taken from the King James Version of the Bible. Hebrew and Greek definitions are derived from the Strong's and Cruden's Concordances, unless otherwise noted. Dictionary references are extracted from the 1828 Webster's Dictionary by Noah Webster.

WestBow Press books may be ordered through booksellers or by contacting:

WestBow Press
A Division of Thomas Nelson
1663 Liberty Drive
Bloomington, IN 47403
www.westbowpress.com
1-(866) 928-1240

ISBN: 978-1-4497-5685-7 (hc)
ISBN: 978-1-4497-5684-0 (sc)
ISBN: 978-1-4497-5683-3 (e)

Library of Congress Control Number: 2012910893

Printed in the United States of America

WestBow Press rev. date: 07/09/2012

Table of Contents

List of Illustrations

Acknowledgements

To the great men and women who knew the Truth before
I was even born,

To Alli, Erin and Dean, who made the Truth understandable,

To Toy and Murrel, who urged me onward, devouring the Truth,

To my parents, David and Nona Grant, who taught me the
Truth and how to find it,

To my wife, Cheryl, and our daughters, Elisa and Sarah,
who walk with me, sharing the Truth,

To two churches that love the Truth, and those that have walked
with me in love,

To my dear friends and companions in the faith that also love the Truth,

To Stan and Robin, my brother and sister in the Truth,

To Jim and Sandy, Blaine and Christine, Tiffany and Luke, and Sharon,
who minister the Truth,

And most of all, to our Lord Jesus Christ, the Truth, and the revealer of
hidden riches,

I offer my most sincere thanks and blessing.

May this humble sacrifice be a revelation as you discover the Truth.

Soli Dei Gloria.

CHAPTER 1

Is America In The Bible?

I could hardly believe my ears. I was listening to a respected pastor, known nationwide for his patriotism and love for the United States. He was being interviewed on national television, and the host asked him specifically if the United States was mentioned in the Bible. His answer?

"The United States of America is not in the Bible."

The host pressed him again, almost amazed himself.

"Do you mean to tell me that the United States, this great nation in history, is not mentioned in the Bible?"

"That's right."

"What makes you say that," the host queried further?

"Because I said so," came the blunt response.

Perhaps it shouldn't be surprising that this leader in Christian ministry had no response for his television interviewer, but it is a problem. This pastor is respected, and commands respect, and yet he maintains that America is not found in the Bible. Did America just get lucky? The implications are staggering.

What do you believe? Where did America come from? How did she become so great? She feeds the world, possesses the bulk of all global wealth, sends missionaries worldwide to preach the gospel, has troops on more than 900 military bases to try and help in global conflicts and disasters. Is this a fluke?

Let's Think This Through

Let's consider for a moment the icon that has become the United States of America. For thousands of years the world existed in much the same way. Wooden, wind-powered ships carried our forefathers to the shores of this great land where they used primitive tools to build their rough-hewn houses. They planted their crops using single-furrow plows, and eked out a living drawn from the land.

However, in a matter of a few generations, things changed. Early American colonists chose to build a society on a covenant with Almighty God and Jesus Christ. Through this foundation, they created the United States of America. This nation dominated the earth within a matter of a few short centuries. Developments in technology, inventions and innovation have revolutionized life around the world. The United States is the only nation in the world that has put a man upon the moon, twelve of them in fact. She has a higher standard of living than the vast majority of the world and a more stable form of government than every other nation known to man. Books such as "The 5,000 Year Leap" have been written to try and discover the principles that made America great. She has been a leader in law, justice, innovation, morality . . . the list goes on and on. Has God been looking the other way?

Does God care about nations? Is America on His radar? As my brother Stan asks, did we hit the "lucky nation jackpot," and end up living the good life by coincidence? If we did, then God is not fair, nor just. But that's not His style. Surely He must know who we are.

She Is In The Shadows

There are a couple of beliefs out there today that place America in the "shadows" of the Bible. One of them simply lumps the United States together with the other heathen nations of the world. Many Christians believe that ultimately these nations will come under the rule of someone they call the "antiChrist," and the reign of terror against God's people will be bloody and painful. Most Christians really don't care where America is, because they hope to hit an "eject" button and be raptured off of this earth when Christ returns (hopefully before all the carnage begins). Therefore, most of them really don't care where America is and the role she plays under God. However, if there is no "rapture," there is very little hope of escaping this horrific period. I suspect they might care, then.

If America is not in the Bible, then God already hates her. She has no reason to be blessed, and is more than likely under God's wrath just like other heathen nations of the world. Every Christian should probably avoid involvement with an evil, heathen nation, and should not seek to do anything above winning individual people to Christ. Prolonging the life of such a nation would be against the will of God.

Is She The Great Whore?

Some Christians think the United States is in the Bible, but God refers to her by a different name. She is not called America; instead she is "Babylon." These Christians think the "whore of Babylon" found in the book of Revelation applies to the U.S.A. She is entirely evil, a harlot and seductress, and good for nothing. She is globalism and social progressivism on steroids and should be despised by all.

If God has changed the United States into "Babylon," then once again, God hates her. He despises her. In fact, He commands His people to flee from Babylon in the book of Revelation! Therefore, every Christian that believes in this scenario should actively consider how to leave the United States, because if they do not, they will face God's wrath themselves.

If the United States is this "great whore," singled out by God for judgment and destruction as her end, Christians should also not be involved in any type of government, or work that would prolong her life. This too, would be against God's will and would incur God's wrath.

Oops!

However, there are problems with these beliefs.

First, most Christians that say they believe these things don't live like they believe them. They have chosen a belief system of lazy convenience instead of truly digging into God's Word. Most of the folks that believe this are "rapturists," who believe God is going to eject them off the planet, and therefore, it really doesn't matter. But when it comes to government, politics, taxes, abortions and many other issues, they fight tooth and nail to try and do what is right in God's sight. You can't have it both ways. Either you believe this nation is damned, or you don't.

Second, God never changes the name of His people due to a behavior. This is a problem for the "Babylon" crowd. Consider for a moment my name. It is Steven Grant. I can be good and bring honor to my name (and my heritage), or I can be evil and dishonor my name. But it doesn't *change* my name. God does not single out a nation and call her Babylon, when she has been America before that. While it is true that many of the names of the nations have been changed or translated into a different language by mankind through time, God has not changed their names because of their nature. In fact, when Jesus Christ pronounced judgment upon the Jews (Matthew 23:38; Luke 13:35), He said, "Behold, your house is left unto you desolate." They were known as the House of Judah, or the Jews. He caused them to endure suffering and pain, as a Father would punish a rebellious child, but God did not change their name!

Third, some say that we are blessed as a nation because we have supported the Jews, but the United States was blessed long before the Jewish State of Israel became a nation in 1948! Many Old and New Testament Scriptures demonstrating God's sovereignty over nations would have to be ignored. Consider God's prophecy about Cyrus the king of Babylon in the Old Testament. (Isaiah 44:28; Isaiah 45:1-4) God spoke over this king's life and foreknew he would enable the House of Judah to return and build the temple under his reign. Others such as Assyrian leaders Benhadad and Naaman were anointed to be king even though they did not bless the Jews; rather they harmed them! If God only works in the prophetic realm with those that bless the Jews, this contradicts that completely.

Fourth, the United States of America has become a global superpower in such a short time that it is impossible this occurred without the intentional, divine hand of God. As the book "The 5,000 Year Leap" states, when the early pilgrims settled on the eastern shores of the United States, life was being lived much as it had during the previous 5,000 years. True, there were innovations and technological advances to a certain extent, but ships were still rowed or powered by wind and sail. Crops were still planted by a single-furrow plow, and high-speed transportation consisted of riding animals, or being drawn in a carriage pulled by them. Then, from the late 1700's to the present day, huge leaps in technology, invention, law, recognition of individual rights, and other advances occurred, led by the United States of America. If God did not have His hand in this globally-transforming propulsion forward, led by one nation on earth, the atheists are right. There is no god.

Could it be, that many in today's Christian circles (and even patriotic circles) don't know the truth? Where did America come from? Does the Bible have something to say?

Another Quote

Charles A.L. Totten is a great American patriot. He came from a venerated military family and was the Professor of Military Science and Tactics at Yale University in the 1800's. A godly Christian man, Totten had much to say about the Bible.

Professor Totten said, *"I can never be too thankful to Almighty God that in my youth He used the late Professor Wilson (a Yale Theology Professor) to show to me the difference between the two houses. The very understanding is the key by which almost the entire Bible becomes intelligible, and I cannot state too strongly that the man who has not yet seen that the Israel of the Scriptures is totally distinct from the Jewish people is yet in the very infancy, the mere alphabet of Biblical study and that to this day 7/8ths of the Bible is shut to his understanding."*

Now consider this. Dr. Totten is speaking about the United States of America. Reread the quote. Did you note the word "America" in his text? No. But it's there. Totten had been trained under Yale Theology Professor Benjamin Wilson, and had received his understanding from this excellent theologian. Yale President Ezra Stiles had personally recruited Wilson because of his beliefs about the United States of America and their correlation to the Bible. They are quite different than today's beliefs, aren't they! According to Professor Totten, 7/8ths of the Bible rests on the revelation waiting to be discovered. Our forefathers believed the United States was sovereignly chosen by God and they anchored their faith and progress as a nation to this truth.

So who is right? Were our forefathers correct, or is contemporary Christianity right? We can't have it both ways and we must discover the truth. It is one of the greatest truths worth discovering. But it takes some digging and some time. As you turn the pages of this book, you will learn new things about the Bible and history that will make your heart come alive! And you will discover that like Esther in the Bible, we were born to the kingdom for such a time as this.

And speaking of time, let's take a look at that very issue.

CHAPTER 2

America's Time In The Last Days

"What time is it?" If I were to ask you what time it is, you would undoubtedly look at a watch, telephone or clock to give me an answer. If we were scheduling an event, we might refer to a calendar. We might discuss seasons, holidays and special events in light of the time.

Ecclesiastes 3:1-8 [1]*To every thing there is a season, and a time to every purpose under the heaven:* [2]*A time to be born, and a time to die; a time to plant, and a time to pluck up that which is planted;* [3]*A time to kill, and a time to heal; a time to break down, and a time to build up;* [4]*A time to weep, and a time to laugh; a time to mourn, and a time to dance;* [5]*A time to cast away stones, and a time to gather stones together; a time to embrace, and a time to refrain from embracing;* [6]*A time to get, and a time to lose; a time to keep, and a time to cast away;* [7]*A time to rend, and a time to sew; a time to keep silence, and a time to speak;* [8]*A time to love, and a time to hate; a time of war, and a time of peace.*

Did you notice all of the significant times mentioned in this passage? Birth and death are fairly important! So is peace-time and war. If we behaved like we were celebrating when someone died, we would be in trouble! It would be equally unfitting to weep and grieve at the birth of a wonderful child. So, understanding the times helps us to know how to live, believe and apply various Scriptures appropriately. This is how we can understand various passages of Scripture that can seemingly be in conflict at times. We should be people of peace, but if we are in a time of war, we must search out and understand what God's word says about that season.

But I Thought . . .

You might say, *"but I thought this book was about America in the Bible."* You are right. It is. However, the United States of America began as a group of settlements and colonies in the early 1600's, which is only 400 years ago. She has existed as a nation at the time of this writing for less than 250 years. So America's place in Scripture will have ancient roots, but her time to be revealed on the world stage will be in the last days.

The United States of America is populated by people from all over the world. The majority of her inhabitants and ideology came from a time much farther back than just the last few decades. In one sense, America is one of the strangest nations on earth. China is populated by Chinese, Scotland by the Scots. But the United States of America is a melting pot, with people that came from somewhere. But where?

Every person on earth is an original descendent of the sons of Noah; Shem, Ham and Japheth. We are either Shemites, Hamites, or Japhethites, or a variation of these sons today. This dates back to the flood, which goes *way* back in time! If we are going to study the roots of America in the Bible, then we must connect the dots from way-back-then, to right-here-now. And in order to do that, we must deal with time as it is addressed in the Bible.

So, Back To Time

Everybody uses the art of forecasting on a regular basis in life. We all look at weather forecasts in order to know how to dress for various seasons and weather patterns. We look at our spending so we can pay our bills. We also pay for regular oil changes in vehicles, school fees for students, and shop for various holidays and birthdays. Life has cycles and we use information we gather from past years and credible sources to work through current events.

Why shouldn't we do that with the Word of God as well? Christianity is far larger than a study of our personal salvation. Our eternal life begins with receiving Jesus Christ into our heart and having Him work His new life within us. Christ is the doorway to eternal life. But there is a whole house to be explored inside that door!

Proverbs 25:2 says *"It is the glory of God to conceal a thing; but the honour of kings is to search out a matter."* Apparently God hides things from us if we merely skim the surface. He loves it when we dig into His

Word. A group of men in the city of Berea took God seriously in the New Testament, and God commended them. Acts 17:11 states, *"These were more noble than those in Thessalonica, in that they received the word with all readiness of mind, and searched the scriptures daily, whether those things were so."*

So Do You Have The Time?

With that in mind, I need to warn you. The first part of this chapter may seem boring, fragmented and completely unrelated to this book . . . unless you are willing to be patient. We are unwrapping a mystery together, one that has been unfolding for thousands of years. You are an archaeologist on an historic dig. A fragment of bone or shard of pottery may speak volumes, or it can be casually discarded due to the untrained eye. We will begin with a study of ordinary numbers in the Bible and the meanings behind them. We will also ask the question, "when will Christ return?" As we jump in together, stick with me. You will be rewarded in your search.

What We Will *Not* Do

Let's be clear. I have NO intention of predicting the return of Jesus Christ to this earth. Matthew 25:13 says, *"Watch therefore, for ye know neither the day nor the hour wherein the Son of man cometh."* However, we can be discerning of the season we are in, and the Bible actually commands we study those and learn them well.

You may say, "Well, if I live right and serve God I will be prepared for anything I may face." Really? Can we ignore the Scriptures and understanding, just relying on God alone to speak with us? Consider these passages:

- 1 Thessalonians 5:1-3—*But of the times and the seasons, bretheren, ye have no need that I write unto you. For yourselves know perfectly that the day of the Lord so cometh as a thief in the night. For when they shall say, Peace and safety; then sudden destruction cometh upon them, as travail upon a woman with child; and they shall not escape.*

- Luke 21:36—*Watch ye therefore, and pray always, that ye may be accounted worthy to escape all these things that shall come to pass, and to stand before the Son of man.*
- Ephesians 5:15-17—*See then that ye walk circumspectly, not as fools, but as wise, redeeming the time, because the days are evil. Wherefore be ye not unwise, but understanding what the will of the Lord is . . .*
- Matthew 16:3b— . . . *ye can discern the face of the sky; but can ye not discern the signs of the times?*

Apparently you and I *must* discern the signs of the times, as commanded by Jesus Christ Himself.

- Timing is critical to successful buying and selling. Buy low, sell high.
- Timing is critical for protection. Noah discerned, while the majority of the world around him did not.
- Timing is critical to our Christian walk and behavior. As God's children, His Spirit lives within us. He has given us His Word, the Bible. It has been authenticated more than any other book on earth. With the Word of God and the Holy Spirit to guide us we can discern the times.

Can We Really Know?

According to Christ and His Apostles you and I can know the times we live in. This is exciting! Every generation has a purpose to fulfill. The nations have plans and times before Almighty God, and we can live in the light instead of in darkness.

- 1 Thessalonians 5:4-10 [4]*But ye, brethren, are not in darkness, that that day should overtake you as a thief.* [5]*Ye are all the children of light, and the children of the day: we are not of the night, nor of darkness.* [6]*Therefore let us not sleep, as do others; but let us watch and be sober.* [7]*For they that sleep sleep in the night; and they that be drunken are drunken in the night.* [8]*But let us, who are of the day, be sober, putting on the breastplate of faith and love; and for an helmet, the hope of salvation.* [9]*For God hath not appointed us to wrath, but to obtain salvation by our Lord Jesus Christ, [10]Who died for us, that, whether we wake or sleep, we should live together with him.*

Did you catch some of those points the Apostle Paul made? We can be so aware of the times, we will be prepared and alert. We are children of light; not darkness. Most of the world will not recognize the things we will be given as we study these truths. But we can have God's best as we understand God's timings and His purposes for nations, including the United States of America. Based on timing and what God intends to do with America, we can know how to live our lives! Let the excitement begin!

Seven Signs

There are seven signs that have frequently been used to understand what God is doing. They are:

1. Signs in nature (seasons, natural disasters, sun, moon, stars, etc.);
2. Signs in society (as it was in the days of Noah);
3. Signs in technology (in the last days men will run to and fro and knowledge shall be increased);
4. Signs in the global church (the 7 churches in Revelation, persecution, revivals or the lack thereof);
5. Signs in the Tribes of Israel (more on that, later);
6. Signs in world events (new age, one-world government, global trade);
7. Signs in prophecy (types in fulfilled prophecy, watching for unfulfilled events to come to pass).

However, there are also milestones in God's prophetic calendar that we will study today. *"Prophetic calendar,"* you say? Yes. God has created one and it is found in Scripture. Let's start in Second Peter.

- 2 Peter 3:3-8—*Knowing this first, that there shall come in the last days scoffers, walking after their own lusts, and saying, Where is the promise of his coming? for since the fathers fell asleep, all things continue as they were from the beginning of creation. For this they willingly are ignorant of, that by the word of God the heavens were of old, and the earth standing out of the water and in the water: whereby the world that then was, being overflowed with water, perished: but the heavens and the earth, which are now, by the same word are kept in store, reserved unto fire against the day of judgment and perdition of ungodly men. But, beloved, be not ignorant of this one thing, that one day is with the Lord as a thousand years, and a thousand years as one day.*

Notice a few things in this passage.

- **First**, scoffers will attempt to make every day and every season alike, so that no attention is given to the last days and return of Christ. They don't want people to realize the end times as forecasted in Scripture.
- **Second**, they will forget the importance of the creation story and timeline. In fact, they will use their own arrogance and perhaps pseudo-science to attack God's story of creation. They may try to replace it with something far inferior, and yet more widely recognized.
- **Third**, they will also cease to regard critical events (such as the flood) as critical to teaching, thinking and preparedness. They will insist that all things just move along at a steady pace and that no catyclismic events (e.g., the flood) occurred or will occur in the future.
- **Fourth**, *one thing* must be remembered. One day is with the Lord as a thousand years, and a thousand years as one day.

Was this fourth point merely poetic thinking? If we believe that Scripture is truly God-breathed and inspired by the Holy Spirit, perhaps we should take a closer look at that. Let's correlate it to another Scripture.

- Psalms 90:4—*For a thousand years in thy sight are but as yesterday when it is past, and as a watch in the night.*

Here again, God correlates 1,000 years with one day. Interesting! But how does this connect with the flood and creation back in 2 Peter? Could it be that God was giving us clues? Clues to a hidden timeframe? Now consider this. According to Genesis 1:1-31 and Genesis 2:1-2, God spent 6 days creating the worlds and on the seventh day, God rested. Notice the pattern; six days to create and the seventh to rest.

The Numbers Six And Seven.

These patterns related to the numbers six and seven are also noted in the book of the Revelation. For example, in Revelation 13:18, the number six is linked to mankind and the last days "mark of the beast." Six is connected with commerce and work, and buying and selling.

The number seven is also seen in the book of the Revelation. There are seven churches, seven seals, seven trumpets and seven bowls or vials. In Revelation 11:15 the seventh trumpet is sounded and great voices in heaven say *"The kingdoms of this world are become the kingdoms of our Lord, and of his Christ; and he shall reign for ever and ever."*

In Revelation 16:17 the seventh bowl is poured out and a great voice comes out of the temple of heaven, from the throne, saying, *"It is done."* Based on these two Scriptures, the number seven represents divine completion, when the labor of man is finished and the rest of God begins.

So now based on 2 Peter we can connect the numbers 1,000, six and seven together in some type of a reference point. We can add them, subtract them, multiply them, or divide. How do they intersect? In order for this study to be more than speculation, there must be something else in the Bible that will connect the dots, so to speak.

After creation we know that mankind fell. Since that time we have entered into the age of redemption. God has spent this entire age redeeming humanity. How long will this age of redemption last? To answer this, let's look two more numbers in Scripture that were introduced by Rev. W. H. Offiler in his book, "God And His Bible." They are the numbers 120 and 50.

120—Signifies the end of all flesh.

- Genesis 6:3—Man's days are going to be limited to 120 years.

- Deuteronomy 34:7—Moses' fleshly life ceased at age 120. God buried him and resurrected him to be used during the Great Tribulation (Deuteronomy 34:5-6, Luke 9:30, Jude 1:9).
- II Chronicles 5:11-14—120 priests sounded 120 trumpets in one accord at the dedication of Solomon's temple. The glory of God filled the temple and no man could even stand to minister. It was a ceasing of flesh in ministry.
- Acts 1:15; Acts 2:1-13—120 were filled with the Holy Spirit. Fleshly ministry and an earthly priesthood gives way to ministry in the Holy Ghost, as He fills the lives of believers everywhere.

50—Signifies Jubilee; celebration, debts cancelled, freedom from oppression.

- Leviticus 25:10-17—Jubilees were proclaimed every 50th year.
- Isaiah 61:1-3—Jesus came in a Jubilee year to set the captives free!

It's interesting that these two numbers were introduced to God's children during the time after the flood, when God began to redeem mankind. For example, after Moses nobody lived to be more than 120 years old just as God had stated back in Genesis 6:3. And the jubilees were so significant that God judged the Israelites for not keeping them as a 50 year rest-year in their land. They were forced to spend time in captivity based on the years they had not kept. Jeremiah prophesied this fact, and its fulfillment is found in 2 Chronicles 36:21.

As we "play" with these numbers, what shall we do with them? We know they are significant to God, but what should they mean to us? Shall we add them? Divide them against each other perhaps? What about subtraction? All have been considered. But when these two numbers, 120 and 50 are multiplied together, something wonderful happens!

When 120 is multiplied by 50 . . . .

- 120 x 50 = 6,000

Exciting, isn't it! No?! Did you catch the correlation? You see, we are doing something more than merely multiplying numbers. Remember, we are looking at how numbers in the Bible intersect with each other and what these interactions mean. So when 120 and 50 multiplied together equal 6,000, is there a correlation? Yes!

Let's look back now at the earlier numbers. They were six, seven, and 1,000. An obvious correlation would be to multiply six by 1,000. Does it match?

- 6 x 1,000 = 6,000
- 120 x 50 = 6,000

Is this a mistake? No! Now, let's look at what this could mean in Scriptures.

- 6 x 1,000 = *six one-thousand year days* in God's calendar of redemption! Remember, in 2 Peter it spoke of the day of the Lord being 1,000 years.
  - o From Adam to Noah—Approx. 2,000 years (2 days).
  - o From Noah/Abraham to Jesus—Approx. 2,000 years (2 days).
  - o From Jesus to the present time—Approx. 2,000 years (2 days).

How many days did God spend creating the heavens and the earth? Six. Was this pattern alluded to in 2 Peter? Yes! Wasn't this pattern commanded by God to be the one thing that we remember in the study of that passage? Absolutely! Could this be the reason? Is there still another validating piece of evidence?

The Seventh Day

So far we have made a couple of exciting discoveries. We found out that God had revealed a divine secret in 2 Peter about a timeline in the earth today. He further showed us that this redemptive timeline is double-verified by multiplying 6 x 1,000, and 120 x 50 to reach the same answer: 6,000. But what about the number seven?

According to Genesis 1 and 2, the Lord rested on the seventh day, enjoying the fruit of His labors and fellowshipping with Adam and Eve. Revelation tells us that the number seven signifies the end. Things are wrapped up whenever we see that divine number. But there is still another Scripture in Revelation to consider.

- Revelation 20:4 [4]*And I saw thrones, and they sat upon them, and judgment was given unto them: and I saw the souls of them that were beheaded for the witness of Jesus, and for the word of God, and which had not worshipped the beast, neither his image, neither had received his mark upon their foreheads, or in their hands; and they lived and reigned with Christ a thousand years.*

Revelation 20:1-6 dwells specifically on a certain time period that is a very specific length. It is 1,000 years, and is known by many as the term, "The Millennium" for that reason. How does this intersect with the other numbers?

- 7 x 1,000 = 7,000

Do you see it? The addition of a Millennium, a 1,000 year time period at the close of 6,000 years of redemption creates a perfect "week" of God's redemption. He will spend 6,000 years redeeming those in mankind that want to serve Him, and will enjoy a magnificent 1,000 year reign at rest and peace with those that love Him. This is God's redemptive week.

God's Redemptive Week

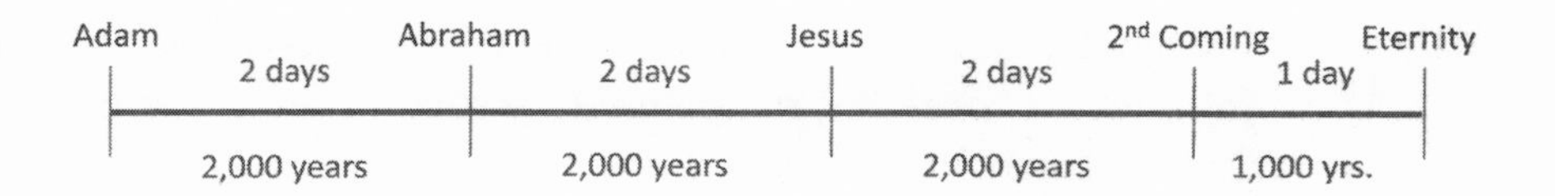

There may be those that are skeptical and consider this to be mere play with numbers to manipulate the mind. God expected this! He gave us even more intersecting material so that we could have a perfect understanding of His times and seasons! Shall we look a little deeper?

God's Three Eternal Witnesses

There is a very interesting passage in the Epistle of 1 John.

- 1 John 5:7-8—*For there are three that bear record in heaven, the Father, the Word, and the Holy Ghost; and these three are one. And there are three that bear witness in earth, the Spirit, and the water, and the blood; and these three agree in one.*

This is fascinating! First, we note that God has given us three record-keepers or eternal witnesses that are in heaven. They are, the Father, the Word (Jesus Christ is the Word incarnate according to John 1:14), and the Holy Ghost. They are all present throughout history, but each one plays a unique role during various epochs of time. As you look at the following Scriptures, note how they interact with each other, with one rising to the forefront in various eras.

The Father

The Father is featured predominantly in the first 2,000 year period.

- Genesis 3:14-24—God judged the fall of mankind due to Adam and Eve's sin, and paved the way for Jesus to come.
- Genesis 4:9-16—God judged Cain for murdering Abel, his brother.
- Genesis 6:17—God saw mankind's wickedness and poured out the Flood of water upon the earth, judging all of humanity.
- Genesis 8:22—The Lord accepted Noah's animal sacrifice, thus paving the way for the next dispensation, that of Jesus and the shedding of sacrificial blood.

The Word (Jesus)

While Jesus Christ was not on the earth as a man until the close of the next 2,000 year period, the imprints of His sacrificial work are everywhere!

- Genesis 22:1-14—Isaac was offered up by Abraham, at God's command, as a type of Jesus. Christ later offered Himself, submitting to the Father, as a sacrifice for the sins of mankind.
- Exodus 12:2-6—The sacrificing of the passover lamb is instituted . . . . another type of Jesus. Note that during this celebration, the sacrificial lamb was taken from the herd early on the 10th day of the month and was killed the evening of the 14th day of the month. So the lamb was set aside in a holding pen, for 4 days. From Adam to Christ's sacrifice was approximately 4,000 years, or four one-thousand year days.
    - o Revelation 13:8 specifies that Christ the sacrificial lamb was slain from the foundation of the world! This would be a time period of 4,000 years from the fall of mankind to Calvary.

- Isaiah 53—This chapter clearly depicts Christ as a sacrificial lamb, dying for our sin, in this prophesy about the Messiah.
    - o NOTE: Other types of Jesus Christ include: Chief Shepherd (1 Peter 5:4), the rock that followed them (1 Corinthians 10:1-4), the King of glory (Psalm 24:7-10; 1 Corinthians 2:8; James 2:1).

- Matthew 1:21-23—Jesus was given His Name because it means "Savior." He was and is the Savior of the world.
- John 1:14—*And the Word was made flesh and dwelt among us (and we beheld his glory, the glory as of the only begotten of the Father,) full of grace and truth.*
    - o Jesus is the living Word of God; the entire Bible personified. This is why He is recognized as "the Word" in 1 John 5:7.

- John 1:29—John the baptist identifies Jesus Christ: "Behold the lamb of God . . ."
- Mark 15:25-26—They crucified Him. Jesus Christ died for our sins.
- Matthew 3:11—John the baptist identified Jesus as the baptizer with the Holy Ghost. Just as the Father accepted Noah's animal sacrifice, paving the way for the next 2,000 year dispensation, so Christ promised the Holy Spirit, to usher in His work during the next epoch of time.

The Holy Ghost

The third heavenly witness found in 1 John 5:7 is the Holy Ghost. Just as the Father and the Word transcend time, so the Holy Ghost is preexisting and eternal. However, His primary work began when Christ the lamb of God's work on earth was finished.

- Genesis 1:2—The Spirit of God (the Holy Ghost) was moving upon the waters during the creation of the earth.
- Exodus 30:22-33—The anointing oil, used on the priest, prophet and king denoted the Holy Spirit coming upon those that occupied these specific offices. However, the Holy Ghost did not fill every man during this time.
- Joel 2:28—The outpouring of the Holy Spirit was foretold to those in that era, so that they might know that God would finish His work completely.
- John 16:7—Jesus declared to His disciples that it was expedient or necessary that He depart. He said that the Comforter, or the Holy Ghost would not come until He departed. But He would send the Comforter to us.
- John 14:16-17; 26—Jesus Christ said that He would send a Comforter that would abide with us forever. This Spirit is truth, whom the world cannot receive. Jesus specified that this Comforter is called the Holy Ghost (verse 26).
- Acts 2:17-18—In the last days the Holy Spirit is poured out. This had never occurred during the previous 4,000 years of time. Since this outpouring happened during the last dispensation of 2,000 years, it is rightfully called the "last days."

- Acts 1:5; Acts 2:1-4—The final dispensation of the Holy Ghost begins and continues through our present day.

How amazing! These three witnesses, the Father, the Word (Jesus Christ), and the Holy Ghost are actively involved in redeeming mankind throughout this period God has established for redemption. Each one reveals Himself especially during a specific era, but they all are one. Their goal is redemption and the establishment of a Covenant Kingdom on earth.

Then 1 John goes further! He also states that there are three witnesses, or signs, that God has used on earth to point the way to redemption.

The Three Earthly Witnesses

The three earthly witnesses are recorded in 1 John 5:8. They are, the water, the blood and the Spirit. Now we all know that just as God in His Triune form has been around forever, these three earthly witness would be present on the earth during the entire age. However, as the Father, the Word and the Spirit each had an epoch of time where they were particularly noted, the same should hold true for these witnesses as well.

The Water

- Genesis 1:2—The first record of the earth notes that the Spirit of God moved upon the face of the waters. This water-oriented world was significant to God during this era.
- Genesis 2:4-6—Mist watered the entire earth until the flood came. Water was the greatest element noted consistently during the first 2,000 years.
- Genesis 6:17—Water (e.g., the flood) is used as the first universal tool of Judgement of mankind.
- Luke 17:27—Jesus acknowledged the use of the flood to judge and purify the earth via the flood.
- I Corinthians 10:1-2—The Israelites are baptized in the Red Sea. Although this occurred outside the first 2,000 years, it

still denotes the importance of water as a testimony or witness upon the face of the earth.

In the Old Covenant time God often moved through miracles related to water. If you wish, study out the following: Water from the Rock or Meribah (Exodus 17:7 and Numbers 20:13), Waters of Marah (Exodus 15:23), Waters of Separation (Numbers 19:21), Waters of Jordan (Joshua 3; 2 Kings 2:6; 2 Kings 5:10; Matthew 3:13), etc. All of these waters during Israel's travels signified the use of water to purge, to try and to cleanse the Israelites.

The Blood

Water was a dominant feature during the first 2,000 year time period, but the blood was not. In fact, Abel's animal sacrifice (Genesis 4:4) is the only animal sacrifice recorded during the first 2,000 years of mankind. All other sacrifices occurred after the flood had cleansed the earth. Although water was mentioned during the next 2,000 years, it was the blood that dominated the era.

- Genesis 8:20-22—Noah offered an animal, or blood sacrifice to God after leaving the ark. God accepted this sacrifice, but there was no other sacrifice recorded until Abraham entered into covenant with Almighty God.
- Genesis 15—In this passage God established his covenant with Abram. At God's instruction, Abram killed animals and God accepted his sacrifice as the beginnings of His covenant with Abram's seed.
- Exodus 12:2-6—The passover is instituted with all of the tribes of Israel. The male, firstborn Lamb was kept for four days in a holding pen before being slain. Again, this represented 4-1,000 year periods, and was fulfilled when Christ was crucified as the Lamb of God, 4,000 years after the fall of Adam and Eve.
- Numbers 15—This chapter focused completely on the rigors and exacting standards involved in animal sacrifice. These sacrifices were performed regularly by the people, the priests and the Levites, until the time of Christ.

- Mark 15:25-26—Jesus is crucified. The ultimate sacrifice and testimony is once again saved for the end of this 2,000 year dispensation.

The Spirit

The Holy Spirit was specifically mentioned as both a heavenly witness and an earthly witness in 1 John. The Holy Spirit is the manifested presence of God in the lives of men, and therefore serves as a bridge between God and mankind.

- Luke 4:18-19—Jesus Christ proclaimed the Spirit of the Lord was upon Him. And The Holy Spirit is now within the world drawing us to Christ, and living in the lives of believers until Christ returns.
- John 4:24—Christ said the time was coming when true believers must worship the Father in spirit and in truth. Worship was not an act of penance or good deeds, but a change in the spirit. God's Spirit came to change our lives.
- Romans 8:26—The Spirit helps our infirmities.
- James 5:7—James indicated the latter (or ending rain) of the Spirit would be mighty!

What are the odds of these earthly witnesses and the three Eternal witnesses interacting and functioning with the same type of clarity during a specific 6,000 year period? It would be astronomical! God Himself would have to orchestrate this type of divine order. Therefore, these three earthly witnesses, the water, the blood and the Spirit have been signposts to mankind on the earth. Through history and in our contemporary times, God uses these markers so that man is without excuse. They all point the way to God. There is yet another passage that we can study, with three more signs from God Himself. Speaking of "astronomical" evidence . . .

Three Heavenly Witnesses

- Genesis 1:14—*And God said, Let there be lights in the firmament of the heaven to divide the day from the night; and let them be for signs, and for seasons, and for days, and years.*

Christians agree that God Himself created the heavenly bodies, the sun, moon and stars. We use them for calendars the world over. God told us to use them for days and years. We also use them (as He foretold) for predicting seasons. The first use God ordained for the heavenly bodies were for signs! Now this is not astrology, nor studying the zodiac. We do not worship the heavenly bodies, but we should observe what they signify and how God has used them for His glory.

The Sun

The primary body of glory in the heaven is the sun. As we mentioned before, these bodies were created for signs, seasons, days and years. There are other Scriptures that tell us these things as well.

- Psalm 19:1-4—The heavens declare the glory of God.
- I Timothy 6:15-16—Paul the apostle writes that Jesus now dwells in the light which no man can see . . . . it is God Himself! This is represented by the sun.
- Psalm 84:11—The Lord God is a Sun and Shield.
- Matthew 24:29—The sun will be darkened in the last days.
- Luke 23:44—The sun was darkened for 3 hours during Christ's crucifixion.

The sun is the brightest body seen by man. It has a great impact on our climate and lifestyles. Solar flares can alter life on earth with one burst of energy. The sun is a vivid parallel to many facets of God the Father. Just as no man can look on the face of God and live, no one can gaze upon the face of the sun and retain their eyesight. It is far too glorious to behold in our flesh. Many idolatrous cultures have worshipped the creation more than the creator. Because of this we note that many have worshipped the sun, moon or stars as substitutes. While the sun is a sign of God, we worship God Himself and merely recognize this sign that points toward Him in its proper context.

The Moon

Just as Christ reflects the glory of the Father, so the moon reflects the light of the sun in the darkest of times. Jesus Christ, the Word, shines in darkness and darkness does not comprehend it (John 1:5).

- John 6:38—Jesus said that he came to do the will of the Father. The moon reflects the glory of the sun.
- Isaiah 52:14—Jesus' visage was marred. The moon has been a target, a point of attack for both mankind and lunar objects. It has also been a shield to the earth, protecting us from asteroids and other debris hurtling through space. It is a "scarred body," that literally protects mankind by taking the punishment in itself.
- Revelation 6:12—The moon turns to blood . . . . parallel to Jesus shedding His blood on Calvary.

The moon has been battered and bruised to protect the earth from the punishment of asteroids and other lunar objects. So too, Jesus Christ took our punishment and our sin. In the last days the moon will be turned to the appearance of blood, a final witness and sign to the eternal, cleansing blood of Jesus.

The Stars

The stars are a heavenly witness to the leading of the Holy Spirit. They are there day and night whether we recognize them or not. They lead those that are hungry for truth, they shine in darkness, and they crown God's people.

- Matthew 2:1-2—The wise men were led to Jesus by a star. No man can come to God except the spirit draws him.
- Genesis 15:5-6—Stars are linked with Abraham's seed. They cannot be numbered for multitude. The Holy Spirit is omnipresent, ever present. Everywhere.
- Revelation 1:16—Jesus holds seven stars of the seven churches in His Hand. It is the Holy Spirit's anointing upon each church.

- Revelation 12:1—A woman is clothed with the sun, standing on the moon, crowned with 12 stars. This is the bride of Christ. She is clothed with the glory of God, standing upon the Rock Jesus Christ, and anointed to reign with the power of the Holy Spirit!

Just as God the Father is represented by the sun, Jesus Christ is represented by the moon, and the Holy Spirit is also represented in the heavens by stars.

Do Not Worship Symbols!

The Word of God is very clear. We are to only worship God. Therefore, these symbols, as glorious as they may be, are merely shadows of the truth, designed to reveal Almighty God to us. Deuteronomy 17:2-5 says we must not worship the sun, moon and stars, and Deuteronomy 4:15-19 commands us to refrain from making images of these and other items. This must be kept in proper context in order to be pleasing to God.

The Combined View

When all of the witnesses are displayed together, the entire earth is without excuse. During the *first 2,000* years the glory of God was reflected in the sun. This created celestial worship around the world of the sun-god. Water was the predominating element and God the Father was prominent.

During the *next 2,000* year period moon worship emerged. Blood and animal sacrifice was also prevalent. Both of these elements were meant to foretell the ultimate sacrifice, Jesus Christ, who would take away the sin of the world. This was also the era when the Bible, the written Word of God emerged and the Old Testament writings were canonized.

The *latest 2,000* year period from the time of Christ up until present days has been the time of the Holy Spirit. As stated in Acts 2:17, these are the last days. There is a hunger today for the supernatural power of God. The stars are also erroneously worshipped by some today, with astrological symbols and predictions published in every major newspaper in the world.

A combined chart of all of these witnesses could perhaps look as follows:

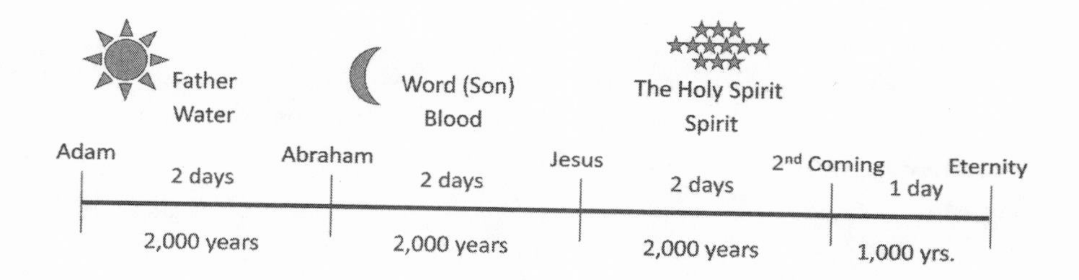

So Far

We have now taken a handful of numbers (6, 7, 1,000, 50, and 120) and their associated Scriptures. We have laid them against other Scriptures that show us nine witnesses that will be active during a specific time period (three Eternal Witnesses, three earthly witnesses, and three heavenly witnesses). The odds of all of this material coming together to form a perfect, understandable view of God's calendar of events are essentially impossible and thus amazing. But if we are going to be looking at times and seasons and the implications of God's prophecies over nations within that context, we must examine every angle.

What About Calendar Discrepancies?

Valid questions have been asked about calendar discrepancies and potential errors in calculating timeframes. This author freely acknowledges these issues. However, God provides the answer. His calendar is perfect, but mankind's calendars are not. There are Scriptures and other data that confirm this.

First, there is at least a four-to-eight year discrepancy in the calculations of Christ's birth. This is widely known and accepted.

Furthermore, the Jewish calendar in use throughout Old Testament times was a 360 day calendar. Today, we use a 365 day calendar in Western culture, with an additional day thrown in on leap years! God has been well aware of this fact!

- Daniel 7:25 *"And he shall speak great words against the most High, and shall wear out the saints of the most High, and think to change times and laws: and they shall be given into his hand until a time and times and the dividing of time."*

This passage says that in the last days laws would be changed to deviate from God's holy ways. However, it also says that mankind would change times, or calendars! God Himself forecast this variation in time.

Not only will mankind change calendars, but God changes the times. Daniel 2:21 says that *"he (God) changeth the times and the seasons: he removeth kings, and setteth up kings: he giveth wisdom unto the wise, and knowledge to them that know understanding."*

Furthermore, in Acts 1:6-7, when the disciples gathered to Christ, they had questions about the times. Christ's response to them is worthy of note. *"When they therefore were come together, they asked of him, saying, Lord, wilt thou at this time restore again the kingdom to Israel? And he said unto them, it is not for you to know the times or the seasons, which the Father hath put in his own power."*

The disciples were not reprimanded over their questions about the Kingdom of Israel. Instead, Jesus reminded them personally that God Himself had various times and seasons under His power; His jurisdiction.

Why would God do this? There may be several reasons. God is sovereign and has the right to reserve this under His own knowledge and power. Secondly, He knows that man would pride Himself too greatly on knowing every little detail. This would put man in the place of God (and it is a place that many men have found themselves to be in). Good men and women have wrongly predicted the second coming of Christ and have fallen in their pride. They failed to recognize the fact that the day and hour is reserved for God Himself.

Another reason God may have obscured the specific day and hour is because He wants followers that are devoted to Him regardless of the time. How many would be saved the day before His coming if they knew He was to return? (I suspect there would be many of us.) He wants followers that love Him regardless of the season, and has purposely obscured the day and hour of His return. *These are the times and the seasons which the Father has put in His own power.*

Let us contrast this with the words of the Apostle Paul, in 1 Thessalonians 5:1-3. *"But of the times and the seasons, brethren, ye have no need that I write unto you. For yourselves know perfectly that the day of the Lord so cometh as a thief in the night. For when they shall say, Peace and safety; then sudden destruction cometh upon them, as travail upon a woman with child; and they shall not escape."*

Does 1 Thessalonians 5 contradict Acts 1? Absolutely not. The date and time of Christ's return is reserved unto the Father alone. It is a very narrow band, an event with a specific date on God's calendar. However, God does want His children to understand the times. This is why it is critical to understand the times, as we mentioned earlier. As we are students of the Bible, God reveals Himself to us. We can know God's timings and His ways over the nations. This includes America. There is still more He has for us to understand before we begin to take a hard look at how God has formed America and placed her in this specific time in history.

The Greatest Revelation Is At The End!

We have made the case that God has patterns in His redemptive week. Let's look at another significant sign. During the ***first 2,000*** years, the witness of water was prevalent. Dew watered the earth on a daily basis and many think the earth was largely tropical and stable in it's weather patterns. However, at the close of this era the fountains of the deep were broken up and the windows of heaven also poured water upon the earth. The earth went from dew, to deluge, in one cataclysmic event.

During this time, the future leadership of the next epoch were also being prepared for the new "move of God." Noah, his wife, their sons and their wives were selected by God and blessed for their obedience. Because of their preparation for what God had said, they were protected and blessed. They weathered the turbulence of the time and replenished the earth after the flood.

During the ***second 2,000*** years, the earthly witness involved the shedding of blood. Millions of animals were sacrificed to atone for sin. Thousands of these sacrifices are mentioned in the Old Testament and it marked man's need for an eternal solution. At the close of this timeframe Jesus Christ, the Lamb of God, gave His life and shed His blood as the ultimate sacrifice for sin. Nothing else could come close to Jesus' blood as the pure and spotless Lamb. Again, it was an event unmatched in human history.

Once again, the future leadership for the next era was prepared during the closing days of the waning dispensation. The disciples and followers of Jesus Christ grew up in the old "society," but were personally taught by Jesus Christ about things to come. They were tested by the events of the crucifixion and resurrection, to emerge as the leaders of the next era in history.

If This Pattern Holds True . . .

The ***last 2,000*** year period prior to the millennial reign of Christ may well be drawing to a close. This is the era of the Holy Spirit. On the day of Pentecost, the Holy Spirit was poured out and freely offered to every believer in Christ Jesus as Savior and King. God's Holy Spirit was sent into the world to gather the heathen and gentiles to be grafted into God's Israel, as wild branches united with the Abrahamic covenant. The Holy Spirit has been in operation since the birth of the early church. However, if this pattern holds true, the greatest, most exciting days are just ahead of us!

Although God had created Adam and Eve and their seed, by the time the flood came, the majority were complacent and self-centered. God destroyed them, sparing Noah, the one that heard His voice. During Christ's time on earth God's covenant people had once again become complacent and self-centered, despite the fact that they were under God's Abrahamic covenant. God raised up a fresh group, and many of the others went on to their own destruction.

Today God is also looking for disciples with fresh eyes, open hearts, and ears that will hear what the Spirit is saying. Do not believe for one moment that just because you attend a church, are a good person in your community, and know a few fundamentals of the Christian faith, you are automatically going to catch on to the "new thing" that God does at the end of this age. God's operations always seem to be radical to the mainstream. Noah was strange and the disciples were hated. It will take a commitment on your part (and mine) to embrace the fresh revelation of the Holy Spirit at the end of this age.

This study is a part of that truth. It may not correlate to a few of the things you have learned in the past. Stick with it. You will soon see truths in the Word of God you have never seen before. And it will be well worth your while. Your eyes will be opened to new wonders in Christ. You will begin to live your Christian life in a much different way.

But remember. Just as Noah and his family, and the disciples of Jesus Christ, you may be mocked and in the minority. God will train you and prepare you to reign with Him. In these last days there will be times of tribulation, and yet there will also be divine protection for those that listen to the Spirit of God. The greatest witness is at the close of each era, and today is no exception. We are in the last days. The signs are everywhere. Are you ready?

God's Redemptive Week

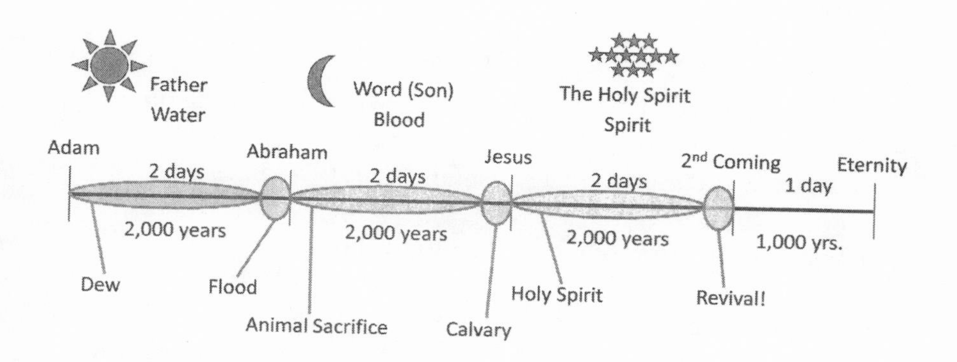

God's Prophetic "List"

There are many things on God's prophetic "list" that will still occur during this last timeframe. Luke 23:8-11; 25-26 lists several events, and they include

- Wars,
- Rumors of wars,
- Nation rising against nation and kingdom against kingdom,
- Perplexity in people's lives,
- Famine and pestilence,
- Persecution,
- Earthquakes,
- The sea and waves roaring (tsunamis, floods, hurricanes, etc.), and
- Signs in the sun, moon and stars.

God's Redemptive Week

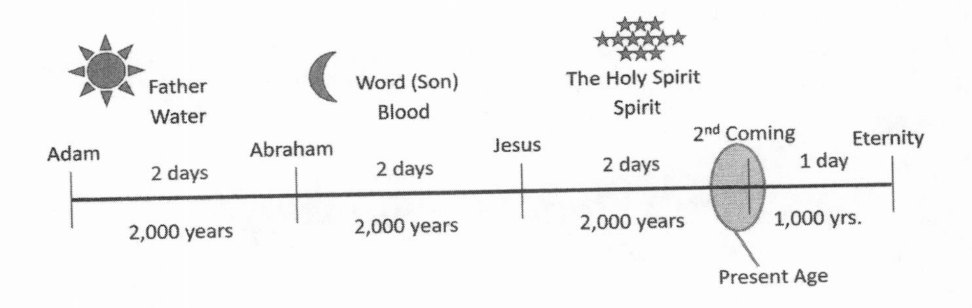

All of this will happen, coinciding with the revelation of the son of perdition, and a global war among ideologies that pit Islam, Communism and globalism against Christianity and capitalism.

The Danger Of Missing God's Prophetic Timing

We have already written about various sects that have tried to predict the second coming of Christ. If they would have studied the chapter you are reading now, they could have avoided the error of their predictions. You see, they often chose to focus on only one event or individual, instead of looking carefully at all of the seven signs we discussed earlier. These signs must flow together for us to properly discern the times and seasons.

These inaccurate "predictions" haven't just hurt the ungodly. They have also alienated the church from God's prophetic Word (which is more than a third of His Scriptures). Today many churches have degenerated to the lowest common denominator. Many churches say very little about prophecy, current events, and how they correlate to our lives and nations. These churches choose to focus on the gospel of the individual. They talk about personal salvation and forgiveness, and how to live a Christian life.

Other churches may elevate their teaching into marriage and ethical conduct in our personal lifestyles. But quite frankly, Jesus didn't preach the gospel of the individual. He preached the gospel of the Kingdom. The gospel enables us to be a part of the Kingdom, but the kingdom of self is not the gospel.

Today, many Christians are wrongly deluded into thinking that as long as they live a good Christian life, that's all they need to know. What do you hear taught from most pulpits? Does the teaching move beyond personal or family application? If it doesn't touch government, prophecy, economics, and business as well, it could be shallow at best, or at worst it could be dangerous. *Every* New Testament epistle deals with prophecy. Jesus chose to present it to His disciples on the eve of His death. It was that important to Him. He also spent time immediately before His ascension to the Father dealing with the subject. Therefore, the study of the times and seasons of the Lord isn't optional; it is necessary.

Consider what would have happened to Noah and his family if they had avoided prophetic things. What would have happened to those that chose to ignore the prophetic events in the land of Egypt as Moses stood before Pharaoh. They could claim to be "God's chosen people" but they would have experienced destruction just like the heathen even if they had been living upright and moral lives. Jesus likened the last days to the days of Noah. Therefore, it could be life-threatening to ignore what God says about these last days. We must know what time it is, where we stand in light of the Scriptures, and what we must do to follow God in these days.

Where do we go from here?

Since the United States of America is a nation that God established in the last days, we had to address her time in God's history. Although she may be a "new" nation, her people came from somewhere. All Americans have descendents with a past. How does this factor in. At this point, you may have more questions than answers. You may be asking questions about whether this chapter even matters. Believe me, it does. God has a role for the United States to play in His grand scheme.

Now that we have a better understanding of time, let's return to the journey. What about America? Does she have a role to play in the last days? Let's find out. To do so, we must return to the root of the revelation . . . in Genesis.

CHAPTER 3

The Book Of Beginnings

If Bible prophecy will be fulfilled (and, based on past history, we know it most certainly will come to pass), it is important that we know the answers to two questions:

1. Where does America stand in God's timetable, and
2. How does America fit?

We answered question one in the second chapter. Now, it is time to move on and answer question number two.

First, let me refer you back to the quote (from chapter one) shared by Yale Professor Charles A.L. Totten, concerning the study we are about to undertake.

> *"I can never be too thankful to Almighty God that in my youth He used the late Professor Wilson to show to me the difference between the two houses. The very understanding is the key by which almost the entire Bible becomes intelligible, and I cannot state too strongly that the man who has not yet seen that the Israel of the Scriptures is totally distinct from the Jewish people is yet in the very infancy, the mere alphabet of Biblical study and that to this day 7/8ths of the Bible is shut to his understanding."*

He said that without the information you are about to learn, 7/8ths of the Bible will be shut to your understanding! That is a significant statement.

I do believe what we are about to study. This prophetic truth will reveal things that will happen in the United States of America and abroad. Since revelation is progressive, much more will be revealed about this as time goes on. However, the core teachings will remain the same.

I will present my case, much as a lawyer would present a case to a judge or jury. Evidence is critical if the prosecution intends to win a case. I intend to provide that evidence through this study, using the sure Word of prophecy, the Word of God. You must evaluate the evidence. You may choose to agree or disagree with the teachings. If you choose to believe something different, I would challenge you to base it solely on the Word of God. Scripture must support the truth. We cannot rely on philosophy, denominational doctrine, and most certainly not tradition or what you *want* to believe based on emotion or feelings. With those ground rules set forth, let's begin by asking a few questions:

1. What country has fed more people than any other?
2. What country has loaned more money to other nations and peoples than any other?
3. What nation has sent more missionaries to foreign fields than any other?
4. What nation has been known as a "Christian" nation, more than any other?
5. Has our nation, the United States of America, been blessed? If so, by whom? Why?

The answers to these questions are found in and around one nation: The United States of America. According to United Nations and other data-gathering services, this one nation produces more than 30 percent of the world's output in goods and services at the time of this writing, despite exporting jobs, spending money, and forgiving untold millions in debts owed by other nations and groups. Is this blessing simply happenstance? Are we a "fluke?" Did we just hit the "lucky nation" jackpot? If God is the God of precision and accuracy we believe Him to be, this cannot be the case. How then, does the USA fit in Bible prophecy?

To understand how and where America fits, we must go to the book of Genesis (which means beginnings). We must be accurate in interpreting the beginnings of Bible prophecy or else we will be far off the mark in hitting the target at the end. Anyone who has fired a gun or handled a bow and arrow will understand this principle. The slightest movement of the weapon, when fired, will result in the bullet (or arrow) being several inches or even feet off target. So it is with God's Word. If we are not aligned perfectly at the origins of God's great plans and promises in Genesis, then we will be miles off at the target, at the end of our age.

Thus, we begin with Genesis. There are incredible prophecies here which are often overlooked, but which have significant impact on today's world and international happenings. It will be worth your patience! You will be challenged to read most of Genesis as you read through this book. Take your time. Discern my commentary in this book and judge it for accuracy. You will discover new revelations about the ancient book of Genesis you have never seen before, if you will dig into it with fresh eyes and a hunger for God. We will begin in Genesis chapter 9.

Shemites, Hamites and Japhethites

According to Scripture, every person alive on earth today came from one family. That family was the family of Noah and his three sons.

Genesis 9:1, Genesis 10. Noah was commanded to replenish the earth after the flood. This occurred through his three sons and their wives. The sons names were Shem, Ham and Japheth. Much prophetic study links back to Genesis chapters 9 and 10.

While this might seem obvious to those that believe the Bible, scientific discoveries and DNA testing also point back to common ancestry. Today, every Asian, Caucasian, Black and other race finds its roots in this family of faith.

The issue of names and how they evolve also finds its origins in this passage. Each person on the face of the earth is either a Japhethite, a Hamite, or a Shemite. This author personally knew one woman whose grandmother had referred to her as a "daughter of Ham." The Jews today are known as "Semites," which is a hybrid version of "Shemite." Why? Because they descended from the line of Shem, Noah's son. The term "anti-Semetic" has its origins in this lineage. The term means that you are racially motivated to dislike the descendents of Shem.

Through this one issue alone we also see that terms adjust and evolve over time.

The Origin Of The Hebrews

One of Shem's descendents was a man named Eber. Eber (also known as Iber, or Heber) was also well known enough to have his name abbreviated in later days. His descendents became known as Heberites, Hebrews, Ebereans and by other "morphed" changes of his name. Again, we must understand that linguistics change over time. If we understand this, then names, locations and tribal terms can reveal a great deal through history.

Heber's most notable descendent is found in Genesis 12 and this is where our story truly begins. This man's name? Abram.

Abram

Genesis 12:1-7 [1]*Now the LORD had said unto Abram, Get thee out of thy country, and from thy kindred, and from thy father's house, unto a land that I will show thee:* [2]*And I will make of thee a great nation, and I will bless thee, and make thy name great; and thou shalt be a blessing:* [3]*And I will bless them that bless thee, and curse him that curseth thee: and in thee shall all families of the earth be blessed.*

[4]*So Abram departed, as the LORD had spoken unto him; and Lot went with him: and Abram was seventy and five years old when he departed out of Haran.* [5]*And Abram took Sarai his wife, and Lot his brother's son, and all their substance that they had gathered, and the souls that they had gotten in Haran; and they went forth to go into the land of Canaan; and into the land of Canaan they came.*

[6]*And Abram passed through the land unto the place of Sichem, unto the plain of Moreh. And the Canaanite was then in the land.* [7]*And the LORD appeared unto Abram, and said, Unto thy seed will I give this land: and there builded he an altar unto the LORD, who appeared unto him.*

Let's note a few things in this passage. First, God revealed Himself to Abram, but he was not from a godly family. In fact it is thought that Abram's father Terah was the inventor or creator of teraphim (which means "household idol"). Abram was found to be hungry for a relationship with God.

Abram was a Shemite and a Hebrew. What did God speak to him?

- Verse 1. God told Abram to leave his homeland and relatives. This is the first record of the Lord God speaking with Abram and giving him a promise.
- Verse 2. God promised to make OUT OF (not all of) Abram a great nation. He will bless him, make his name great, and that he will be a blessing to others.
- Verse 3. *"I will bless them who bless you, and curse them who curse you."* The whole earth will be blessed because of Abram. They will also be cursed based on how they treat Abram and his posterity. NOTE: This verse has been constantly linked to how the nations of the world treat the Jews and the Jewish State of Israel. While it is true that the Jews and Abram's lineage (begotten through Isaac) are to be blessed, the Jews are only a part of Abram's seed. This verse is not solely meant to "bless the Jews." You will see that unfold as we progress.
- Verses 4-6. Abram obeyed God and left with his family and goods. These include his father, his nephew lot, and his wife Sarai.
- Verse 7. When Abram passed through the land of Canaan, God promised that land to Abram's seed in future days.

As with most prophecy, there is a physical as well as a spiritual interpretation. The covenant is physical, as well as spiritual, and deals with Abram's descendents. Since Abram and Sarai were childless at this point, this promise must be fulfilled in later events.

The life of Abram is critical for a few reasons. First, Abram was the father of faith (Romans 4:16) recognized in the New Testament as the one that would bring forth Jesus Christ as Savior and Lord. This would fulfill every spiritual prophecy for a coming Messiah.

However, God also promised physical blessing and property rights to Abram's seed, based on Abram's relationship with God Himself. This is the title deed to the Jewish State of Israel and their claim to the land of the Bible. It is also the root of blessing and cursing over all the nations of the world. If a nation is blessed, they must somehow be connected to

Abram and His seed. If they are cursed, they have despised Abram and/ or Abram's God. We will be able to note graphic examples of this as we move forward through Genesis and other books of the Bible.

Abram's God Gives Wealth

As Abram continued to follow God, the Lord blessed Him. Abram's travels took him into Egypt and now as Abram moved onward he was greatly blessed. In fact, the blessing of God in a tangible, physical way proved to be a problem for the families of Abram and Lot.

Genesis 13:1-13 *[1]And Abram went up out of Egypt, he, and his wife, and all that he had, and Lot with him, into the south. [2]And Abram was very rich in cattle, in silver, and in gold. [3]And he went on his journeys from the south even to Bethel, unto the place where his tent had been at the beginning, between Bethel and Hai; [4]Unto the place of the altar, which he had made there at the first: and there Abram called on the name of the LORD.*

[5]And Lot also, which went with Abram, had flocks, and herds, and tents. [6]And the land was not able to bear them, that they might dwell together: for their substance was great, so that they could not dwell together. [7]And there was a strife between the herdmen of Abram's cattle and the herdmen of Lot's cattle: and the Canaanite and the Perizzite dwelled then in the land. [8]And Abram said unto Lot, Let there be no strife, I pray thee, between me and thee, and between my herdmen and thy herdmen; for we be brethren. [9]Is not the whole land before thee? separate thyself, I pray thee, from me: if thou wilt take the left hand, then I will go to the right; or if thou depart to the right hand, then I will go to the left.

[10]And Lot lifted up his eyes, and beheld all the plain of Jordan, that it was well watered every where, before the LORD destroyed Sodom and Gomorrah, even as the garden of the LORD, like the land of Egypt, as thou comest unto Zoar. [11]Then Lot chose him all the plain of Jordan; and Lot journeyed east: and they separated themselves the one from the other. [12]Abram dwelled in the land of Canaan, and Lot dwelled in the cities of the plain, and pitched his tent toward Sodom. [13]But the men of Sodom were wicked and sinners before the LORD exceedingly.

Let us observe a few details here before we move on with the story. First, God's blessing upon Abram's life is so tangible that he has become wealthy. Lot also became blessed simply because he lived with Abram and followed what Abram did in his godly lifestlye.

Abram has distanced himself from his family and heritage by this time. Terah, his father, is dead and Abram has moved on. In this passage he leaves Egypt and goes to the area of present-day Bethel (which means House of God, in Hebrew). There, Abram offers sacrifice unto Almighty God and calls on His Name.

Because of the sheer volume of God's blessing upon Abram and Lot's herds, strife erupts between their herdsmen over pasture and water for the livestock. Abram generously offers to Lot the first pick of the land before them. Lot liked what he could see. He chose the plain of Jordan, where the city of Sodom was located. Sodom was already extremely wicked, but that didn't phase Lot. He chose his land in proximity to the present evils of the world and chose to live in them based on his reasoning and natural senses. This left Abram with no recourse but to call on God.

Genesis 13:14-18 *[14]And the LORD said unto Abram, after that Lot was separated from him, Lift up now thine eyes, and look from the place where thou art northward, and southward, and eastward, and westward: [15]For all the land which thou seest, to thee will I give it, and to thy seed for ever. [16]And I will make thy seed as the dust of the earth: so that if a man can number the dust of the earth, then shall thy seed also be numbered. [17]Arise, walk through the land in the length of it and in the breadth of it; for I will give it unto thee. [18]Then Abram removed his tent, and came and dwelt in the plain of Mamre, which is in Hebron, and built there an altar unto the LORD.*

After Lot separated from Abram, God spoke again to Abram. The promises God gave were significant in their scope.

First, God ordered Abram to stand and look to the north, the south, the east and the west. God promised Abram that He would sovereignly give all of the land Abram saw (using his location as an epicenter) and to Abram's seed forever. This included the land that Lot had just possessed. God was not pleased with Lot's attraction to the world, and the immoral, self-indulgent society. While Lot chose a fertile plain, God promised it to Abram's seed in the future.

Then God gave an even more amazing promise to Abram. In verse 16 God promised that Abram's seed would be as the dust of the earth, virtually impossible to be numbered because of their fruitfulness!

However, at this point Abram and Sarai are still childless. This will take a miracle from God.

Many have said that this prophecy to Abram was fulfilled through Jesus Christ and His spiritual seed. Galatians 3:29 says *"and if ye be Christ's, then are ye Abraham's seed and heirs according to the promise."* It is completely true that God grafts every Christian believer into the seed of Abraham. However, God was speaking in a physical context here as well. We must be careful to not spiritualize physical prophecies.

In verse 17 God commanded Abram to rise up and walk the land he has seen as a step of faith, knowing that his physical seed will possess every bit of it in the future. Abram walked this literal land as an inheritance for an earthly people. Later, he walked spiritual Canaan land, the place where God dwells. This is the spiritual inheritance of all Christians.

God Confirms His Promise

When God makes a promise to man, He intends to keep it. Therefore, we must understand that God will confirm what He says so that we can trust Him. God's promises may appear to be slow in coming, and we can be tested. Still, God wants us to know He is telling the truth. So He appeared to Abram once again in Genesis 15.

Genesis 15:1-6 [1]*After these things the word of the LORD came unto Abram in a vision, saying, Fear not, Abram: I am thy shield, and thy exceeding great reward.*

[2]*And Abram said, Lord GOD, what wilt thou give me, seeing I go childless, and the steward of my house is this Eliezer of Damascus?* [3]*And Abram said, Behold, to me thou hast given no seed: and, lo, one born in my house is mine heir.* [4]*And, behold, the word of the LORD came unto him, saying, This shall not be thine heir; but he that shall come forth out of thine own bowels shall be thine heir.* [5]*And he brought him forth abroad, and said, Look now toward heaven, and tell the stars, if thou be able to number them: and he said unto him, So shall thy seed be.* [6]*And he believed in the LORD; and he counted it to him for righteousness.*

This heavenly vision of God speaking directly with Abram gives Abram the opportunity to have a dialogue with God. Abram was concerned about the future and about his destiny. But God assured him that he was not to fear; God Himself was his shield or protector. He was also going to reward Abram in a very great manner.

In verses 2 and 3 Abram reveals the source of his concern. He has no child. If he and Sarai die, the child of Eliezer (a servant from Damascus) would become his heir since he had been born in Abram's house. All of the great wealth, as well as all of the land God promised to Abram would then fall into the hands of this servant and his family. This was not to be the case.

Verses 4 and 5 reveal God's intentions and confirm what He has said previously. God specifies that Eliezer's son will not be the heir. Instead, God will give Abram a physical heir that will come from his bowels. Then God brings Abram forth to look at the night sky. God says that Abram's seed will be as numerous as the stars of the heaven!

Abram believes God's promise as a physical reality (verse 6). In fact, this so settles Abram's mind that he never brings up the issue with God again! It is evident that both Abram and God know that they are speaking about a literal promise and a literal seed. The spiritual seed is also an accepted factor, but we must recognize this as a promise God intended to manifest in physical form on the earth.

So tangible is this promise of God, that Abram makes an animal sacrifice to Almighty God, and God moves through that sacrifice as a pillar of fire. God foretells Abram about the future when his seed will be in captivity, in Egypt, and even specifies the number of years of this captivity. This is a physical promise to a literal people that will come forth in the future.

But There's A Problem

As Abram's life continues both he and Sarai continue to get old! In fact, the New Testament says that Sarai's womb was "dead." She could not bear children at all. So, Sarai came up with a plan.

Genesis 16 *[1]Now Sarai Abram's wife bare him no children: and she had an handmaid, an Egyptian, whose name was Hagar. [2]And Sarai said unto Abram, Behold now, the LORD hath restrained me from bearing: I pray thee, go in unto my maid; it may be that I may obtain children by her. And Abram hearkened to the voice of Sarai. [3]And Sarai Abram's wife took*

Hagar her maid the Egyptian, after Abram had dwelt ten years in the land of Canaan, and gave her to her husband Abram to be his wife.

[4]And he went in unto Hagar, and she conceived: and when she saw that she had conceived, her mistress was despised in her eyes. [5]And Sarai said unto Abram, My wrong be upon thee: I have given my maid into thy bosom; and when she saw that she had conceived, I was despised in her eyes: the LORD judge between me and thee. [6]But Abram said unto Sarai, Behold, thy maid is in thy hand; do to her as it pleaseth thee. And when Sarai dealt hardly with her, she fled from her face.

[7]And the angel of the LORD found her by a fountain of water in the wilderness, by the fountain in the way to Shur. [8]And he said, Hagar, Sarai's maid, whence camest thou? and whither wilt thou go? And she said, I flee from the face of my mistress Sarai. [9]And the angel of the LORD said unto her, Return to thy mistress, and submit thyself under her hands.

[10]And the angel of the LORD said unto her, I will multiply thy seed exceedingly, that it shall not be numbered for multitude. [11]And the angel of the LORD said unto her, Behold, thou art with child, and shalt bear a son, and shalt call his name Ishmael; because the LORD hath heard thy affliction. [12]And he will be a wild man; his hand will be against every man, and every man's hand against him; and he shall dwell in the presence of all his brethren. [13]And she called the name of the LORD that spake unto her, Thou God seest me: for she said, Have I also here looked after him that seeth me? [14]Wherefore the well was called Beerlahairoi; behold, it is between Kadesh and Bered.

[15]And Hagar bare Abram a son: and Abram called his son's name, which Hagar bare, Ishmael. [16]And Abram was fourscore and six years old, when Hagar bare Ishmael to Abram.

Apparently God has spoken to Abram, but He hasn't spoken to Sarai. It has now been 10 years since they departed Ur, and they are still childless. Abram is 85 and Sarai is 75 years old. But Sarai has a plan. She recommends to Abram that he conceive a child with her handmaid, Hagar, an Egyptian. Abram agrees to this proposition and soon Hagar is pregnant!

Once Hagar is pregnant, Sarai sees the folly in her decision. She discusses this with Abram and he decides to be as non-confrontive as possible. This was a pattern in Abram's life, and illustrates the fact that while Abram's faith was strong, his personal life wasn't necessarily the same! Sarai turns on Hagar and becomes harsh in her dealings with her long-time handmaid. Hagar flees into the wilderness, alone and expecting Abram's child.

While Hagar struggles in the wilderness, the Angel of the Lord meets her and gives her a promise. She is to return to Abram and Sarai and God will give her a blessed child. His name will be called Ishmael, a son, and he will be multiplied greatly. In fact, his seed would be great, numberless in multitude! Therefore Hagar obeys the voice of God and returns.

At the time appointed, Hagar gives birth to a son. He is named Ishmael, which means "God will hear." Abram now has a son. Is he the promised child?

If Ishmael is the promised child, then the Arab-bloc nations are truly the promised seed of God today. God had other promises for Ishmael simply because he was a son of Abram. Let's look at these for a moment.

The Arab Nations

Many believe that Ishmael is the father of the Arab peoples (including most Arabs). Here are the characteristics God Himself said would come out of Ishmael's lineage.

<u>Verse 12</u>

- He will be a wild man, one that runs wild such as a wild ass in the wilderness.
- His hand will be against every man. He will be warlike and even fight against those that are closest to him because he lives for the battle and the conflict. His seed will be a people of conflict.
- Every man's hand will also be against Ishmael's seed. He will be disliked and attacked because of his hatred and complete insolence toward others. Ishmael will not be tolerant.
- He shall dwell in the presence of all his bretheren. Ishmael is a tribal people, living in clans and kingdoms. There will be strife among them, but they won't spread out. Instead, they will occupy a specific region of the world.

<u>Genesis 17</u> also includes a promise about Ishmael in <u>verse 20</u>.

- Ishmael will be blessed by God. He will be fruitful and will multiply greatly.
- He will father twelve princes (in the arabic, the word sheik means prince). Ishmael will be a great nation.
- However, he will not be a recipient of the covenant blessing. God has reserved that for someone else.

Based on these identifying features alone, it is most likely the case that the Arab-bloc nations are descendents of Ishmael. They have been clannish, nomadic, and have always been warlike, even among themselves. The religion they espouse to this day, Islam, is a religion of conquest and constant war despite being advertised as a religion of peace. God's blessing is upon them, and we see it today with their oil riches. However, they have not obtained the covenant blessing from Almighty God. They may receive it spiritually by embracing Jesus Christ as Savior and Lord, but their physical seed was not intended to carry on God's blessing in the earth.

Well, we have answered our question. Is Ishmael the promised heir? No. He is blessed, but there is more to come.

God Makes A Covenant With Abram

When we read through the Bible, we often fail to consider the span of time God uses to work in people's lives. Abram was 86 years old when Ishmael was born (chapter 16). However, when we pick up Abram's story again in chapter 17, he is now 99 years old. Twenty-four years have passed since he and Sarai departed from Ur. Hagar's son Ishmael is now 13 years old. But God is intent on keeping His word with Abram. In fact, as we will soon see, God intends to magnify His Word to a greater degree than ever before. Let's take this next chapter in sections. It is loaded with God's revelation for us today.

Genesis 17:1-2 [1]*And when Abram was ninety years old and nine, the LORD appeared to Abram, and said unto him, I am the Almighty God; walk before me, and be thou perfect.* [2]*And I will make my covenant between me and thee, and will multiply thee exceedingly.*

God appears to Abram when he is at an advanced age. He announces Himself and commands Abram to walk in a perfect, mature way before

Him. Then he announces something He has never done before. God is going to make covenant with an ordinary man!

Normally covenants are made between equal parties. Neighboring countries, clans or families may cut covenant, and align themselves together. But in this case God, the King of kings, chose to make a covenant with one man, a human and frail man at that!

When covenants were made, this meant that each party was then obligated to the other by a blood oath. There was usually a ceremony, sealed with a blood sacrifice and drinking pledges. Each party pledged everything they possessed to the other party. If there was war, they would defend each other to the death. This covenant was the most serious contract that could possibly be made, and God chose to make it with Abram.

God mentions the conditions of His covenant throughout the rest of this chapter. In fact, He specifies this covenant thirteen separate times! And God now reveals the terms and conditions that He has foreordained.

Genesis 17:3-7 [3]*And Abram fell on his face: and God talked with him, saying,*

[4]*As for me, behold, my covenant is with thee, and thou shalt be a father of many nations.* [5]*Neither shall thy name any more be called Abram, but thy name shall be Abraham; for a father of many nations have I made thee.* [6]*And I will make thee exceeding fruitful, and I will make nations of thee, and kings shall come out of thee.*

[7]*And I will establish my covenant between me and thee and thy seed after thee in their generations for an everlasting covenant, to be a God unto thee, and to thy seed after thee.*

As Abram bows before God Almighty, the Lord announces that His covenant will be made with Abram. Nobody else will receive this covenant blessing, despite the fact that there are now dozens of nations and people groups scatted throughout the world. God specifies the fact that His covenant, the covenant of God's blessing and favor, is bestowed solely upon Abram.

The next thing Abram hears God speak, is the fact that he is to be the father of many nations! This is astonishing! It is also a very interesting term in Hebrew. The term for "many" in Hebrew is "hamon," which has a couple of major meanings. First, it means "many, or a multitude." God's promise is for multiplication, abundance, and plurality of nations.

The Hebrew term for nations is "gowy." This term means "foreign nations, Gentiles, nationalities, and ethnic groups." Abraham is not going to be the father of one nation, but many! And these ethnicities or people will not be known as "Jews," but also as "Gentiles."

Then, God changes Abram's name to denote His promise. The term Abram means "high or lofty father," denoting honor. However, God now changes his name to Abraham, which means "father of a great multitude."

God reiterates this in verse 6, when He states that He will make Abraham (His new name) exceeding fruitful. Again, God says that He will make nations (plural, multiple) come out of Abraham. This Hebrew word specifically indicates there will be foreign nations, Gentile nations and people will come from Abraham. Kings will come from him as well!

If this is not enough for Abraham to fathom, God then adds a more fantastic touch. In verse 7, God promises that He will not merely establish His covenant with Abraham alone, but He will renew it with his seed in their generations. In fact, God specifies that with every generation He will make this an everlasting covenant, to be a God unto them, and for them to be His people!

We have traversed seven verses of this chapter, and already the Almighty God has made promises that must be fulfilled in our days! If God keeps His Word (and He does), then Abraham's everlasting covenant with Him must still be in effect today. This means that in the world today there are multiple nations of the world that can claim Abraham as their father. It also means that God's physical blessing upon Abraham and His seed is still possible today, especially when Abraham's seed keeps covenant with Almighty God as a nation, and puts their trust in Him. But there is more!

Genesis 17:8-9 *[8]And I will give unto thee, and to thy seed after thee, the land wherein thou art a stranger, all the land of Canaan, for an everlasting possession; and I will be their God. [9]And God said unto Abraham, Thou shalt keep my covenant therefore, thou, and thy seed after thee in their generations.*

God now promises the entire land of Canaan to Abraham's seed for an everlasting possession. This is the title deed to the land! Once again, we must acknowledge the fact that this covenant promise is not spiritual, but literal. God commanded Abraham's seed to keep covenant with Him, and He would ensure that they inherited the land of Canaan forever! It does not belong to anyone else! Period.

Genesis 17:10-14 [10]*This is my covenant, which ye shall keep, between me and you and thy seed after thee; Every man child among you shall be circumcised.* [11]*And ye shall circumcise the flesh of your foreskin; and it shall be a token of the covenant betwixt me and you.* [12]*And he that is eight days old shall be circumcised among you, every man child in your generations, he that is born in the house, or bought with money of any stranger, which is not of thy seed.* [13]*He that is born in thy house, and he that is bought with thy money, must needs be circumcised: and my covenant shall be in your flesh for an everlasting covenant.* [14]*And the uncircumcised man child whose flesh of his foreskin is not circumcised, that soul shall be cut off from his people; he hath broken my covenant.*

Since God has made these eternal promises to Abraham and to his seed, He now has the right to demand something of Abraham. God requires that Abraham and every male child be circumcised in their flesh. This cutting in their flesh represents a physical separation from every culture around them. They will be different in every area. They will be set apart, because they are in covenant with God. And God expects that their flesh will be impacted, and their lives will be severed from the ways of the world around them.

Genesis 17:15-16 [15]*And God said unto Abraham, As for Sarai thy wife, thou shalt not call her name Sarai, but Sarah shall her name be.* [16]*And I will bless her, and give thee a son also of her: yea, I will bless her, and she shall be a mother of nations; kings of people shall be of her.*

There are those today that would try to argue the point that the covenant specified up to this point belonged to Abraham and subsequently to his son Ishmael, who was born through Hagar. However, as stated earlier, God had other plans. And he reveals them now.

Not only did God change Abram's name to Abraham, He now changes Sarai's name to Sarah. The term Sarai means "dominant" or "captain," perhaps denoting her temperament and attitudes up to this point. 1 Peter 3:6 says that Sarah obeyed Abraham, calling him "Lord," or master. It is likely her attitude and temperament had to change over time for God to open His hand of blessing to her. But now God gives her a new name. Sarah. It means "noble lady, princess, queen." Sarah will be the woman through whom God will bring forth the covenant people; not Hagar.

God specifies that it is Sarah that will be a mother of nations. This nullifies any allegations that the multitude of nations could come through both Ishmael and any other seed to come. The promises of God are reserved for the seed of Abraham and Sarah alone. Kings of people will be of her. God is very specific.

Because of this Abraham falls on his face in near disbelief. God has promised him a son through Sarah, and they are well advanced in age. However, his heart is tender toward his son Ishmael. He wants God to bless him as well.

Genesis 17:17-20 [17]*Then Abraham fell upon his face, and laughed, and said in his heart, Shall a child be born unto him that is an hundred years old? and shall Sarah, that is ninety years old, bear?* [18]*And Abraham said unto God, O that Ishmael might live before thee!* [19]*And God said, Sarah thy wife shall bear thee a son indeed; and thou shalt call his name Isaac: and I will establish my covenant with him for an everlasting covenant, and with his seed after him.* [20]*And as for Ishmael, I have heard thee: Behold, I have blessed him, and will make him fruitful, and will multiply him exceedingly; twelve princes shall he beget, and I will make him a great nation.*

God responds to Abraham's request kindly. However, he knows that Ishmael will not continue to follow Him. So He blesses Ishmael and his seed with the promises we have discussed earlier. But then God answers Abraham's concerns with a very direct statement. God's everlasting covenant will be established through Abraham and Sarah. Sarah will bring forth a son and they will call His name Isaac; a God-appointed name.

Genesis 17:21-22 [21]*But my covenant will I establish with Isaac, which Sarah shall bear unto thee at this set time in the next year.* [22]*And he left off talking with him, and God went up from Abraham.*

God's eternal covenant will be established with Isaac. This is God's final answer, and He ends the conversation on that point. According to Genesis 21:12 and Genesis 22:1-2, Isaac is the only son that God recognized as carrying the covenant blessing. And it is a significant blessing that changes the faces of the world.

According to Deuteronomy 32:8, God sets the boundaries of the nations of the world. However, He first predetermined the size and scope of the nations that would come forth and populate the world . . . through Isaac! This cannot be spiritualized, nor can it be explained by the existence of only the Jews.

Consider this. The Arab people are a group roughly 260 million in number, while the Jews are a group of less than 20 million worldwide. If God promised that Abraham's seed would be as the sand of the sea or the stars of the heaven and promised fulfillment of that through Isaac, how is it that they are outnumbered by the tribes of Ishmael?

Many people try to spiritualize this and count Christian believers around the world as the seed of Abraham. However, Ishmael's seed is largely Islamic. This is one of the largest religions in the world, far larger than Judaism. If we compare spiritual to spiritual, again this does not make sense.

The facts are these. God promised to bless Abraham and Sarah with a multitude of nations—not just one nation, but many. Abraham's very name denotes this. These people would determine the boundaries of other nations of the world by their very size and scope. The foundations of this promise are very small, being fulfilled in one person at a time. But by the time we get to the end of days, we must see how God reveals His covenant in the nations of the world. If we do not, we have missed what God has spoken in Genesis 17. How does the United States of America fit into this? Let's continue.

Isaac Is Born

From Genesis 12 through 17 the years probably lagged in Abraham's life. Twenty-four years passed during that season. However, in chapter 17 God made a covenant with Abraham, and now it was time to fulfill it. During this time, Abraham traveled southward, claiming the land God had promised him (chapter 20). God also visited Abraham and reconfirmed His covenant with him (chapter 18). He also told Abraham about His plans to destroy Sodom. This was fulfilled shortly thereafter (chapter 19). Now it was time for the promise!

Genesis 21:1-4 [1]*And the LORD visited Sarah as he had said, and the LORD did unto Sarah as he had spoken.* [2]*For Sarah conceived, and bare*

Abraham a son in his old age, at the set time of which God had spoken to him. [3]*And Abraham called the name of his son that was born unto him, whom Sarah bare to him, Isaac.* [4]*And Abraham circumcised his son Isaac being eight days old, as God had commanded him.*

What a time of celebration for Abraham and Sarah! They had waited all their lives for a child, and God has rewarded them with a child and with an everlasting covenant. To honor God, Abraham names his son Isaac. He also has him circumcised as God commanded.

A Line In The Sand

Not everyone was happy that God's covenant was going to be established through Isaac. Abraham's other son Ishmael was caught mocking Isaac. And Sarah didn't like it.

Genesis 21:9-21 [9]*And Sarah saw the son of Hagar the Egyptian, which she had born unto Abraham, mocking.* [10]*Wherefore she said unto Abraham, Cast out this bondwoman and her son: for the son of this bondwoman shall not be heir with my son, even with Isaac.* [11]*And the thing was very grievous in Abraham's sight because of his son.* [12]*And God said unto Abraham, Let it not be grievous in thy sight because of the lad, and because of thy bondwoman; in all that Sarah hath said unto thee, hearken unto her voice; for in Isaac shall thy seed be called.* [13]*And also of the son of the bondwoman will I make a nation, because he is thy seed.*

[14]*And Abraham rose up early in the morning, and took bread, and a bottle of water, and gave it unto Hagar, putting it on her shoulder, and the child, and sent her away: and she departed, and wandered in the wilderness of Beersheba.* [15]*And the water was spent in the bottle, and she cast the child under one of the shrubs.* [16]*And she went, and sat her down over against him a good way off, as it were a bowshot: for she said, Let me not see the death of the child. And she sat over against him, and lift up her voice, and wept.* [17]*And God heard the voice of the lad; and the angel of God called to Hagar out of heaven, and said unto her, What aileth thee, Hagar? fear not; for God hath heard the voice of the lad where he is.* [18]*Arise, lift up the lad, and hold him in thine hand; for I will make him a great nation.* [19]*And God opened her eyes, and she saw a well of water; and she went, and filled the bottle with water, and gave the lad drink.* [20]*And God was with the lad; and he grew, and dwelt in the wilderness, and became an archer.* [21]*And he*

dwelt in the wilderness of Paran: and his mother took him a wife out of the land of Egypt.

Although God cared for Ishmael and kept His promise to Abraham, from this point forward there was strife between the two brothers. Hagar did not seek out someone connected to Abraham or God's covenant as a wife for Ishmael. She didn't seek God for direction despite His guidance in her life, and the life of her son up to this point. Instead, she selected someone like herself, to become Ishmael's mate. And from this point forward it became increasingly clear that there were two types of people being established on the face of the earth. There were those that were under God's covenant and blessing, and those that were not.

Just How Serious Is This?

God was so serious about establishing His covenant with man that he put Abraham through what could be the ultimate test of trust. He challenged him to sacrifice Isaac in obedience to His command.

Genesis 24:1-14 [1]*And it came to pass after these things, that God did tempt Abraham, and said unto him, Abraham: and he said, Behold, here I am.* [2]*And he said, Take now thy son, thine only son Isaac, whom thou lovest, and get thee into the land of Moriah; and offer him there for a burnt offering upon one of the mountains which I will tell thee of.*

[3]*And Abraham rose up early in the morning, and saddled his ass, and took two of his young men with him, and Isaac his son, and clave the wood for the burnt offering, and rose up, and went unto the place of which God had told him.* [4]*Then on the third day Abraham lifted up his eyes, and saw the place afar off.* [5]*And Abraham said unto his young men, Abide ye here with the ass; and I and the lad will go yonder and worship, and come again to you.* [6]*And Abraham took the wood of the burnt offering, and laid it upon Isaac his son; and he took the fire in his hand, and a knife; and they went both of them together.* [7]*And Isaac spake unto Abraham his father, and said, My father: and he said, Here am I, my son. And he said, Behold the fire and the wood: but where is the lamb for a burnt offering?* [8]*And Abraham said, My son, God will provide himself a lamb for a burnt offering: so they went both of them together.* [9]*And they came to the place which God had told him of; and Abraham built an altar there, and laid the wood in order, and bound Isaac his son, and laid him on the altar upon the wood.* [10]*And Abraham stretched forth his hand, and took the knife to slay his son.*

[11]And the angel of the LORD called unto him out of heaven, and said, Abraham, Abraham: and he said, Here am I. [12]And he said, Lay not thine hand upon the lad, neither do thou any thing unto him: for now I know that thou fearest God, seeing thou hast not withheld thy son, thine only son from me. [13]And Abraham lifted up his eyes, and looked, and behold behind him a ram caught in a thicket by his horns: and Abraham went and took the ram, and offered him up for a burnt offering in the stead of his son. [14]And Abraham called the name of that place Jehovahjireh: as it is said to this day, In the mount of the LORD it shall be seen.

Many have questioned why God would put Abraham through such a grueling requirement. But in reality, the answer was simple. God was looking for a people He could trust. God would determine the boundaries of nations based on Abraham's seed. The Savior of the World, Jesus Christ, would be brought forth from Abraham's seed. Nations and people would be blessed and others cursed based on this one issue—the covenant between God and man. No wonder God tested Abraham's faith!

Did you notice what God said in verse 2? It's important. When God was speaking to Abraham, He referred to Abraham's son Isaac as his "only son." This is significant because in God's eyes there was only one covenant child. Isaac was the only son of the covenant and God intended to pass the covenant blessing on through him.

We see that Abraham was faithful to God. He "passed" God's integrity test, and as a result, God was pleased. But there was still more to come.

Genesis 22:15-18 *[15]And the angel of the LORD called unto Abraham out of heaven the second time, [16]And said, By myself have I sworn, saith the LORD, for because thou hast done this thing, and hast not withheld thy son, thine only son: [17]That in blessing I will bless thee, and in multiplying I will multiply thy seed as the stars of the heaven, and as the sand which is upon the sea shore; and thy seed shall possess the gate of his enemies; [18]And in thy seed shall all the nations of the earth be blessed; because thou hast obeyed my voice.*

Passing The Covenant

When the angel of the Lord called out to Abraham it is apparent that Isaac was also present. They were both on the mountain, and had offered up the Lord's substitute sacrifice together. Isaac had just witnessed his father's radical commitment to a covenant with Almighty God. He had also seen God's provision in response to Abraham's faith. Now the baton was being passed from father to son. Isaac was also made a recipient of God's covenant knowledge and blessing.

In fact, this promise correlates to God's promise to Abraham found in Genesis 21:12, where God told Abraham that " . . . in Isaac shall thy seed be called." In other words, the blessing would flow through Isaac. But the covenant people would also be referred to in time as *"Isaac's sons."* This would become a part of their heritage.

Once again God referred to Isaac as Abraham's "only son." Now God reaffirms His covenant with Abraham in the presence of Isaac. He promises His divine blessing on Abraham's life and lineage. God promises that He will multiply Abraham's seed as the stars of the heaven and as the sand of the sea. God further promises that Abraham's seed will have military might and supremacy. They will possess the gate of their enemies.

The term "possess" in the Hebrew (H3423) means, *"to occupy (be driving out previous tenants, and possessing in their place); by implication to seize, to rob, to inherit; also to expel, to impoverish, to ruin."* In other words, God had just promised to Abraham and Isaac the future ability for their seed to be dominant in the world among the nations. The nations that sprang from them would become world superpowers in terms of military might, colonization, and supremacy! Abraham's seed would not merely come into empty lands. They would expel those that were there before them, as the Lord gave them land to inherit.

Back To Our Question

A few pages back we asked a simple question. "Is America in the Bible?" Some have denied the fact. However, a deeper study of the Word of God has led us to Genesis 22. If God has promised military might and global dominance to those that are His literal covenant children, wouldn't it be reasonable to assume that we should be able to find them in the world today?

Many will argue that the Jewish State of Israel is the military superpower in the Middle East, and rightfully so. They have sprung out of Abraham. They are not mighty because of their intelligence, size, or personal strength. Their might has come from God's promise to Abraham as their father. But if God merely stopped by fulfilling His promises solely in the Jews, He could be accused of being small-minded and unfaithful to His Word. Many nations have helped the Jews through the years, and they rely on others (particularly the United States) for allegiance and defense of their land.

Logic then dictates that God could not have been speaking in Genesis 22 about the Jews alone as fulfillment of this passage. Who else would be a nation that is a military superpower, a conquering, colonizing people, and a nation that is blessed above all others? Let's continue.

Death And Possession

Genesis 23 may not seem like a spiritual passage at all. But to God, it anchors yet another part of His covenant promise. Abraham's wife, Sarah, has died. After 127 earthly years, she has met the Lord face to face. She has raised up Isaac, now 37 years old, and her work is done. But Abraham is still technically a wanderer, a man without a country. Where will he bury his wife?

Abraham confronted this issue while living near present-day Hebron. Chapter 23 delineates the fact that Abraham met with the local tribes and purchased property in that area, including a cave to use as a burial site, and a nearby field. He was grossly overcharged in the transaction. However, this passage proves that Abraham lived in this region nearly 4,000 years ago. The other tribes are gone; they left neither legacy nor lineage. But the seed of Abraham is the oldest-known people-group to inhabit the land of Canaan in the Middle-East. This passage is their title deed to the land.

If God's promises are relegated to merely receiving spiritual blessings from Christ, this would not be important. People could serve God anywhere in the world, and His blessing upon their lives would be universal. While every individual, nation, tribe and tongue can receive Jesus Christ as Savior and King, there is a clear and distinct difference in how blessing is imparted to them based on where they live. God has a physical people that are descendents of Abraham. Their lands are blessed. They are not spiritual blessings; they are physical gifts from God. God still has a covenant people that are a literal, physical people. (If this were not true, Paul would not have addressed this in Romans 9.) As we follow God's covenant blessings and the trail begun in Genesis, we then have an accurate understanding of what God is doing in the earth today.

Marriage Under The Covenant Blessing

Ishmael had not continued to follow God. With his mother's help (Hagar), he had selected an Egyptian woman as his wife (Genesis 21:21). This woman was likely an idol-worshipper and Ishmael's choice in his mate denoted his lack of respect for Almighty God. No mention is made of Ishmael seeking out his father Abraham while he was yet living. He would be blessed, but he had abandoned his heritage in God.

While God's followers were very few, God foreknew those that would follow Him. Isaac, the covenant son, was now 40 years old. His mother, Sarah, had been dead for three years. And while Isaac was still single, God had a mate already selected that would be a joint-heir of the covenant blessing as his wife.

Genesis 24:1-9 [1]*And Abraham was old, and well stricken in age: and the LORD had blessed Abraham in all things.* [2]*And Abraham said unto his eldest servant of his house, that ruled over all that he had, Put, I pray thee, thy hand under my thigh:* [3]*And I will make thee swear by the LORD, the God of heaven, and the God of the earth, that thou shalt not take a wife unto my son of the daughters of the Canaanites, among whom I dwell:* [4]*But thou shalt go unto my country, and to my kindred, and take a wife unto my son Isaac.* [5]*And the servant said unto him, Peradventure the woman will not be willing to follow me unto this land: must I needs bring thy son again unto the land from whence thou camest?* [6]*And Abraham said unto him, Beware thou that thou bring not my son thither again.* [7]*The LORD God of heaven, which took me from my father's house, and from the land of my kindred, and which spake unto me, and that sware unto me, saying, Unto thy seed will I give this land; he shall send his angel before thee, and thou shalt take a wife unto my son from thence.* [8]*And if the woman will not be willing to follow thee, then thou shalt be clear from this my oath: only bring not my son thither again.* [9]*And the servant put his hand under the thigh of Abraham his master, and sware to him concerning that matter.*

Marriage between close family members had not yet been banned by God. Perhaps it was because genetic mutations were not as prevalent, or other reasons unknown to us. Whatever the case, Abraham directed his servant to find a wife for his 40-year-old son, Isaac. This wife was not to be from the Canaanites, but from the Semites. She was to be a descendent of Shem, and a Hebrew from Abraham's kin. This kept heathen influence out of the covenant lineage.

Genesis 24:10-20 [10]*And the servant took ten camels of the camels of his master, and departed; for all the goods of his master were in his hand: and he arose, and went to Mesopotamia, unto the city of Nahor.* [11]*And he made his camels to kneel down without the city by a well of water at the time of the evening, even the time that women go out to draw water.* [12]*And he said, O LORD God of my master Abraham, I pray thee, send me good speed this day, and show kindness unto my master Abraham.* [13]*Behold, I stand here by the well of water; and the daughters of the men of the city come out to draw water:* [14]*And let it come to pass, that the damsel to whom I shall say, Let down thy pitcher, I pray thee, that I may drink; and she shall say, Drink, and I will give thy camels drink also: let the same be she that thou hast appointed for thy servant Isaac; and thereby shall I know that thou hast showed kindness unto my master.* [15]*And it came to pass, before he had done speaking, that, behold, Rebekah came out, who was born to Bethuel, son of Milcah, the wife of Nahor, Abraham's brother, with her pitcher upon her shoulder.* [16]*And the damsel was very fair to look upon, a virgin, neither had any man known her: and she went down to the well, and filled her pitcher, and came up.* [17]*And the servant ran to meet her, and said, Let me, I pray thee, drink a little water of thy pitcher.* [18]*And she said, Drink, my lord: and she hasted, and let down her pitcher upon her hand, and gave him drink.* [19]*And when she had done giving him drink, she said, I will draw water for thy camels also, until they have done drinking.* [20]*And she hasted, and emptied her pitcher into the trough, and ran again unto the well to draw water, and drew for all his camels.*

Abraham's chief servant traveled a great distance back to the region of Abraham's ancestry. It is possible he had never been there himself. But God led him directly to the city of Abraham's family. On the outskirts of town, the servant asks God for divine guidance. He asks for a woman to come out of the city and offer to provide water for his thirsty camels! This would be a very difficult task, and through it he would discern whether this woman was selected by God. And God answered by choosing the right woman. But was she of the right lineage?

Genesis 24:22-31 [22]*And it came to pass, as the camels had done drinking, that the man took a golden earring of half a shekel weight, and two bracelets for her hands of ten shekels weight of gold;* [23]*And said, Whose daughter art thou? tell me, I pray thee: is there room in thy father's house for us to lodge in?* [24]*And she said unto him, I am the daughter of Bethuel the son of Milcah, which she bare unto Nahor.* [25]*She said moreover unto him, We have both straw and provender enough, and room to lodge in.* [26]*And the man bowed down his head, and worshipped the LORD.* [27]*And he said, Blessed be the LORD God of my master Abraham, who hath not left destitute my master of his mercy and his truth: I being in the way, the LORD led me to the house of my master's brethren.* [28]*And the damsel ran, and told them of her mother's house these things.*

[29]*And Rebekah had a brother, and his name was Laban: and Laban ran out unto the man, unto the well.* [30]*And it came to pass, when he saw the earring and bracelets upon his sister's hands, and when he heard the words of Rebekah his sister, saying, Thus spake the man unto me; that he came unto the man; and, behold, he stood by the camels at the well.* [31]*And he said, Come in, thou blessed of the LORD; wherefore standest thou without? for I have prepared the house, and room for the camels.*

Was this coincidence, or was this the hand of God? This woman, Rebekah, was not a distant relative of Abraham. She was his neice! God had brought the servant to the right city, selected the right woman, and had brought them into contact immediately. Now it was time for the servant to state the purpose of his mission.

Genesis 24: 34-53 [34]*And he said, I am Abraham's servant.* [35]*And the LORD hath blessed my master greatly; and he is become great: and he hath given him flocks, and herds, and silver, and gold, and menservants, and maidservants, and camels, and asses.* [36]*And Sarah my master's wife bare a son to my master when she was old: and unto him hath he given all that he hath.* [37]*And my master made me swear, saying, Thou shalt not take a wife to my son of the daughters of the Canaanites, in whose land I dwell:* [38]*But thou shalt go unto my father's house, and to my kindred, and take a wife unto my son.* [39]*And I said unto my master, Peradventure the woman will not follow me.* [40]*And he said unto me, The LORD, before whom I walk, will send his angel with thee, and prosper thy way; and thou shalt take a wife for my son of my kindred, and of my father's house:* [41]*Then shalt thou be clear from this my oath, when thou comest to my kindred; and if they give not thee one, thou shalt be clear from my oath.* [42]*And I came this day* *unto the well, and said, O LORD God of my master Abraham, if now thou do prosper my way which I go:* [43]*Behold, I stand by the well of water; and it shall come to pass, that when the virgin cometh forth to draw water, and I say to her, Give me, I pray thee, a little water of thy pitcher to drink;* [44]*And she say to me, Both drink thou, and I will also draw for thy camels: let the same be the woman whom the LORD hath appointed out for my master's son.* [45]*And before I had done speaking in mine heart, behold, Rebekah came forth with her pitcher on her shoulder; and she went down unto the well, and drew water: and I said unto her, Let me drink, I pray thee.* [46]*And she made haste, and let down her pitcher from her shoulder, and said, Drink, and I will give thy camels drink also: so I drank, and she made the camels drink also.* [47]*And I asked her, and said, Whose daughter art thou? And she said, The daughter of Bethuel, Nahor's son, whom Milcah bare unto him: and I put the earring upon her face, and the bracelets upon her hands.* [48]*And I bowed down my head, and worshipped the LORD, and blessed the LORD God of my master Abraham, which had led me in the right way to take my master's brother's daughter unto his son.* [49]*And now if ye will deal kindly and truly with my master, tell me: and if not, tell me; that I may turn to the right hand, or to the left.* [50]*Then Laban and Bethuel answered and said, The thing proceedeth from the LORD: we cannot speak unto thee bad or good.* [51]*Behold, Rebekah is before thee, take her, and go, and let her be thy master's son's wife, as the LORD hath spoken.* [52]*And it came to pass, that, when Abraham's servant heard their words, he worshipped the LORD, bowing himself to the earth.* [53]*And the servant brought forth jewels of silver, and jewels of gold, and raiment, and gave them to Rebekah: he gave also to her brother and to her mother precious things.*

Although Abraham's family did not participate in the covenant with Almighty God, they recognized the sovereign hand of God in their lives. As Abraham's servant explained the miracle that had occurred, they gave their blessing for Rebekah to return with him, to be married to Isaac. The servant gave them gifts that were quite valuable as well. This no doubt persuaded them as to Abraham's great wealth and the extent of God's blessing in his life.

As the family gave Rebekah into the hand of Abraham's servant, they also bestowed a blessing upon her. It is very interesting, because they did not pursue a covenant relationship with God. However, the blessing upon their daughter would be fulfilled many times over in coming years, after she and Isaac were married.

Genesis 24:59-61 [59]*And they sent away Rebekah their sister, and her nurse, and Abraham's servant, and his men.* [60]*And they blessed Rebekah, and said unto her, Thou art our sister, be thou the mother of thousands of millions, and let thy seed possess the gate of those which hate them.* [61]*And Rebekah arose, and her damsels, and they rode upon the camels, and followed the man: and the servant took Rebekah, and went his way.*

Did you read that? The prophecy to Rebekah was twofold:

- She would be the mother of thousands of millions;
- Her seed would possess the gate of those which hate them.

Rebekah had been blessed by Almighty God, and perhaps she did not yet realize it. But the blessing upon her was exactly like the one pronounced upon her soon-to-be-husband, Isaac.

When this is contrasted to the life of Ishmael, and his selection of a wife, the differences are stark in comparison. One sought out the heritage of his father; the other did not. One desired blessing from His Heavenly Father; the other did not. One took a Semite woman of the same heritage; the other did not. As a result we can understand this fact. God was guarding this covenant relationship. It would grow to be significant in the last days. Thousands of millions would come from Abraham's covenant line.

Genesis 24:62-67 [62]*And Isaac came from the way of the well Lahairoi; for he dwelt in the south country.* [63]*And Isaac went out to meditate in the field at the eventide: and he lifted up his eyes, and saw, and, behold, the camels were coming.* [64]*And Rebekah lifted up her eyes, and when she saw Isaac, she lighted off the camel.* [65]*For she had said unto the servant, What man is this that walketh in the field to meet us? And the servant had said, It is my master: therefore she took a veil, and covered herself.* [66]*And the servant told Isaac all things that he had done.* [67]*And Isaac brought her into his mother Sarah's tent, and took Rebekah, and she became his wife; and he loved her: and Isaac was comforted after his mother's death.*

The Next Generation

God has blessed Abraham with great wealth, an everlasting covenant, and a child that God Himself promised. But now it is time for the covenant blessing to be passed along. Genesis 25 brings out the fact that this covenant family is very imperfect. Yet God had His hand of direction in every event.

Genesis 25:7-10 *[7]And these are the days of the years of Abraham's life which he lived, an hundred threescore and fifteen years. [8]Then Abraham gave up the ghost, and died in a good old age, an old man, and full of years; and was gathered to his people. [9]And his sons Isaac and Ishmael buried him in the cave of Machpelah, in the field of Ephron the son of Zohar the Hittite, which is before Mamre; [10]The field which Abraham purchased of the sons of Heth: there was Abraham buried, and Sarah his wife.*

When Abraham was buried, he was buried in the land God had promised to him and to his seed forever. His sons Isaac and Ishmael were both there to bury him beside Sarah, his covenant wife. This second testimony to the occupation of the land once again proves the right of Abraham's seed to possess that land by inheritance.

Genesis 25:12-18 provides us with insight into Ishmael's life and death. As God promised (in Genesis 17), Ishmael brought forth twelve sons of his own. They migrated into the area of the Arab peninsula and it's adjacent lands near present-day Egypt. God kept His promise to Abraham regarding Ishmael, but he was not the promised, covenant son.

That Problem Shows Up Again

Genesis 25:19-26 *[19]And these are the generations of Isaac, Abraham's son: Abraham begat Isaac: [20]And Isaac was forty years old when he took Rebekah to wife, the daughter of Bethuel the Syrian of Padanaram, the sister to Laban the Syrian. [21]And Isaac entreated the LORD for his wife, because she was barren: and the LORD was entreated of him, and Rebekah his wife conceived. [22]And the children struggled together within her; and she said, If it be so, why am I thus? And she went to inquire of the LORD. [23]And the LORD said unto her, Two nations are in thy womb, and two manner of people shall be separated from thy bowels; and the one people shall be stronger than the other people; and the elder shall serve the younger. [24]And when her days to be delivered were fulfilled, behold, there were twins* *in her womb. [25]And the first came out red, all over like an hairy garment; and they called his name Esau. [26]And after that came his brother out, and his hand took hold on Esau's heel; and his name was called Jacob: and Isaac was threescore years old when she bare them.*

Isaac was 40 years old when he married Rebekah. However, just as Abraham and Sarah had struggled with barrenness in their marriage, so too did Isaac and Rebekah. This was not a short-term problem. Keep in mind the fact that Isaac was the covenant child. God had promised to Abraham and to Isaac that their seed would be as the stars of heaven and as the sand of the sea. God's blessing to Rebekah would be that she would be the mother of thousands of millions. Was God lying? No! He always keeps His Word. So, after more than 19 years of struggling with barrenness, Rebekah conceived.

Rebekah's pregnancy was anything but normal. (God seldom does things in a "normal" manner, because He wants to reveal His divine hand in our lives.) Through the years, Rebekah had obviously seen God bless her husband Isaac as he had prayed. So, she sought the Lord about the difficulties in her pregnancy. And God spoke to her.

- Two nations are in your womb.
- Two manner of people shall be separated from your bowels.
- The one shall be stronger than the other.
- The elder shall serve the younger.

Sure enough. When Rebekah discovered it was time to give birth, she also found herself giving birth . . . to twins! The first one came out. A son, red all over, like a hairy garment. He was named Esau. The second came out, another son. His hand took ahold of Esau's heel, while he was still coming out of the womb. His name was called Jacob.

- Esau means "rough" as in someone that handles life in a rough-and-tumble manner. Esau was also called "Edom," which means "Red" for his color. He was a red-man.
- Jacob means "heel catcher," because of his actions in grabbing Esau's heel as he emerged from the womb. This term of heel catcher became synonomous with the term "supplanter," or someone that takes the place of another. In current terms, he might be called "con artist."

Playing Favorites

Genesis 25:27-28 [27]*And the boys grew: and Esau was a cunning hunter, a man of the field; and Jacob was a plain man, dwelling in tents.* [28]*And Isaac loved Esau, because he did eat of his venison: but Rebekah loved Jacob.*

After 20 years of waiting for children, Isaac and Rebekah were undoubtedly overjoyed to have twin sons. But they both began to favor separate sons in their actions. Isaac loved the outdoors. He loved to work in the fields (Genesis 26:12-22). He even loved to go out and pray and meditate in the outoors (Genesis 24:62-63). Esau developed these tendencies as well, loving hunting, field work, and the outdoors. Jacob was called a "plain man." He was more gentle and preferred the indoors. Perhaps this endeared him to his mother Rebekah, and he became her favorite. This partisan favoring would cause trouble in the future.

Birthright For Sale

Genesis 25:29-34 [29]*And Jacob sod pottage: and Esau came from the field, and he was faint:* [30]*And Esau said to Jacob, Feed me, I pray thee, with that same red pottage; for I am faint: therefore was his name called Edom.* [31]*And Jacob said, Sell me this day thy birthright.* [32]*And Esau said, Behold, I am at the point to die: and what profit shall this birthright do to me?* [33]*And Jacob said, Swear to me this day; and he sware unto him: and he sold his birthright unto Jacob.* [34]*Then Jacob gave Esau bread and pottage of lentiles; and he did eat and drink, and rose up, and went his way: thus Esau despised his birthright.*

As the twin brothers continued to grow, they undoubtedly realized that God's blessing was upon their families. First, they were wealthy! In fact, by the standards of that era, they were wealthy beyond belief, and growing constantly richer. They had probably also been told by their parents of their miraculous births, and of the covenant that was carried by their family, passed down from God to their grandfather Abraham. That was the source of their blessing.

In every family there were two blessings that were given to the children. One was the birthright blessing, and the other was the prophetic blessing. This may not seem important to us, but it was critical to them (and it's more important to us today than we realize). The birthright blessing was given by rite of birth. If a family had four sons, the eldest son was entitled to a "double portion" of the material inheritance when the parents died. Therefore, in a family of 4 sons, the material possions would be divided into 5 equal portions. The eldest son would claim 2 portions by reason of his "birth-right." the remaining 3 sons would each receive one portion for themselves.

One day after Esau and Jacob were grown, Jacob was cooking in the tents. Esau had gone out hunting, but had not captured any game. Hungry and tired, he came into the tent, and Jacob's bean stew was smelling good! When Esau asked Jacob for a bowl of the beans, Jacob offered a deal. He would give the beans to Esau . . . if Esau would sell Jacob the birthright. This conniving deal would give Jacob two portions (out of three) of the material wealth of Isaac and Rebekah, when they died.

What did Esau think of this arrangement? Amazingly enough, he agreed to it. Thinking only with his natural appetites, he decided to give Jacob the bulk of the family inheritance.

- Esau cared less about his covenant blessings than he did his personal appetites.
- Esau sold away his future, for short-term provision.
- Esau wanted to get out and live in the fields, more than he wanted to cultivate and produce wealth and gain from them.
- Jacob was both strategic and conniving. He was looking toward the future.
- Jacob was showing his manipulative colors, even at this age. He would do anything to get what he wanted.
- Jacob would use this trait in the future to get even more of what he wanted.

God Reaffirms His Covenant With Isaac

Isaac and Rebekah were still somewhat nomadic in their lifestyles. Although God had promised the land of Canaan to Abraham and to His seed, Isaac continued to follow the best pasture and water for his herds. Genesis 26 speaks of a famine, and Isaac was tempted to travel to Egypt, to water his flocks and heards along the Nile River. But God had other directions for him.

Genesis 26:1-5 [1]*And there was a famine in the land, beside the first famine that was in the days of Abraham. And Isaac went unto Abimelech king of the Philistines unto Gerar.* [2]*And the LORD appeared unto him, and said, Go not down into Egypt; dwell in the land which I shall tell thee of:* [3]*Sojourn in this land, and I will be with thee, and will bless thee; for unto thee, and unto thy seed, I will give all these countries, and I will perform the oath which I sware unto Abraham thy father;* [4]*And I will make thy seed to multiply as the stars of heaven, and will give unto thy seed all these countries; and in thy seed shall all the nations of the earth be blessed;* [5]*Because that Abraham obeyed my voice, and kept my charge, my commandments, my statutes, and my laws.*

God spoke to Isaac during this time of famine, commanding Isaac to remain in the land He had provided. While everyone else would leave because of the famine, Isaac was commanded to stay. Here, God reiterated his covenant, and told Isaac that he would be blessed. God said:

- Stay in this land. I will be with you, and give this land, and all these countries to you and to your seed.
- I will make your seed to multiply as the stars of heaven.
- I will give these countries to your seed.
- In your seed shall all the nations of the earth be blessed.
- Because Abraham kept my statutes and obeyed me.

Notice how God's promise to Isaac compares to His promise to Abraham. Isaac would have the land. His seed would become innumerable. These things would happen in the future, to future generations. The blessing was due to the fact that Isaac was walking in Abraham's covenant with God. But God repeated Himself to Isaac just a matter of years later.

Genesis 26:23-24 [23]*And he went up from thence to Beersheba.* [24]*And the LORD appeared unto him the same night, and said, I am the God of Abraham thy father: fear not, for I am with thee, and will bless thee, and multiply thy seed for my servant Abraham's sake.*

God spoke to each generation more than once, so that His covenant blessing would be established. Under the covenant, Isaac and

Rebekah grew and prospered. Esau and Jacob also thrived under God's covenant. But once again a pattern emerged between the two that was very similar to the one that occurred between Ishmael and Isaac many years before.

Esau Takes Wives

Genesis 26:34-35 *[34]And Esau was forty years old when he took to wife Judith the daughter of Beeri the Hittite, and Bashemath the daughter of Elon the Hittite: [35]Which were a grief of mind unto Isaac and to Rebekah.*

Like Ishmael before him, Esau had a way of doing things on his own. There is no record of him seeking the counsel of his family in the matter of choosing a wife. When he selected his wives, he chose non-Semitic women. They were Hittites, of the tribes that lived in the land. They caused a great deal of bitterness and strife in the house with Isaac and Rebekah. Ultimately, Esau may have discovered the error of his ways. He later married a third wife (Genesis 28:8-9) that was a descendent of Ishmael, but even this was not pleasing to the family. Esau had begun to lose his grip on God's covenant blessing, because he didn't take the covenant seriously. He made decisions for himself alone.

Jacob Steals The Family Blessing

God did not bless Abraham and his family because they were perfect. Abraham failed several times in his walk with God as well as in the way he behaved in life. But he kept believing God and trusting Him. God was pleased with this. So when we read about his family, we will note the fact that the family was messed up in several areas! One area we alluded to previously was the problem that Isaac and Rebekah had, in playing favorites with their sons. Isaac preferred Esau, and Jacob was preferred by Rebekah. This was about to become a major problem within the family.

Genesis 27:1-4 *[1]And it came to pass, that when Isaac was old, and his eyes were dim, so that he could not see, he called Esau his eldest son, and said unto him, My son: and he said unto him, Behold, here am I. [2]And he said, Behold now, I am old, I know not the day of my death: [3]Now therefore take, I pray thee, thy weapons, thy quiver and thy bow, and go* *out to the field, and take me some venison;* [4]*And make me savoury meat, such as I love, and bring it to me, that I may eat; that my soul may bless thee before I die.*

Isaac had aged to the point that he was now going blind. He felt it was time to bestow the blessing upon his sons, and he intended to give the greater measure of blessing to Esau.

The Blessing

This blessing may seem insignificant to many today, but to Abraham and Isaac as carriers of the covenant, this prophetic blessing (or curse) was critical to their success or failure. They believed that when this time came, they would speak God's prophetic words directly to the heart of their children, and these words would carry onward infinitely into the generations that would succeed them. Normally this blessing was carried out with the entire family gathered around, and the patriarch (father) would call forth each of the children one-by-one. He would place his right hand upon their head or shoulder, and prophesy God's blessing or curse over their life and the lives of their children. It was a sacred time.

Isaac was preparing his heart. Despite Esau's headstrong ways, he wanted him to have God's greater blessing. Esau had despised the birthright and had chosen his wives indiscriminately. But because Isaac favored his eldest son, his judgment was clouded. Now he sent his son into the field to hunt a deer. He wanted to eat his favorite meal, Esau's prepared venison, before he blessed him. At this point Isaac was thinking only in this direction. It seems that no significant blessing was prepared for his second-son, Jacob.

The Con Game

Genesis 27:5-17 [5]*And Rebekah heard when Isaac spake to Esau his son. And Esau went to the field to hunt for venison, and to bring it.*

[6]*And Rebekah spake unto Jacob her son, saying, Behold, I heard thy father speak unto Esau thy brother, saying,* [7]*Bring me venison, and make me savoury meat, that I may eat, and bless thee before the LORD before my death.* [8]*Now therefore, my son, obey my voice according to that which I command thee.* [9]*Go now to the flock, and fetch me from thence two good kids of the goats; and I will make them savoury meat for thy father, such as*

he loveth: [10]*And thou shalt bring it to thy father, that he may eat, and that he may bless thee before his death.* [11]*And Jacob said to Rebekah his mother, Behold, Esau my brother is a hairy man, and I am a smooth man:* [12]*My father peradventure will feel me, and I shall seem to him as a deceiver; and I shall bring a curse upon me, and not a blessing.* [13]*And his mother said unto him, Upon me be thy curse, my son: only obey my voice, and go fetch me them.* [14]*And he went, and fetched, and brought them to his mother: and his mother made savoury meat, such as his father loved.* [15]*And Rebekah took goodly raiment of her eldest son Esau, which were with her in the house, and put them upon Jacob her younger son:* [16]*And she put the skins of the kids of the goats upon his hands, and upon the smooth of his neck:* [17]*And she gave the savoury meat and the bread, which she had prepared, into the hand of her son Jacob.*

But there was trouble in the tent! Rebekah heard Isaac call for Esau, and tell him of the plans to impart the prophetic blessing to him. But she loved Jacob more than Esau! She wanted him to have the blessing instead. Rebecca undoubtedly remembered the blessing that had been imparted to her by her family when she left to marry Isaac. She knew that God had given these children to them, and that God had told her that Jacob would be the son of destiny (while he was still in her womb). So, she decided to help God out.

Calling Jacob, she told him to get two goat kids, and bring them to her. She would prepare them in such a way that they would be loved by her husband, Isaac. Perhaps his sense of taste was impaired by this time and he could not discern between meats. Rebekah would also smuggle some of Esau's clothing to Jacob, and he would wear it in to serve meat to his father. But Jacob knew of a greater problem. You see, Esau was very hairy. Jacob was not. In fact, he was smooth and had very little body hair! If Isaac detected this con job, he would curse Jacob forever! Rebekah was so determined, she told Jacob that she would take any curse that was given to him upon her own life; so great was her determination to see Jacob receive this prophetic blessing. The game was on! And Jacob did as his mother commanded. Now it was time to take the meat into his blind father, Isaac.

Genesis 27:18-27 [18]*And he came unto his father, and said, My father: and he said, Here am I; who art thou, my son?* [19]*And Jacob said unto his father, I am Esau thy firstborn; I have done according as thou badest me: arise, I pray thee, sit and eat of my venison, that thy soul may bless me.*

[20]And Isaac said unto his son, How is it that thou hast found it so quickly, my son? And he said, Because the LORD thy God brought it to me. [21]And Isaac said unto Jacob, Come near, I pray thee, that I may feel thee, my son, whether thou be my very son Esau or not. [22]And Jacob went near unto Isaac his father; and he felt him, and said, The voice is Jacob's voice, but the hands are the hands of Esau. [23]And he discerned him not, because his hands were hairy, as his brother Esau's hands: so he blessed him. [24]And he said, Art thou my very son Esau? And he said, I am. [25]And he said, Bring it near to me, and I will eat of my son's venison, that my soul may bless thee. And he brought it near to him, and he did eat: and he brought him wine, and he drank. [26]And his father Isaac said unto him, Come near now, and kiss me, my son. [27]And he came near, and kissed him: and he smelled the smell of his raiment, and blessed him, and said, See, the smell of my son is as the smell of a field which the LORD hath blessed:

Jacob entered his father's tent and presented himself with the meat. Isaac was surprised. He wanted to know who it was. Jacob begins to lie.

- "I am Esau, your firstborn."
- "I did what you wanted me to do."
- "Get up. Eat my venison and bless me."

But Isaac is not so sure.

- "How is it that you were able to kill a deer so quickly?"

Jacob lies again.

- "Because the Lord your God (notice Jacob did not say that the Lord was his God at this point) brought it to me!"

Isaac is blind, but he is not foolish. He wants to check things out a bit more before he imparts the blessing to his son.

- "Come closer. I want to feel you. I know that you are a hairy man, and I want to make sure it is you, Esau."

Jacob came and perhaps knelt before his father. Isaac leaned forward. He feels the goatskin Rebekah has draped over Jacob's neck, and touches the backs of his hands. Rebekah has placed goatskin there, too. He is puzzled.

- "Your voice sounds like Jacob's voice, but your hands are like Esau's.
- "Are you Esau?"

Jacob replies.

- "I am."

Isaac now has Jacob serve him the food, which he eats with pleasure. Then he has Jacob come forward for one more test as he prepares to speak prophetic blessing over him. Isaac leans in and smells Jacob's clothes.

- "Yes, your clothes smell like the fields. You are a wilderness man, my son."

The fix is in.

The Covenant Blessing Imparted To Jacob

Genesis 27:28-29 [28]*Therefore God give thee of the dew of heaven, and the fatness of the earth, and plenty of corn and wine:* [29]*Let people serve thee, and nations bow down to thee: be lord over thy brethren, and let thy mother's sons bow down to thee: cursed be every one that curseth thee, and blessed be he that blesseth thee.*

The blessing Isaac now prophesies over Jacob is both brief and powerful. It is loaded with significance, and carries with it the framework of the entire covenant blessing God had bestowed upon Abraham and Isaac. In it God provides:

- blessings of nature with supernatural moisture and well-balanced growing seasons.

- excellent pasture and crop-lands. (This was essential to cultivate both food and wealth that the covenant people would need.)
- insulation from famine and desolation in every way.
- Other people would be servants to Jacob and to his seed.
- Nations would bow down and serve those that would come out of Jacob.
- Jacob would also be the Lord, or chief-ruler, over his brethren. (Isaac had obviously intended that Esau's lineage rule over Jacob and his line).
- Jacob's reach would also extend to rule over his mother's side of the family. In short, every people group in the world would have to bow down to Jacob's seed.
- Cursed be every one that curses you, and blessed is he that blesses you!

After receiving this powerful, prophetic word from his father, Jacob scrambles from the tent. He is now the most-blessed man in the world.

Esau Returns

Genesis 27:30-38 [30]*And it came to pass, as soon as Isaac had made an end of blessing Jacob, and Jacob was yet scarce gone out from the presence of Isaac his father, that Esau his brother came in from his hunting.* [31]*And he also had made savoury meat, and brought it unto his father, and said unto his father, Let my father arise, and eat of his son's venison, that thy soul may bless me.* [32]*And Isaac his father said unto him, Who art thou? And he said, I am thy son, thy firstborn Esau.* [33]*And Isaac trembled very exceedingly, and said, Who? where is he that hath taken venison, and brought it me, and I have eaten of all before thou camest, and have blessed him? yea, and he shall be blessed.* [34]*And when Esau heard the words of his father, he cried with a great and exceeding bitter cry, and said unto his father, Bless me, even me also, O my father.* [35]*And he said, Thy brother came with subtlety, and hath taken away thy blessing.* [36]*And he said, Is not he rightly named Jacob? for he hath supplanted me these two times: he took away my birthright; and, behold, now he hath taken away my blessing. And he said, Hast thou not reserved a blessing for me?* [37]*And Isaac answered and said unto Esau, Behold, I have made him thy lord, and all his brethren* *have I given to him for servants; and with corn and wine have I sustained him: and what shall I do now unto thee, my son?* [38]*And Esau said unto his father, Hast thou but one blessing, my father? bless me, even me also, O my father. And Esau lifted up his voice, and wept.*

No sooner had Jacob left, then Esau showed up! Blythely ignorant of his brother's treachery, Esau has located a deer, prepared the venison, and now enters the tent to serve his father. But Isaac's reaction lets him know immediately that he has been swindled by his own brother. Isaac's trembling words, questioning who he is, and asking about the person that was just in the tent receiving the blessing are enough.

Esau is torn to his very core. He has lived his entire life hearing about the covenant blessing, and as his father's favorite, he undoubtedly expected to be the chief recipient of its honor. Esau literally screams bitterly before his father. "Bless me, even me also, O my father."

Isaac's response is telling about the magnitude of the blessing Jacob now owns. He tells Esau that Jacob will be his lord and master, and Esau will serve him. He says that Jacob will be the one that has God's blessing for wealth and material goods. And it breaks Esau's heart.

The agony in the tent must have been unbearable. Isaac realizes that Jacob, the supplanter, is appropriately named. He has swindled Esau out of his birthright, and now he has taken his blessing as well. Esau, the rugged outdoorsman, lays before his father in the tent, broken and sobbing, begging his father for one prophetic blessing. And in this tragic scene, God speaks.

Genesis 27:39-40 [39]*And Isaac his father answered and said unto him, Behold, thy dwelling shall be the fatness of the earth, and of the dew of heaven from above;* [40]*And by thy sword shalt thou live, and shalt serve thy brother; and it shall come to pass when thou shalt have the dominion, that thou shalt break his yoke from off thy neck.*

Notice the promise God gives to Esau. He tells him:

- His dwelling shall be the fatness of the earth. Oil is a fatty substance. Could it be that much of the oil wealth and industry would come into the hands of Esau's seed?
- He would live under the dew of heaven from above. In other words, much of his existence would be outdoors, perhaps nomadic in nature.

- Esau's seed would be warlike, violent, and live by the sword. (NOTE: Esau would later marry a daughter of Ishmael, another warlike soul. Their union through the years would produce the very foundation for Islam; a religion that is based on conquest, the sword and war.)
- And when Esau has dominion, or domination in the world, he would break the yoke of Jacob's control and dominion over his lands and tribes.

Esau's blessing is nothing like Jacob's. However, it is significant and deserves attention in the prophetic realm. Through the prophecies given to Esau and Ishmael we see the emergence of the Islamic, Middle-East coalition that controls much of the world's oil production. These people still carry a hatred for Jacob's seed, and hate his dominion wherever it is. They long to control their own destiny and chart their own course. The roots of this relationship with the world were prophesied by God in a tent, with Isaac as God's spokesman.

The Plot To Kill Jacob

Genesis 27:41-45 *[41]And Esau hated Jacob because of the blessing wherewith his father blessed him: and Esau said in his heart, The days of mourning for my father are at hand; then will I slay my brother Jacob. [42]And these words of Esau her elder son were told to Rebekah: and she sent and called Jacob her younger son, and said unto him, Behold, thy brother Esau, as touching thee, doth comfort himself, purposing to kill thee. [43]Now therefore, my son, obey my voice; and arise, flee thou to Laban my brother to Haran; [44]And tarry with him a few days, until thy brother's fury turn away; [45]Until thy brother's anger turn away from thee, and he forget that which thou hast done to him: then I will send, and fetch thee from thence: why should I be deprived also of you both in one day?*

As you can imagine, the tension around the house was high after this event. Esau couldn't keep his hatred for his brother a secret, and told someone about his long-term plans. He knew that Isaac was old and feeble, and expected him to die soon. As soon as he was dead, Esau was going to kill Jacob. But once again word got back to Rebekah about Esau's plans. Once again, she hatched a plan of her own, and told Jacob about her intentions. She would send him away to her brother Laban's house, where she was raised. She would send him under the pretext of finding a proper wife, but it would actually be done to protect Jacob's life. It was time for her to go to her husband, Isaac.

Jacob Is Sent Away

Genesis 27:46 [46]*And Rebekah said to Isaac, I am weary of my life because of the daughters of Heth: if Jacob take a wife of the daughters of Heth, such as these which are of the daughters of the land, what good shall my life do me?*

It was true that Esau's wives were not liked by Isaac or Rebekah. But this was only a pretext. What would Isaac do with this information? He may not have seen Jacob since the swindled blessing had been given. How would he handle Jacob the next time they met? Would Isaac curse his youngest son? Would he shun him forever? God knew, but it was time that Jacob found out.

More Than Just A Story

Stories like this make for great reading. They are dramatic, filled with human pathos, and the characters are flawed. We must remember that these stories are true. God allowed these events to happen so that His covenant with Abraham and Isaac would continue on to the next generation. While Esau was casual about life (he treated his birthright, his marriages and perhaps other issues lightly), Jacob was not. He intensely craved the blessing, so much so, that he was willing to lie, cheat and steal to get it. While man looked on the outward appearance and natural birth order, God was looking in Jacob's heart. True, God would have to deal with Jacob. But in Jacob, God had the raw material that was needed to advance God's covenant forward.

This covenant blessing is not merely a casual thing to God, nor should it be to us. If we take the time to study this out, we will understand the fact that God's covenant with Abraham is still in effect today. Many Pastors use Isaac's words to Jacob when they refer to the Jews. They say that we will be blessed if we bless the Jews, and will be cursed if we curse them. Is this true? Is it relegated to the Jews alone? These are questions we need to answer in coming chapters. With that, let's move on.

CHAPTER 4

Israel Rising

Sometimes God doesn't seem to make sense. More than two thousand years after the fall of man, a man named Abram gets his attention. This man is a Shem-ite, a descendent of Shem (Noah's son), and also a descendent of Shem's progeny—Heber. Thus, he will be known as a Semite and a Hebrew. God also makes a covenant with Abram and changes his name to Abraham, which means "Father of a great multitude," or "Father of many nations." But in God's covenant with Abraham (and Sarah), He specifies that His covenant blessing will only be passed on through their son Isaac.

After Isaac reaches adulthood, God ratifies the original covenant with Isaac (not Esau), and becomes known as the God of Abraham and Isaac. Isaac and Rebekah marry and bear twin sons, Esau and Jacob. Esau is a rugged outdoorsman, his father's pride and joy. Jacob is mother's favorite and an indoorsman. He is also a swindler. But when it comes time for God's covenant blessing to be passed along, who gets it? Jacob!

You may wonder what this has to do with the United States of America and Bible prophecy, but it actually has a direct connection. We asked a few questions to begin chapter 3, and we haven't answered them yet. But our assumptions are these: in order for such a nation as America to exist, it must have the intentional help and blessing of Almighty God. It may even have connections to Jacob's personality, in that it may be a conniving and greedy people at times. But that does not change its identity or its origins. God deals with behavior over a period of time, with His covenant people. So, back to America. Where did this nation come from? What linkage does the Bible establish between ancient Israel and our present time? Let's continue to study in the book of beginnings, Genesis, and follow the path forward through history.

Doomed Or Not Doomed?

When we last left the covenant story, Jacob had just swindled his brother Esau out of the covenant blessing that was due him. Jacob had conned Esau out of the blessing of material prosperity, the birthright, a few years prior. But this covenant blessing was the big one! This was God's promise, the crown jewel of the family. Isaac had intended to pass it to Esau, but Jacob had taken advantage of his father's blindness. Pretending to be Esau, he crept into his father's tent and received the incredible prophecies of God, taking them for himself.

Esau was so angry with Jacob, he plotted to kill him. But Rebekah, their mother, had other plans. Jacob was her favorite, and she wanted to get him out of town. So she approached Isaac and requested that Jacob be sent away to her relatives. Isaac agreed. But there was still the matter of the con game. Would Isaac curse Jacob for his evil ways when they met? Would Jacob live the rest of his life under a curse?

Genesis 28:1-5 [1]*And Isaac called Jacob, and blessed him, and charged him, and said unto him, Thou shalt not take a wife of the daughters of Canaan.* [2]*Arise, go to Padanaram, to the house of Bethuel thy mother's father; and take thee a wife from thence of the daughters of Laban thy mother's brother.* [3]*And God Almighty bless thee, and make thee fruitful, and multiply thee, that thou mayest be a multitude of people;* [4]*And give thee the blessing of Abraham, to thee, and to thy seed with thee; that thou mayest inherit the land wherein thou art a stranger, which God gave unto Abraham.* [5]*And Isaac sent away Jacob: and he went to Padanaram unto Laban, son of Bethuel the Syrian, the brother of Rebekah, Jacob's and Esau's mother.*

Jacob must have trembled when his father sent for him. But what did Isaac do when they met? He blessed Jacob! According to Hebrew custom, Jacob knelt before his father and received God's blessing from Isaac! Isaac had known God his entire life. He met the God of the Covenant on a mountain of sacrifice, when his own father, Abraham, was prepared to offer him as a sacrifice before God! God intervened that day, and Isaac heard His voice. He knew that this covenant relationship with God was larger than His understanding. He understood that God had allowed Jacob to receive the full measure of blessing; not Esau. He was prepared to trust God.

Isaac blessed Jacob. Probably laying his hands upon Jacob's head or shoulders, he spoke God's blessing and covenant promises over his son. Then he commanded him to return to Rebekah's homeland and select a wife from his mother's family members. (Once again God was ensuring that the covenant would be guarded, even through marriage to fellow Semites.) Then Isaac pronounced a specific covenant blessing upon Jacob alone.

- God Almighty bless thee.
- May He make you fruitful and multiply you.
- You will be a multitude of people.
- The blessing of Abraham will be given to you by God, and to your seed with you.
- You will inherit the land God has promised to Abraham and His seed.

And with that, Isaac sent Jacob away. Undoubtedly Esau heard about the blessing and was troubled. He had already married two women from local tribes against his parent's wishes. Now, in an attempt to curry favor with his family he selected a third wife, one who was a descendent of Ishmael. But it did no good. Both the covenant blessing of Almighty God and the birthright blessing of material wealth had gone with Jacob.

What Does God Think?

Genesis 28:10-22 [10]*And Jacob went out from Beersheba, and went toward Haran.* [11]*And he lighted upon a certain place, and tarried there all night, because the sun was set; and he took of the stones of that place, and put them for his pillows, and lay down in that place to sleep.* [12]*And he dreamed, and behold a ladder set up on the earth, and the top of it reached to heaven: and behold the angels of God ascending and descending on it.* [13]*And, behold, the LORD stood above it, and said, I am the LORD God of Abraham thy father, and the God of Isaac: the land whereon thou liest, to thee will I give it, and to thy seed;* [14]*And thy seed shall be as the dust of the earth, and thou shalt spread abroad to the west, and to the east, and to the* *north, and to the south: and in thee and in thy seed shall all the families of the earth be blessed.* [15]*And, behold, I am with thee, and will keep thee in all places whither thou goest, and will bring thee again into this land; for I will not leave thee, until I have done that which I have spoken to thee of.*

[16]*And Jacob awaked out of his sleep, and he said, Surely the LORD is in this place; and I knew it not.* [17]*And he was afraid, and said, How dreadful is this place! this is none other but the house of God, and this is the gate of heaven.* [18]*And Jacob rose up early in the morning, and took the stone that he had put for his pillows, and set it up for a pillar, and poured oil upon the top of it.* [19]*And he called the name of that place Bethel: but the name of that city was called Luz at the first.* [20]*And Jacob vowed a vow, saying, If God will be with me, and will keep me in this way that I go, and will give me bread to eat, and raiment to put on,* [21]*So that I come again to my father's house in peace; then shall the LORD be my God:* [22]*And this stone, which I have set for a pillar, shall be God's house: and of all that thou shalt give me I will surely give the tenth unto thee.*

After Jacob departed from his family, he traveled by himself toward Haran. However, Jacob was far from alone. That night, God gave Jacob a divine dream. And He spoke to him about his destiny. The dream Jacob had consisted of a ladder reaching from earth to heaven, and the angels of God ascended and descended on this ladder. The messengers of God were in contact with Jacob! Then, God spoke!

- I am the Lord, God of Abraham your father, and the God of Isaac.
- The land where you are sleeping will be given to you and your seed.
- Your seed shall be as the dust of the earth.
- You shall spread abroad, north, south, east and west.
- In you and in your seed all the families of the earth shall be blessed!

Did you notice the consistent pattern? God's promise to Jacob is basically the same as He promised to Abraham and Isaac. But now it is expanded! Not only has God promised that physical land to Jacob's seed, but now He has stated that Jacob's seed would spread abroad. They would migrate and be a multitude of nations, just as God promised Abraham. The covenant would bless the world with material wealth and blessing through Jacob's seed. Not only has Isaac blessed his son, but God Himself has sanctioned and blessed Jacob as the bearer of His covenant. Despite his conniving ways, God sees Jacobs heart and has accepted him.

Jacob Responds To God

This dream scared Jacob so badly, he awoke! He called the place the house of God, and the gate of heaven. Obviously shaken, he knew that he must respond to God's blessing on his life.

- Jacob took one of the stones used for his sleeping area or pillow.
- He set it up and anointed it with oil as a pillar or pillow stone.
- He called it Beth-El, the House of God.
- He made a vow to God: if God will keep me and protect my way, and give me what I need to live so that I can return to my father's house in peace, the Lord shall be my God.
- This pillow stone shall be God's house, a symbol of the covenant.
- I will give ten percent of all my material goods to God as well.

The covenant promise has moved to the next generation! God has now ratified His covenant with Abraham, Isaac and Jacob. Each time it has become larger and more powerful. God will spend the next several years refining Jacob's life, but to God Almighty, Jacob is His chosen vessel. There is no other nation or people on earth that will be blessed like his seed.

Genesis 29:1-14 [1]*Then Jacob went on his journey, and came into the land of the people of the east.* [2]*And he looked, and behold a well in the field, and, lo, there were three flocks of sheep lying by it; for out of that well they watered the flocks: and a great stone was upon the well's mouth.* [3]*And thither were all the flocks gathered: and they rolled the stone from the well's mouth, and watered the sheep, and put the stone again upon the well's mouth in his place.* [4]*And Jacob said unto them, My brethren, whence be ye? And they said, Of Haran are we.* [5]*And he said unto them, Know ye Laban the son of Nahor? And they said, We know him.* [6]*And he said unto them, Is* *he well? And they said, He is well: and, behold, Rachel his daughter cometh with the sheep. [7]And he said, Lo, it is yet high day, neither is it time that the cattle should be gathered together: water ye the sheep, and go and feed them. [8]And they said, We cannot, until all the flocks be gathered together, and till they roll the stone from the well's mouth; then we water the sheep.*

[9]And while he yet spake with them, Rachel came with her father's sheep: for she kept them. [10]And it came to pass, when Jacob saw Rachel the daughter of Laban his mother's brother, and the sheep of Laban his mother's brother, that Jacob went near, and rolled the stone from the well's mouth, and watered the flock of Laban his mother's brother. [11]And Jacob kissed Rachel, and lifted up his voice, and wept. [12]And Jacob told Rachel that he was her father's brother, and that he was Rebekah's son: and she ran and told her father. [13]And it came to pass, when Laban heard the tidings of Jacob his sister's son, that he ran to meet him, and embraced him, and kissed him, and brought him to his house. And he told Laban all these things. [14]And Laban said to him, Surely thou art my bone and my flesh. And he abode with him the space of a month.

The journey from Canaan to Haran took several months, and was 8-900 miles in distance. When Jacob arrived he was treated like a king. Rebekah's brother Laban welcomed him immediately and began to speculate as to how he might put Jacob to work.

The Con Artist Is Conned Himself

Genesis 29:15-30 *[15]And Laban said unto Jacob, Because thou art my brother, shouldest thou therefore serve me for nought? tell me, what shall thy wages be? [16]And Laban had two daughters: the name of the elder was Leah, and the name of the younger was Rachel. [17]Leah was tender eyed; but Rachel was beautiful and well favoured. [18]And Jacob loved Rachel; and said, I will serve thee seven years for Rachel thy younger daughter. [19]And Laban said, It is better that I give her to thee, than that I should give her to another man: abide with me. [20]And Jacob served seven years for Rachel; and they seemed unto him but a few days, for the love he had to her. [21]And Jacob said unto Laban, Give me my wife, for my days are fulfilled, that I may go in unto her. [22]And Laban gathered together all the men of the place, and made a feast. [23]And it came to pass in the evening, that he took Leah his daughter, and brought her to him; and he went in unto her. [24]And Laban gave unto his daughter Leah Zilpah his maid for an* *handmaid. [25]And it came to pass, that in the morning, behold, it was Leah: and he said to Laban, What is this thou hast done unto me? did not I serve with thee for Rachel? wherefore then hast thou beguiled me? [26]And Laban said, It must not be so done in our country, to give the younger before the firstborn. [27]Fulfil her week, and we will give thee this also for the service which thou shalt serve with me yet seven other years. [28]And Jacob did so, and fulfilled her week: and he gave him Rachel his daughter to wife also. [29]And Laban gave to Rachel his daughter Bilhah his handmaid to be her maid. [30]And he went in also unto Rachel, and he loved also Rachel more than Leah, and served with him yet seven other years.*

When Laban discovered the fact that Jacob intended to stay in the region for a while, he began scheming. After all, his sister Rebekah (Jacob's mother) had helped Jacob con Isaac into blessing Jacob over Esau. It was in their blood, and Laban was no exception.

Jacob had become infatuated with Laban's youngest daughter, Rachel. She was a real beauty, and Jacob wanted to marry her. So he agreed to work for Laban for 7 years, in exchange for her hand in marriage. On the night of the marriage, there was undoubtedly music, dancing, and perhaps more than a little wine flowing. In the darkness and under the Middle-Eastern veils, Laban pulled a switch. Rachel's older sister Leah was not as lovely, and may not have had any suitors for her hand. It was Leah that Laban led to the marriage tent that night, and Jacob bought the lie in the darkness! After a night of marital bliss, presumably with Rachel, Jacob awoke to discover he had spent the night . . . with Leah! He was mad!

Storming out of the tent, Jacob confronted his new father-in-law. He accused Laban of intentionally deluding him, but Laban passed it off as a tribal custom. The older daughter must marry first, was his claim. But Jacob could have Rachel as his wife, too. He only needed to work another 7 years as a servant to Laban, to fulfill her pledge. Reluctantly, Jacob agreed.

Although God's hand of blessing was on Jacob's life, God did not intend to allow Jacob to continue to swindle and cheat his way into blessing. God promised to be his blessing, and that was enough. Jacob had moral sins in his life that had to be dealt with, and God was doing just that. For the next 20 years, God allowed Jacob to live in Laban's tents, and deal with the repercussions of his marriages to two sisters. Whew! Can you imagine what he was about to face?

Sibling Rivalry

Genesis 29:31-35 *[31]And when the LORD saw that Leah was hated, he opened her womb: but Rachel was barren. [32]And Leah conceived, and bare a son, and she called his name Reuben: for she said, Surely the LORD hath looked upon my affliction; now therefore my husband will love me. [33]And she conceived again, and bare a son; and said, Because the LORD hath heard that I was hated, he hath therefore given me this son also: and she called his name Simeon. [34]And she conceived again, and bare a son; and said, Now this time will my husband be joined unto me, because I have born him three sons: therefore was his name called Levi. [35]And she conceived again, and bare a son: and she said, Now will I praise the LORD: therefore she called his name Judah; and left bearing.*

God understands the thoughts and intents of the heart. Apparently God cared for Leah, despite the fact that Rachel was Jacob's favorite. So he opened Leah's womb. A wife that would bear children (especially sons) was considered a special blessing to a man. Jacob's firstborn did not come from Rachel but from Leah, and so did Jacob's next three sons. Isaac's prophecy over his son to be fruitful and multiply in his generation had been fulfilled. This was a token gesture by God that He was watching over Jacob and would fulfill His covenant with his seed.

Genesis 30:1-21 *[1]And when Rachel saw that she bare Jacob no children, Rachel envied her sister; and said unto Jacob, Give me children, or else I die. [2]And Jacob's anger was kindled against Rachel: and he said, Am I in God's stead, who hath withheld from thee the fruit of the womb? [3]And she said, Behold my maid Bilhah, go in unto her; and she shall bear upon my knees, that I may also have children by her. [4]And she gave him Bilhah her handmaid to wife: and Jacob went in unto her. [5]And Bilhah conceived, and bare Jacob a son. [6]And Rachel said, God hath judged me, and hath also heard my voice, and hath given me a son: therefore called she his name Dan. [7]And Bilhah Rachel's maid conceived again, and bare Jacob a second son. [8]And Rachel said, With great wrestlings have I wrestled with my sister, and I have prevailed: and she called his name Naphtali. [9]When Leah saw that she had left bearing, she took Zilpah her maid, and gave her Jacob to wife. [10]And Zilpah Leah's maid bare Jacob a son. [11]And Leah said, A troop cometh: and she called his name Gad. [12]And Zilpah Leah's maid bare Jacob a second son. [13]And Leah said, Happy am I, for the daughters will call me blessed: and she called his name Asher.*

[14]And Reuben went in the days of wheat harvest, and found mandrakes in the field, and brought them unto his mother Leah. Then Rachel said to Leah, Give me, I pray thee, of thy son's mandrakes. [15]And she said unto her, Is it a small matter that thou hast taken my husband? and wouldest thou take away my son's mandrakes also? And Rachel said, Therefore he shall lie with thee to night for thy son's mandrakes. [16]And Jacob came out of the field in the evening, and Leah went out to meet him, and said, Thou must come in unto me; for surely I have hired thee with my son's mandrakes. And he lay with her that night. [17]And God hearkened unto Leah, and she conceived, and bare Jacob the fifth son. [18]And Leah said, God hath given me my hire, because I have given my maiden to my husband: and she called his name Issachar. [19]And Leah conceived again, and bare Jacob the sixth son. [20]And Leah said, God hath endued me with a good dowry; now will my husband dwell with me, because I have born him six sons: and she called his name Zebulun. [21]And afterwards she bare a daughter, and called her name Dinah.

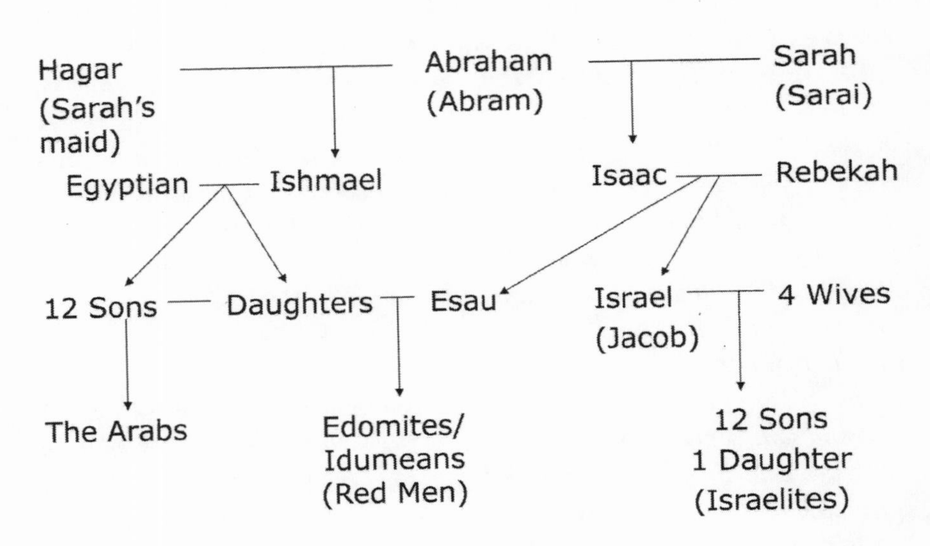

Jacob has a problem! His favorite wife Rachel is barren, while her older sister Leah (also Jacob's wife) is giving birth with no problem! So Rachel desperately approaches Jacob. "Give me children, or else I'm going to die," she demands! Jacob is no help at all. He gets mad. So Rachel begins a competition. She gives her handmaid Bilhah to Jacob as his wife/concubine, so that she can be a surrogate and perhaps Rachel can indirectly have children through her! But Leah is watching!

Leah decides that two can play that game. She gives her handmaid Zilpah to Jacob as a wife/concubine. Now Jacob has four wives, and has to keep them all satisfied. Within a very short period of time three of them are pregnant by Jacob, and his family is exploding! Soon, Jacob's family expands to a total of eleven children: 6 sons and a daughter by Leah, and two sons apiece from both Bilhah and Zilpah! The long-awaited prophecy of multiplication given to Abraham and Isaac is now being fulfilled, but Rachel is still barren.

Genesis 30:22-24 [22]*And God remembered Rachel, and God hearkened to her, and opened her womb.* [23]*And she conceived, and bare a son; and said, God hath taken away my reproach:* [24]*And she called his name Joseph; and said, The LORD shall add to me another son.*

Rachel was the woman that tended to cling to her father Laban's idolatrous ways. In fact, she would later steal her father's household idols when they moved, and take them with her (unbeknownst to Jacob). But her barrenness had brought her to a place of brokenness. Finally, she called on the Almighty God. When she did, God heard her, and gave her a son. She called his name Joseph. Rachel was thrilled, but knew that God would give her another child as well. This was her claim before Almighty God. But until that time, Joseph became Jacob's favorite out of his 11 sons.

Jacob's Business Ventures

Jacob spent fourteen years working as an indentured servant to his father-in-law, Laban. Now that his time was through, he wanted to return to his father's house. Laban had other ideas. He persuaded Jacob to remain and manage his flocks and herds. Jacob agreed to do this for a price. He would take the speckled and grizzled animals. (It was thought at that time that solid-colored animals were stronger genetically.) Laban agreed. During the next seven years, Jacob managed the herds and engineered their breeding cycles so that his animals were stronger and larger than Laban's. Jacob's wealth increased as Laban's herds languished. (Genesis 30:25-43) God's covenant blessing was being revealed in Jacob's children and in his physical wealth. But his spirit was still conniving and deceitful.

Genesis 31:1-3; 13 [1]*And he heard the words of Laban's sons, saying, Jacob hath taken away all that was our father's; and of that which was our father's hath he gotten all this glory.* [2]*And Jacob beheld the countenance of Laban, and, behold, it was not toward him as before.* [3]*And the LORD said unto Jacob, Return unto the land of thy fathers, and to thy kindred; and I will be with thee.*

[13]*I am the God of Bethel, where thou anointedst the pillar, and where thou vowedst a vow unto me: now arise, get thee out from this land, and return unto the land of thy kindred.*

Through the years, Laban's sons (and Jacob's brothers-in-law) became increasingly angry at Jacob's business dealings. They saw their father's fortunes (and their inheritance) declining, and Jacob's wealth increasing. Jacob started to hear the rumbles of discontent. It was then that he also heard the voice of God once again. God commanded Jacob to return to his Father Isaac's house after more than 20 years away. God also promised Jacob that it would be well.

Jacob presented this to his wives, and they consented to go with Jacob. They knew God's blessing was with Jacob. Rachel's prayers for a child had been answered, and everything Jacob touched was blessed. They also acknowledged their father's cutthroat and deceptive ways, in selling them and spending their dowries. They were ready to go. (Genesis 31:14-16)

Once again Jacob decided to try and play the role of deceiver. He didn't tell Laban he was going; he merely left when Laban was out in the fields himself. When Laban found out his general manager had absconded with his daughters and possibly with some of his herds, he was enraged. He set off in hot pursuit. However, God appeared to Laban in a dream and commanded him to treat Jacob kindly. This forced Laban into a corner, and he parted company with Jacob in peace. But before they parted, there was one issue that had to be resolved. Laban's household idols were missing!

Jacob may have been a deceiver, but he was not an idolator. He claimed to worship Almighty God alone, so he emphatically denied all wrongdoing. Unbeknownst to Jacob, however, Rachel had stolen them! She hid them in her tent, and sat on them when her father searched the premises, claiming to be in the middle of her menstrual time. Laban never found the idols, and Rachel kept them. And in the end, Laban bade his daughters farewell and returned home.

Jacob Faces Himself

Genesis 32:1-8 [1]*And Jacob went on his way, and the angels of God met him.* [2]*And when Jacob saw them, he said, This is God's host: and he called the name of that place Mahanaim.*

[3]*And Jacob sent messengers before him to Esau his brother unto the land of Seir, the country of Edom.* [4]*And he commanded them, saying, Thus shall ye speak unto my lord Esau; Thy servant Jacob saith thus, I have sojourned with Laban, and stayed there until now:* [5]*And I have oxen, and asses, flocks, and menservants, and womenservants: and I have sent to tell my lord, that I may find grace in thy sight.* [6]*And the messengers returned to Jacob, saying, We came to thy brother Esau, and also he cometh to meet thee, and four hundred men with him.* [7]*Then Jacob was greatly afraid and distressed: and he divided the people that was with him, and the flocks, and herds, and the camels, into two bands;* [8]*And said, If Esau come to the one company, and smite it, then the other company which is left shall escape.*

As Jacob was on the road, God made sure he started to encounter signs that He was going ahead of him. So God allowed Jacob to encounter angels, heavenly messengers of God. Jacob acknowledged this, and decided to try and put out feelers to see how his brother Esau would receive him after all of those years apart. Jacob's message was conciliatory and humble. But what he received back was enough to make him run. Esau was coming to meet him, but he was bringing 400 men with him. This sounded like war!

Although God had assured Jacob that He was going ahead of him, Jacob tried to manipulate things once again. He divided his flocks, herds, and even the families that were with him. He split them up into smaller groups so that if one group was attacked, the others would be far enough away from the battle to escape. He had it figured out . . . or so he thought.

Genesis 32:9-12 [9]*And Jacob said, O God of my father Abraham, and God of my father Isaac, the LORD which saidst unto me, Return unto thy country, and to thy kindred, and I will deal well with thee:* [10]*I am not worthy of the least of all the mercies, and of all the truth, which thou hast showed unto thy servant; for with my staff I passed over this Jordan; and* *now I am become two bands. [11]Deliver me, I pray thee, from the hand of my brother, from the hand of Esau: for I fear him, lest he will come and smite me, and the mother with the children. [12]And thou saidst, I will surely do thee good, and make thy seed as the sand of the sea, which cannot be numbered for multitude.*

Finally, in desperation, Jacob did the thing he had avoided for years. He prayed. His plea to God is wonderful in its design.

- Jacob reminded God that He was the God of Abraham and Isaac, his predecessors.
- He also reminded God that he was obeying His command in returning to the land. God had also assured Jacob that things would go well, and Jacob wanted God to remember that!
- Then Jacob humbled himself before God and stated his unworthiness. The con artist was feeling the pressure of the moment.
- He asked for God to deliver him from Esau's hand. "I fear him," Jacob confessed.
- Then Jacob reminded God of His covenant promise. "God, you said you would do good to me and make my seed as the sand of the sea." He was holding God to His Word.

Ever the strategist, Jacob then arose from prayer and decided to create a "present" for his brother, Esau. He elaborately staged several groups of servants to meet Esau before Jacob and the family came on the scene. Each of these servants was to present Esau with a flock of rams, camels, asses . . . the list was tremendous. It was all designed to soften the heart of Esau. This was the advance party Esau would meet the next day. Finally Jacob took his wives, eleven sons and servants and forded at Jabbok. But he was still self-serving. He re-crossed the stream and remained on the other side, alone. He had as much natural protection between himself and Esau as possible. But God wanted Jacob's heart.

Genesis 32:24-31 *[24]And Jacob was left alone; and there wrestled a man with him until the breaking of the day. [25]And when he saw that he prevailed not against him, he touched the hollow of his thigh; and the hollow of Jacob's thigh was out of joint, as he wrestled with him. [26]And he said, Let me go, for the day breaketh. And he said, I will not let thee* *go, except thou bless me.* [27]*And he said unto him, What is thy name? And he said, Jacob.* [28]*And he said, Thy name shall be called no more Jacob, but Israel: for as a prince hast thou power with God and with men, and hast prevailed.* [29]*And Jacob asked him, and said, Tell me, I pray thee, thy name. And he said, Wherefore is it that thou dost ask after my name? And he blessed him there.* [30]*And Jacob called the name of the place Peniel: for I have seen God face to face, and my life is preserved.* [31]*And as he passed over Penuel the sun rose upon him, and he halted upon his thigh.*

When Jacob was left alone, God met Him there. There came "a man," that wrestled with Jacob. This man was no ordinary man, because he had the stamina to literally wrestle all night. Jacob's night before meeting with Esau was completely sleepless, and filled with exhausted travail. Finally the man "touched" the hollow of Jacob's thigh and knocked it out of joint. Then the unknown man told Jacob to let him go, but Jacob was desperate!

"I will not let you go," he gasps. "I will not let you go unless you bless me." Jacob knows that this man is supernatural, and he is determined to receive God's blessing at all costs.

"What is your name?" comes the voice.

"Jacob." Supplanter. Con artist. That's who Jacob was, and the full measure of his nature. But his heart was still focused on one thing, walking in covenant with God.

"Your name shall no more be called Jacob." You will no longer be a con man.

"Your name shall be called Israel, for as a prince you have power with God and with men, and you have prevailed."

Several significant points are worth noting from this edict.

- **First**, it came from God Himself. God saw through Jacob's nature and knew his tenacity of spirit. Esau had been too casual in claiming God's covenant. Jacob wanted it at all costs.
- **Second**, Israel had power with God. He had gained God's respect because of his ferocious spirit.
- **Third**, God recognized that He was giving Israel and his seed power with mankind, too. Israel's seed would dominate world events as they grew, and this would become more obvious in the last days.

- **Finally**, Jacob had prevailed. His sons would not be known as the sons of Jacob, the con man. Instead, they would be known as the sons of Israel, the prince with God.

As the sun arose and Jacob (or Israel) rose to cross the brook one more time, he was a changed man. He walked with a limp for the rest of his life. It would be a sign of his utter dependence on God alone. Israel would never play the con game again. His character had been reborn. He had been with God. The tribes of Israel would bear his name more than the name of Abraham and Isaac. And they would also be beneficiaries of the blessing.

The Reunion

When Israel and Esau met together in Genesis 33, the reunion was warm and poignant. Esau's men may have been armed for war, but they came in peace. Esau's embrace sealed their reconciliation and the past was put behind them. Esau was still nomadic, and didn't stick around for long. Israel traveled more slowly, to care for the family and the flocks. Arriving in Succoth, Israel built a house and purchased property as his grandfather Abraham before him. (The inhabitants of that day are long-gone, but the sons of Israel still hold title deed to that property and the land around it as proclaimed by Almighty God.)

The turnaround story of Jacob is marked by one significant verse. In Genesis 33:20, Israel did something significant. He had built an altar to God at Bethel when they first met, but had not worshipped God since that time. He was now back in the land God had promised to His seed forever. And he built an alter to God. Was it the God of Abraham and Isaac? No. He called the altar "Ele-lohe-Israel." It meant "God, the God of Israel." God wasn't just for Abraham and Isaac any more. He was now the God of Israel! The covenant had been passed.

Sowing And Reaping

Israel's family had grown up, led by a conniving, scheming father. Galatians 6:7 states, *"Be not deceived; God is not mocked; for whatsoever a man soweth, that shall he also reap."* Israel was now in a covenant relationship with God, but he also had some reaping to do.

Jacob's daughter Dinah was a beautiful woman. Genesis 34 deals with an incident in her life when she was forcibly raped by a Caananite man that lusted after her, and then wanted to marry her. Jacob's sons agreed to the marriage as long as the Caananite tribe was circumcised. The tribe agreed. But while they were healing, Jacob's two sons Simeon and Levi went in and slaughtered all of the men in the tribe to avenge the rape of their sister. This wasn't the only trial Jacob would face in dealing with his family. In fact, the trouble was only beginning, as we shall see.

God Ratifies His Covenant With Israel

Genesis 35:1-4 *[1]And God said unto Jacob, Arise, go up to Bethel, and dwell there: and make there an altar unto God, that appeared unto thee when thou fleddest from the face of Esau thy brother. [2]Then Jacob said unto his household, and to all that were with him, Put away the strange gods that are among you, and be clean, and change your garments: [3]And let us arise, and go up to Bethel; and I will make there an altar unto God, who answered me in the day of my distress, and was with me in the way which I went. [4]And they gave unto Jacob all the strange gods which were in their hand, and all their earrings which were in their ears; and Jacob hid them under the oak which was by Shechem.*

God was taking Jacob (or Israel) back to Bethel, the House of God. This was the place of the stone, where God had met with Jacob as he fled from Esau. God commanded Jacob to return and dwell there, and Jacob obeyed. Jacob also commanded every member of his household to purify their lives in preparation for the journey. They:

- Gave all of their idols to Jacob, to be destroyed;
- Gave Jacob all of their earrings (signs of slavery and attachment to other cultures and religions);
- Changed their garments into fresh, clean clothing, and bathed in preparation for going to Bethel, the House of God.

Jacob built an altar at Bethel (verse 7), and called it "El-Bethel," which means "The God of Bethel." His entire life now revolved around worship of Almighty God, and once again God Himself met with Jacob in that place.

Genesis 35:9-15 [9]*And God appeared unto Jacob again, when he came out of Padanaram, and blessed him.* [10]*And God said unto him, Thy name is Jacob: thy name shall not be called any more Jacob, but Israel shall be thy name: and he called his name Israel.* [11]*And God said unto him, I am God Almighty: be fruitful and multiply; a nation and a company of nations shall be of thee, and kings shall come out of thy loins;* [12]*And the land which I gave Abraham and Isaac, to thee I will give it, and to thy seed after thee will I give the land.* [13]*And God went up from him in the place where he talked with him.* [14]*And Jacob set up a pillar in the place where he talked with him, even a pillar of stone: and he poured a drink offering thereon, and he poured oil thereon.* [15]*And Jacob called the name of the place where God spake with him, Bethel.*

Each time God spoke to Abraham and Isaac, He did so at least twice. We made mention of this in chapter 3, because God always witnesses His covenant in the mouth of two or three. Jacob was no exception. At Bethel, God reiterated His covenant blessing upon Jacob, and once again spoke His new name; Israel!

- Your name is Jacob, but you shall no longer be called that name.
- Your name is now Israel. Prince with God.
- God called his name Israel.

God then gives several more promises to Israel.

- He commands them to be fruitful and multiply. This promise will extend beyond each of the sons, into their progeny.
- IMPORTANT! A nation (singular) and a company of nations (plural) shall be of you!
- Israelites will not be a small enough group to fit into one nation alone! There will be a singular nation! However, there will also be a company, or a cluster, or nations that will be Israelite in heritage. Each of these groups will possess God's covenant blessing!
- Kings shall come out of Israel as well.
- The land of Canaan will become a possession of Israel, as a promise from Almighty God Himself.

Israel is so stirred by God's promise to him that once again he raises up a pillar stone and anoints it. He calls the name of this place, and this pillar stone, Bethel. It is the house of God.

Too Large To Ignore

Do you understand the magnitude of this covenant God was establishing through Abraham, Isaac and Israel? God jealously protected it, and promised it would be established only through certain people. These people would be blessed under God's hand. They would grow to such an extent that the blessing of God could not be contained within one people or nation alone.

Let's fast forward to today for a moment. There are many people today that insist that all of God's natural blessing and covenant commitment is toward the Jews alone. However, this cannot be true! God would have to have lied in Genesis 35. He said Himself that His covenant blessing would spawn more than one nation. God also said that the magnitude of Israel's influence would be larger than could be grasped in one small segment of the world. If this is the case, what has happened to God's covenant blessing today? Who possesses it? How did it get there? What is God doing with it today? Let's study further.

Rachel Dies

Genesis 35:16-20 *16And they journeyed from Bethel; and there was but a little way to come to Ephrath: and Rachel travailed, and she had hard labour. 17And it came to pass, when she was in hard labour, that the midwife said unto her, Fear not; thou shalt have this son also. 18And it came to pass, as her soul was in departing, (for she died) that she called his name Benoni: but his father called him Benjamin. 19And Rachel died, and was buried in the way to Ephrath, which is Bethlehem. 20And Jacob set a pillar upon her grave: that is the pillar of Rachel's grave unto this day.*

Not only did God bless Israel with a new name at Bethel, but He also granted him another son. Rachel was pregnant once again, with her second child. The family journeyed from Bethel, but had to stop because Rachel was in hard labor. As the midwife helped to deliver the child, Rachel named her newborn son with her last breath. "Benoni." Son of my sorrow. Israel would intervene moments later with a new name: "Benjamin." Son of the right hand.

Rachel was Israel's favorite wife. She was beautiful and closest to his heart. But she was also the one that clung to her father's idols the longest. She also clung to natural means rather than God. Sadly, Rachel was the first to die. Israel honored her death with a pillar, a gravestone near present-day Bethlehem.

Firstborn Failure

Genesis 35:21-22 [21]*And Israel journeyed, and spread his tent beyond the tower of Edar.* [22]*And it came to pass, when Israel dwelt in that land, that Reuben went and lay with Bilhah his father's concubine: and Israel heard it. Now the sons of Jacob were twelve:*

One of the interesting patterns that occurred in the covenant family was the repeated failure of the firstborn son. Ishmael was rejected because of his rebellious ways, as was Esau. Reuben was the firstborn son of Israel, born to Leah his wife. Israel also had two handmaid/wives that had been given to him years earlier, and had two sons by each woman. Now Reuben lusted after Bilhah and lay with her. Israel heard about this and it incurred his wrath. Later in Genesis 49, Reuben would pay for his sin against his father.

The Twelve Sons Of Israel

In Israel's mind, his family is complete. He has twelve sons and one daughter. God had further plans that were to be revealed in coming days, but the foundation of the tribes of Israel had been laid. These men would be the recipients to varying degrees of God's covenant blessing.

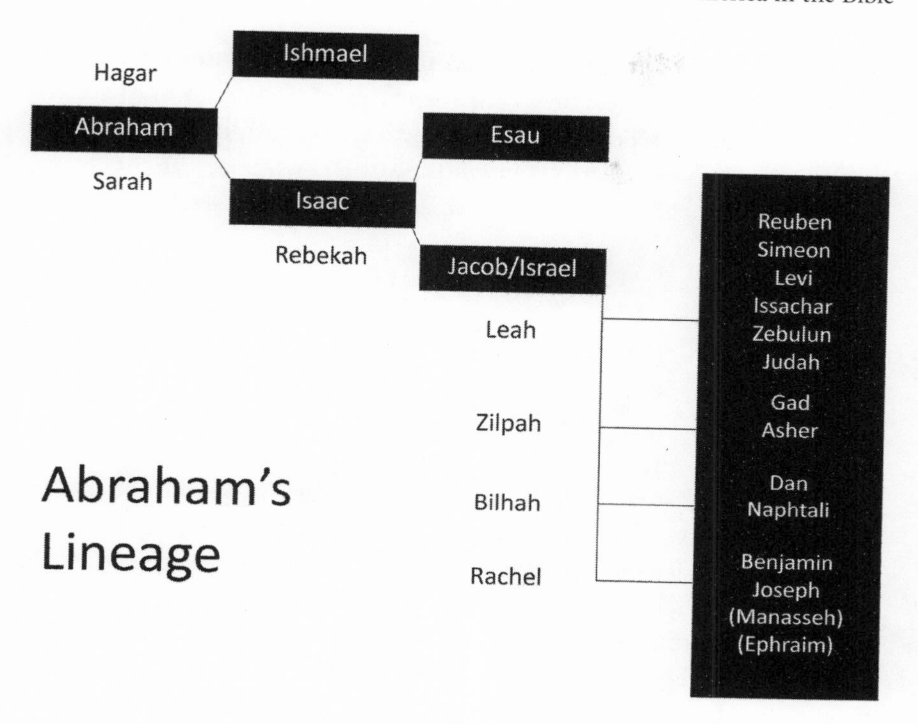

Summary Statements About The Covenant

Before we move ahead, let's look back at some of the incredible promises God has made about His covenant with mankind.

- It is to Abraham's seed, found solely fulfilled in Isaac (Genesis 21:12; Genesis 22:1-2).
- Isaac, in turn, passed it on to Jacob (Israel).
- The covenant people would inherit the land of Canaan (Genesis 12:6-7; Genesis 13:14-15; Genesis 17:8).
- Abraham's seed (in Israel) would grow so large that they would spread abroad (Genesis 28:14).
- Abraham's covenant seed would be many nations (nationalities, ethnic groups, gentiles) (Genesis 17:4,5,6,16; Genesis 35:11).
- They shall be as the stars of the sky, as the sand of the sea (Genesis 13:16; Genesis 15:5; Genesis 22:16-17).

Based on what we have learned in Genesis 35 alone, somewhere in the world today there is a "company" of nations that are literally, physically "Israel's seed!" There must be a literal fulfillment of this, or the Word of God is declared invalid. So then, who are they? Can we know? Yes, we can! Let's go on and discover who they are!

Joseph's Story

The story of Israel's son, Joseph, could fill a book by itself. We will summarize his story since it covers several chapters of Genesis. It is worth reading for several reasons. The issue we will pursue is God's covenant thread through Israel's generations.

Chapter 37 Joseph was the oldest of the two sons borne by Rachel. These two boys were their father's favorites, which the other brothers hated. Israel even had an expensive multi-colored coat made for Joseph, which he wore everywhere. Joseph also dreamed and interpreted dreams. This was apparently a gift from God which made the other brothers hate him even further! Joseph had two dreams that were obvious in their meanings. According to him, God would cause his family including all of his brothers to bow down before him. While his father mildly rebuked him for seeming arrogance, the rest of the brothers despised him for it.

One day, while herding sheep out in the field, the other brothers saw Joseph approaching. Seeing that nobody else was around, they stripped him of his coat, threw him in a pit and plotted to kill him. However, at that time some Midianite traders happened by. Judah suggested they sell Joseph as a slave, pocket the money, dip the coat in blood (to show their father, indicating that Joseph had been killed by a wild animal), and go on. This, they did. The Midianites, in turn, took Joseph into Egypt where they sold him to Potiphar, one of Pharoh's chief men. In their minds, Joseph's dreams were dead.

Judah's Strange Affair

Genesis 38 All of Israel's sons were growing up, and it was obvious they had come from a dysfunctional household. However, God would still flow through them because of His promises to Abraham, Isaac and Israel. Judah was Israel's youngest son borne by his wife, Leah. Now grown, Judah was establishing his own friendships, and befriended Hirah, who lived near Adullam. He also cast his eyes on a local woman of Canaan and had three sons by her: Er, Onan, and Shelah.

By the time we pick up Joseph's story (Genesis 37), Er was a grown man. Judah had picked out his wife from the region where they lived, a woman named Tamar. But the Bible says that Er was wicked, and God killed him! Tamar was now a widow. It was customary that if a woman were widowed, it was the responsibility of his brother to marry her and raise up the lineage. So, Onan reluctantly married Tamar. However, he did not want to have a child by Tamar, because they would be considered "Er's lineage," instead of his own. Onan's rebellion displeased God as well, and Onan died! Now Tamar was widowed twice, after being married to two brothers!

Judah was perplexed. He should have given his youngest son Shelah to Tamar as a husband, but his first two sons had married her and had died. He didn't want to do it. So he made an "excuse," much like his uncle Laban would have done years before. He told Tamar that Shelah was still "too young" to marry. And he sent Tamar home to her father.

After a period of time, Judah's wife died. He mourned for a while and then decided to visit his friend Hiram again. He set out toward Timnath with his sheep-shearers. In the meantime, Tamar had received news of her own, while living as a widow in her father's house. Shelah was now old enough to be married to her, but Judah had "conveniently forgotten." Hearing that Judah was coming into the area, Tamar hatched a scheme of her own. She laid aside her widow's garments, and dressed herself as a prostitute. (Prostitutes covered their faces, to conceal their identities.)

When Judah came down the road to Timnath, there she sat. Waiting. Judah decided he would take advantage of the situation and have a dalliance with this unknown woman. He would pay her well, he said, but he had no payment with him. As collateral, the veiled woman mysteriously offered a deal. She would hold Judah's signet, bracelets and staff, which were the equivalent of his authority. When she was paid, she would return these items. Judah agreed.

After this brief tryst Judah blithely went on his way, sending payment back by the hand of one of his servants. The servant returned with some distracting news. The woman was gone. He had searched, but there were no prostitutes to be found in the area. Judah's signet ring, his bracelets and his staff were also missing. What had happened to the harlot?

Three Months Later

After the shearing season, Judah returned to his tents. Then, disturbing news reached his ears. His daughter-in-law, Tamar, was pregnant! This was a slander to Judah's name of the highest degree. He had not given Shelah, his youngest son, to Tamar as a husband. However, he believed she was completely in the wrong. This child by an unknown father would likely carry on Judah's name, and he was enraged. "Bring her forth, and let her be burned," Judah commanded!

Tamar approached her father-in-law boldly. Was she pregnant? Yes! Had she played the role of harlot. Absolutely! Did she know the father of her child? To Judah's astonishment, she knew his name. She had proof of his identity. With a flourish she produced the evidence. It was a signet ring, bracelets, and a staff! Judah must have been astonished, but he had been caught!

"She has been more righteous than me," he stated. Tamar had remained more faithful to bring forth the covenant lineage than Judah himself. He had avoided giving Shelah his youngest son in marriage to Tamar, and she knew it. But she also knew it was her role to carry forth the family name. Judah did not continue to have marital relations with Tamar, but he accepted her completely. But there was yet another discovery to be made.

Red-Handed

When Tamar finally went into labor the midwife discovered an astonishing fact. Tamar was about to give birth to twins! In the closing moments of delivery, one of the twins pushed his hand through the birth canal and into the world. Excited, the midwife tied a deep red thread around his hand to indicate he had come first. Then the infant hand withdrew! Travail was not yet complete! At last, a baby's head crowned. Pushing into the light, Judah's first grandchild emerged. It was a son! But there was no thread upon his wrist! The one who would be first had been pushed aside! This son was immediately named

"Pharez," which means "a breach" or "a breaking forth." He had broken forth first.

Then the second child emerged, another son. His wrist was fastened with the scarlet thread, but he would not have the blessing of the firstborn son. He was named Zarah, which means "brightness," or "East." Pharez would carry on the blessing of the tribe of Judah. Out of his lineage would spring the kings of the Jews including David, Solomon, and ultimately Jesus Christ, the King of kings.

Zarah would bring forth blessing of his own. His seed would move westward, establishing realms like Zaragossa (Stronghold of Zarah) and Iberia (Land of the Hebrews), before moving north and west again. The people of the red hand would play a pivotal role in history as they met their brothers' seed again in future days.

2 Timothy 3:16a says, *"All Scripture is given by inspiration of God . . ."* Other translations specify graphically that every bit of Scripture is *"God-breathed."* Is this strange story inspired? We must accept God's statement. Yes, it is. What role does it play? First, it paves the way for the covenant lineage of the House of Judah in future days. But it also blazes a trail to the West, where at some point Israel's seed would dwell. It is more than a fable; God put it in His Scriptures for you and me to understand.

Back To Joseph

Genesis 39 Judah was the brother that sold his half-brother Joseph into slavery. The Midianite traders took Joseph into Egypt, where they sold him to the captain of Pharaoh's guard, Potiphar. Stripped of his coat, his title and his family, Joseph's value to the world was relegated to his physical skills and intelligence. However, Genesis 39 states that God was with Joseph. He prospered even as a slave, and quickly rose through the ranks to oversee everything Potiphar had.

Potiphar's wife was paying attention, too. Joseph was young, handsome, and attractive to her. Furthermore, he was a slave, and her husband was master. She seduced Joseph, enticing him with her words and actions day after day. One day she caught him in the house, alone. When she pressed him, Joseph ran from the house leaving his coat in her grasp. Rejected and angry, she framed Joseph. She accused him of attempting to rape her, when the truth was actually the opposite! It was her word against Joseph's statement. Mistress of the household versus slave. Potiphar had no choice but to believe her.

He threw Joseph into Pharaoh's prison, where the enemies of the king were kept. But again, the Lord was with Joseph. He quickly rose through the ranks within the prison, to become second in charge under the hand of the warden. He may have thought at times that God had forgotten him, but the Lord was grooming him for greater things. Joseph's story is the significant story of his generation. His eleven brothers played varying roles in God's unfolding drama, but God had something significant in store for Joseph and his children. It would play a role in fulfilling God's covenant; a role that is significant even to this day.

Dreams In An Egyptian Jail

The prison gates clanged shut behind two new prisoners, and the jail was abuzz with theories. Pharaoh's chief butler and chief baker were in shackles, and since they were the king's official food-tasters, there may have been an attempted coup to subvert the throne by poisoning him. We don't know for sure, but we do know they were committed to Joseph's hand for safekeeping. Then the dreams began.

The chief butler and the chief baker each had a dream that night, but neither of them understood the meaning of what they dreamt. As Joseph approached them, both men were glum and Joseph enquired as to the reasons for their dismay. When told, the solution was obvious to Joseph. Dreams are from God! He can give the dream, and He also gives the interpretation. This explanation opened the hearts of both men, and they recounted their dreams to Joseph. Joseph did not cloak God's interpretations in politically correct terms. The chief butler would be reinstated to his role, Joseph stated. However, the chief baker would die. "Remember me," Joseph pleaded with the butler. "Don't forget me when you are reinstated. I have done nothing wrong." But forget the butler did, and Joseph spent at least another year languishing in jail.

Breakthrough!

Genesis 41 After two full years in prison, Joseph's breakthrough came. This time it was Pharaoh that did the dreaming. He dreamed two similar dreams, and not one of his advisors, priests or soothsayers could tell him what they meant. Finally, the butler remembered! The man in the jail! What was his name? Joseph! Carefully, the butler approached Pharaoh with his news. There was a man that could interpret dreams, and he was very close at hand. He was a prisoner, wrongly imprisoned, and he had told the truth before about his own dream. This was enough information for Pharaoh, who commanded for Joseph to come.

Once again the gates to the prison clattered open, but this time Joseph was summoned to the palace of Pharaoh himself. He barely had time to shave and change his garments before he appeared before the king. When asked if he could interepret dreams, Joseph humbly ascribed any ability to God Himself. Then he listened intently. The dreams Pharaoh recounted were of the same event. There would be seven years of abundance in Egypt, followed by seven years of famine. This was about to begin and God had warned Pharaoh and his people.

Joseph boldly interpreted Pharaoh's dreams and then recommended a prudent course of action that struck a chord with the king. He was elated! Not one of his servants knew the dream, much less what to do. Here was God's man, with the plan of action already in his heart. Pharaoh appointed Joseph on the spot as his second-in-command. (Joseph had been second-in-command in his father's household, in Potiphar's house, in the prison, and now under Pharaoh.)

Psalm 105:17-19 *[17] He sent a man before them, even Joseph, who was sold for a servant: [18] Whose feet they hurt with fetters: he was laid in iron: [19] Until the time that his word came: the word of the LORD tried him. [20] The king sent and loosed him; even the ruler of the people, and let him go free. [21] He made him lord of his house, and ruler of all his substance: [22] To bind his princes at his pleasure; and teach his senators wisdom.*

Pharaoh gave Joseph a new Egyptian name that meant "revealer of secrets." Joseph managed the entire nation, had his own palace, chariot and staff. He had the finest clothing and every amenity that era afforded. He also married a wife, an Egyptian named Asenath! According to the Hebrew historian Josephus, one of the issues Joseph set straight after being appointed by Pharaoh was the story of his "alleged rape" of Potiphar's wife. Joseph returned to Potiphar's house, confronted the woman and gained her confession. After this was resolved Joseph then married . . . Potiphar's daughter, Asenath! What if? What if Joseph would have compromised his morals earlier? What if Joseph would have been willing to live below God's plan for his life? We will never know, but we do know that because of Joseph's steadfast courage, God blessed him and gave him the best of the land. (No mention is made however, about Joseph's interaction with his mother-in-law!)

God also blessed Joseph with two sons of his own. Joseph named his firstborn son Manasseh, which means "forgetting." He was forgetting the past and the pain. When his second son was born, Joseph named him Ephraim, which means "double fruit." Life was good.

The Famine

After the seven years of plenty, God sent a famine upon the entire region. Every nation came to Egypt to buy grain, because the word spread quickly. Joseph had stored up enough for that land and others. It was now time for God to fulfill a prophecy that was 200 years old.

Genesis 42:1-3 *[1]Now when Jacob saw that there was corn in Egypt, Jacob said unto his sons, Why do ye look one upon another? [2]And he said, Behold, I have heard that there is corn in Egypt: get you down thither, and buy for us from thence; that we may live, and not die. [3]And Joseph's ten brethren went down to buy corn in Egypt.*

God had a reason for the famine. The nations of the world languished under intolerable weather conditions and many died. Israel's remaining family was living in the region of Canaan, and their crops were dying, too. It was time to go to Egypt. Jacob called together his 10 oldest sons and sent them down to Egypt to purchase grain and food for the growing clan. Genesis 45:27 tells us there were now 70 members of the family, and they were hungry! Benjamin would not be allowed to go, even though he was now an adult himself. When the brothers had returned with a story of "Joseph's death," Israel's heart had been broken. Joseph had been his favorite, his oldest son by Rachel (his favorite wife). To his knowledge, Benjamin was his only living connection to Rachel, and he would do everything in his power to keep from losing him. The ten sons went to Egypt; Benjamin remained behind with Israel, his father.

Genesis 42 through 47 reveal the details of God's prophetic story. Joseph's brothers did not recognize him; he appeared to be an Egyptian to them. They were shepherds; he was a king. Joseph retained his cloak of secrecy, and caused his brothers to undergo a couple of tests to their integrity. He accused them of being spies, arresting one of them and retaining him in prison. They were to bring back their other brother, Benjamin. Joseph sent the brothers home to meet with their father. Israel finally relented, sending Benjamin with the rest on the next trip. Again Joseph orchestrated a test, planting a valuable goblet in Benjamin's pack and accusing him of stealing. Broken and weeping, the other brothers intervened on Benjamin's behalf.

At last Joseph revealed himself to his brothers. "I am Joseph," he declared. "Does my father yet live?" Joseph's brothers were astonished. Then Joseph revealed God's purpose to his brothers. God had sent Joseph ahead to prepare a place during the time of famine. Now Israel and all of his family were to relocate to Egypt where they would be sustained during the seven lean years and beyond. God was still guarding His covenant people!

After making amends with Joseph, his brothers rushed back to Canaan to share the news with their father Israel. Joseph is alive! He wants us to move to Egypt where he will care for us. God also verified this direction to Israel in a dream.

Israel Goes To Egypt

Genesis 46:2-4 [2]*And God spake unto Israel in the visions of the night, and said, Jacob, Jacob. And he said, Here am I.* [3]*And he said, I am God, the God of thy father: fear not to go down into Egypt; for I will there make of thee a great nation:* [4]*I will go down with thee into Egypt; and I will also surely bring thee up again: and Joseph shall put his hand upon thine eyes.*

God was going to bring Israel into Egypt as a family. But they would emerge as a nation. God had spoken to Abram 200 years before.

Genesis 15:13-14 *And he said unto Abram, Know of a surety that thy seed shall be a stranger in a land that is not theirs, and they shall serve them; and they shall afflict them four hundred years; and also that nation, whom they shall serve, will I judge: and afterward shall they come out with great substance.*

The fulfillment of this promise was beginning in meticulous detail. The Guardian of the covenant was once again leading Israel forward, to develop them as a nation, to strengthen them through service, to enact justice (upon Egypt), and to give the tribes of Israel great wealth and abundance!

God brought Israel and his sons into Egypt. He wept upon Joseph's neck and lived seventeen years beyond that joyful reunion (Genesis 47:28). The prophecies Israel would give to his sons in his dying days are critical to our understanding, and every ounce of this journey testifies to the greatness of Almighty God.

The Adoption

Genesis 48:1-4 *[1]And it came to pass after these things, that one told Joseph, Behold, thy father is sick: and he took with him his two sons, Manasseh and Ephraim. [2]And one told Jacob, and said, Behold, thy son Joseph cometh unto thee: and Israel strengthened himself, and sat upon the bed. [3]And Jacob said unto Joseph, God Almighty appeared unto me at Luz in the land of Canaan, and blessed me, [4]And said unto me, Behold, I will make thee fruitful, and multiply thee, and I will make of thee a multitude of people; and will give this land to thy seed after thee for an everlasting possession.*

Jacob and his sons lived through the time of famine in the region of Goshen, Egypt. Genesis 47:27 tells us they multiplied exceedingly during this time, and their possessions (and wealth) increased dramatically as well. Joseph was second-in-command over all the land of Egypt. Based on scholarly research of Egyptologists such as David Rohl, we now know much of his life. Joseph was an Egyptian outwardly, but maintained his allegiance to the God of Abraham, Isaac and Israel. So when he heard that Jacob, his father, was sick and perhaps near death, he knew it was time to make a journey home.

Joseph's sons Manasseh and Ephraim were now in their late teens or early twenties. They accompanied their father Joseph to Jacob's tent once more. Jacob strengthened himself and sat upon his bed to receive his guests. He began to speak under the inspiration of the Holy Ghost as Joseph entered the room. His words were a solemn reminder of God's covenant to Israel's seed that would last forever.

Jacob told Joseph about his personal encounter with God at Luz (or Bethel), the place of the stone.

- He reiterated God's promise to bless him.
- He would make Israel fruitful, and would multiply him.

- God would make of Israel a multitude of people.
- And God would give the land of Canaan to the Israelites as an everlasting possession.

Then Jacob made a startling proclamation. He said to Joseph, "As of now I am adopting your two sons, Ephraim and Manasseh!"

Genesis 48:5-6 [5]*And now thy two sons, Ephraim and Manasseh, which were born unto thee in the land of Egypt before I came unto thee into Egypt, are mine; as Reuben and Simeon, they shall be mine.* [6]*And thy issue, which thou begettest after them, shall be thine, and shall be called after the name of their brethren in their inheritance.*

Why would Jacob wish to adopt Joseph's two sons? He had twelve sons of his own! Obviously this was a sovereign plan from God's heart; Jacob was being obedient to God's leading. This move would detach Ephraim and Manasseh from Joseph's inheritance rights, and place them directly in line for God's covenant blessing through Jacob (or Israel). They were now considered to be Israelites in every sense of the word.

The Introduction

Genesis 48: 8-12 [8]*And Israel beheld Joseph's sons, and said, Who are these?* [9]*And Joseph said unto his father, They are my sons, whom God hath given me in this place. And he said, Bring them, I pray thee, unto me, and I will bless them.* [10]*Now the eyes of Israel were dim for age, so that he could not see. And he brought them near unto him; and he kissed them, and embraced them.* [11]*And Israel said unto Joseph, I had not thought to see thy face: and, lo, God hath showed me also thy seed.* [12]*And Joseph brought them out from between his knees, and he bowed himself with his face to the earth.*

Jacob's eyes were failing him, as had those of his father, Isaac. He could detect someone else in the room, but he didn't know them. Perhaps he had never met Joseph's sons until this time. Now it was time for introductions to be made. Jacob (or Israel) reached out to Joseph's two sons, embracing them. Joseph bowed before Israel in honor, with his face toward the earth. The tribes of Israel were complete. The last two sons had been added into the covenant.

Israel's Blessing Upon Ephraim And Manasseh

Genesis 48:13-22 [13]*And Joseph took them both, Ephraim in his right hand toward Israel's left hand, and Manasseh in his left hand toward Israel's right hand, and brought them near unto him.* [14]*And Israel stretched out his right hand, and laid it upon Ephraim's head, who was the younger, and his left hand upon Manasseh's head, guiding his hands wittingly; for Manasseh was the firstborn.* [15]*And he blessed Joseph, and said, God, before whom my fathers Abraham and Isaac did walk, the God which fed me all my life long unto this day,* [16]*The Angel which redeemed me from all evil, bless the lads; and let my name be named on them, and the name of my fathers Abraham and Isaac; and let them grow into a multitude in the midst of the earth.* [17]*And when Joseph saw that his father laid his right hand upon the head of Ephraim, it displeased him: and he held up his father's hand, to remove it from Ephraim's head unto Manasseh's head.* [18]*And Joseph said unto his father, Not so, my father: for this is the firstborn; put thy right hand upon his head.* [19]*And his father refused, and said, I know it, my son, I know it: he also shall become a people, and he also shall be great: but truly his younger brother shall be greater than he, and his seed shall become a multitude of nations.* [20]*And he blessed them that day, saying, In thee shall Israel bless, saying, God make thee as Ephraim and as Manasseh: and he set Ephraim before Manasseh.* [21]*And Israel said unto Joseph, Behold, I die: but God shall be with you, and bring you again unto the land of your fathers.* [22]*Moreover I have given to thee one portion above thy brethren, which I took out of the hand of the Amorite with my sword and with my bow.*

Now Joseph arose. Facing Jacob, he placed his sons Manasseh and Ephraim between himself and his father. Manasseh was to Joseph's left (Israel's right), and Ephraim, the youngest, was to Joseph's right and Israel's left hand. The positioning was intentional. It was custom that the right hand bestowed the greater blessing. It denoted strength, power, military might, material blessing, authority in business, family and government, and divine favor. Since Manasseh was the oldest, he was entitled to the blessing of the right hand, or so Joseph thought. Israel now arises from the bed and reaches forward to lay his hands upon his grandsons. Like Abraham to Isaac, and Isaac to Jacob, now the everlasting covenant blessing from Almighty God Himself is about to be imparted once again.

Israel places his left hand upon the eldest, Manasseh. Then he lays his right hand upon Ephraim the younger. Speaking under God's anointing, he blesses their father Joseph and then speaks the divine blessing. *"God, before whom my fathers Abraham and Isaac did walk, the God which fed me all my life long unto this day, the Angel which redeemed me from all evil, bless the lads; and let my name be named on them, and the name of my fathers Abraham and Isaac; and let them grow into a multitude in the midst of the earth."*

What a spectacular impartation! These young men, Ephraim and Manasseh, had just received the impartation of God's covenant blessing. They would be named Israelites, Abraham's sons, and would be known as the sons of Isaac. Joseph, however, was disturbed. Looking up, he saw his father Israel had crossed his hands! The blessing of the right hand was being bestowed upon younger Ephraim, not Manasseh, his firstborn! "Perhaps," he thought, "Israel's eyesight is not good, and he has made a mistake."

Reaching out, Joseph lifted up Israel's right hand from Ephraim's head. As he explained the situation to Israel, Israel became emphatic! "I know it, my son," he replied! This was something intentional. God was at work in a sovereign way, just as He had worked even in the deception of Isaac a generation before.

Then Jacob/Israel revealed God's destiny over Ephraim and Manasseh.

- Manasseh would be a great nation, a great people.
- But Ephraim would become greater than Manasseh in the last days. In fact, Ephraim's seed would become a multitude of nations, a true melting pot of people and cultures like the world had never seen!

Returning to the blessing, Israel reiterated this once again, restating the fact that Ephraim would be the greater people over Manasseh. Then he closed with two final prophetic statements. First, Israel reminded Joseph that God would not keep His people in Egypt, but would return them to Canaan. That was the land God had promised to them forever. Secondly, Israel blessed Joseph (and consequently Ephraim and Manasseh) with a double portion blessing of material goods. The spoils of war were to be his, above all of his brothers. The blessing of Joseph and his sons were nearly beyond belief. Joseph and his sons had won the coveted birthright blessing!

Why Did Joseph Get The Birthright?

God doesn't forget our sins when we do not repent of them. In Genesis 35:22, the seeds for tragedy were sown in the life of one of Israel's sons. Reuben was Israel's oldest son, borne to him by Leah. He was entitled to receive the birthright blessing, that being a double portion of material goods. However, he did the unthinkable; he slept with his father's wife/concubine, Bilhah. Perhaps he thought that since this maid had been given to this father in marriage under questionnable means, she was "available." Maybe he thought his status as firstborn entitled him to do it. Regardless of the reason, Reuben sinned and is never recorded as having repented for his actions. Because of this sin, Jacob/Israel revoked the birthright blessing from Reuben.

1 Chronicles 5:1-2 states, *Now the sons of Reuben the firstborn of Israel, (for he was the firstborn; but, forasmuch as he defiled his father's bed, his birthright was given unto the sons of Joseph the son of Israel; and the genealogy is not to be reckoned after the birthright, for Judah prevailed above his brethren, and of him came the chief ruler; but the birthright was Joseph's:)*

Joseph was Israel's favorite son. Not only would he receive the birthright, he would receive the greatest portion of the spiritual blessing as well. While God reserved specific blessings for other sons (and revoked the blessing from Reuben), the greatest blessing of God was passed to Joseph and his two sons, Ephraim and Manasseh. Furthermore, when God blessed the sons, Ephraim was the recipient of the greater blessing (two-thirds), while Manasseh received less (one third).

These issues are critical factors when one wants to understand Bible prophecy. Nations are blessed or cursed based on God's covenant with Abraham, Isaac and Israel. We will see just how significant God considers this to be when we study a much-avoided chapter . . . next.

In The Last Days

Genesis 48 and **49** are conjoined twins in their context. Chapter 48 contains the prophetic blessing of Israel specifically dealing with his "adopted sons," Ephraim and Manasseh. Chapter 49 addresses his blood borne sons, and deals with their respective futures.

Genesis 49:1-2 [1]*And Jacob called unto his sons, and said, Gather yourselves together, that I may tell you that which shall befall you in the last days.* [2]*Gather yourselves together, and hear, ye sons of Jacob; and hearken unto Israel your father.*

Today most Bible scholars and ministers patently avoid Genesis 49. They simply don't take the time to understand it, but it is loaded with treasure. It is also filled with last-day prophecies that must be understood. This author has heard Genesis 49 taught in a "spiritual" context, where the pastor has spiritualized every portion of this chapter. However, there are prophecies in this chapter that deal with the literal birth of Jesus Christ. There are also prophecies that create entire nations. Others deal with blessings and curses that affect the economies of the world *in the last days*. This cannot be spiritualized.

As Jacob lay dying he summoned his sons together for the blessing upon their lives. He fully understood the magnitude of the occasion; his life had been determined when He received God's blessing from his father Isaac many years before. His opening words to his sons are startling, and very appropriate for today. He said, *"Gather yourselves together, that I may tell you that which shall befall you in the last days."* Notice, he did not talk about what would happen in their relatively short lifespans. He was about to prophesy about the last days.

Nearly 900 years later, the prophet Joel would also prophesy about "the last days." (Joel 2:28-32.) And Acts 2:16-21 (written more than 1,700 years after Jacob's prophecy) states Joel's prophecy was just beginning to be fulfilled. If this is the case, Jacob's prophecies to his sons also began to unfold in that era, and are still being fulfilled today! If we casually move over this chapter, thinking it merely points to God's hand on a few chosen people, we could not be more deceived! God did not invest meticulous detail into the previous 3 generations (Abraham, Isaac and Jacob) for nothing. He had been a jealous guardian of the covenant. Therefore Genesis 49 is very significant to God. It should be to us as well.

Jacob then continued in verse 2 by verifying his dual name. He referred to himself one last time as both Jacob and Israel. One was a name given him signifying his earthly, carnal nature. The other was a name given to him by Almighty God, when he broke free from his sins.

Because of his victory, his children would be known as sons of Israel; prince with God. It was to be a part of their destiny.

This chapter will cover a few of the tribes and touch lightly on a few points regarding the destiny of nations. We will return in a later chapter and address all of them in-depth. However, now we start with Israel's firstborn and the prophecy he received.

Reuben

When Isaac blessed his sons Esau and Jacob, he intended to begin with Esau. However, Jacob supplanted his brother and gained the blessing. As Israel began to prophesy, the brothers were all together, and he called them out by name. There would be no private blessing today. Everybody would hear God's prophetic voice to each one. Everyone knew Reuben was entitled to the blessing of the firstborn. At the very least, this would give him a double portion of the material goods. Today was the day of destiny, but what Reuben heard would change his very life.

Genesis 49:3-4 [3]*Reuben, thou art my firstborn, my might, and the beginning of my strength, the excellency of dignity, and the excellency of power:* [4]*Unstable as water, thou shalt not excel; because thou wentest up to thy father's bed; then defiledst thou it: he went up to my couch.*

Israel began by acknowledging Reuben's excellence and his status as firstborn. He has the power in the natural, and everything should go his way. Suddenly, everything changes! Jacob exposes Reuben's hidden, long-dormant sin.

"You are unstable as water!" The word unstable is a double play on words. Israel tells Reuben he boils and froths like water. But the word also means he is lustful and self-centered. "You shall not excel!" Why? "You went up to your father's bed and defiled it." Reuben had slept with Bilhah. This is no blessing; this is a curse! The birthright has been revoked and Reuben has been left with nothing!

The last days will reveal a people that should have blessing in every conceivable way. Perhaps they have the land, natural resources, and disciplines to excel. Yet something will stand in their way and they shall not excel. We will discover more about Reuben later on. For now all he can do is step aside and watch as his brothers receive their blessings from God.

Judah

Let's drop down a few verses and look at Israel's prophecy to Judah.

Genesis 49:8-10 [8]*Judah, thou art he whom thy brethren shall praise: thy hand shall be in the neck of thine enemies; thy father's children shall bow down before thee.* [9]*Judah is a lion's whelp: from the prey, my son, thou art gone up: he stooped down, he couched as a lion, and as an old lion; who shall rouse him up?* [10]*The sceptre shall not depart from Judah, nor a lawgiver from between his feet, until Shiloh come; and unto him shall the gathering of the people be.*

- Judah would be the tribe that the others would recognize and praise. He would be in the forefront of Israel's descendents and would be known as a direct descendent of Israel.
- Judah's hand would be strong against their enemies.
- The other sons would bow before Judah, and give him honor. He would be known consistently as a chosen people.
- In the last days Judah would be a lion's whelp. A whelp is a young lion cub. However, it also states that Judah would be an old lion! A young and an old lion. How can this be?
- Israel then bestows a high honor upon Judah. He gives Judah the "sceptre" blessing. Israel's kings will be from the tribe of Judah.
- Judah will continue to adhere and respect the Old Testament law, even to the end of the age. A lawgiver will remain between his feet until . . .
- Shiloh. This name was an epithet for Messiah. This is another high honor bestowed upon Judah. The promised Messiah and Savior of the world will come from Judah's descendents. Until that time Judah would adhere to the law of Moses. The tribe of Levi would oversee the animal sacrifices until the ultimate sacrifice of Jesus Christ would take away the sin of the world.
- This Messiah would gather the people, God's Israel, unto Himself in the last days.

Today Judah is none other than the Jewish people. The term Jew is a shortened version of Judah, and will be shown later to be directly linked with this people. While it is true that the enemies of God have tried repeatedly to separate the Jews from the land of promise, God has brought them back to the place He promised to Abraham and His seed forever.

- The Jews are more recognized today than any of the other tribes around the world. Their brothers do praise them as God stated.
- Judah is a military superpower in the Middle East. This is partly due to their armament and technology, but is due in larger part to God's hand upon them in battle. Scenarios such as the raid in Entebbe, the Six Day War, and various forays into Lebanon have shown that God has kept His hand upon the Jews.
- Today the Jewish State of Israel is a lion's whelp, a young nation organized in 1948. However, they are also an ancient nation with roots in the land deeper than any other people presently in existence. They can claim descendency to the time of David at the very least, and no other people group can find any archaeological, literary, or historic evidence that links them to the land in the same way.
- Judah has the sceptre blessing. Beginning with King David, every king of the Jews has been from the tribe of Judah. This dynasty continues today in an amazing fashion that will be discussed in a later chapter.
- The "lion of the tribe of Judah" is Jesus Christ. Jesus, the only Messiah, was a direct descendent of David, the seed of Judah. God foretold this through Israel more than 1,000 years before Jesus was born in the city of David, Bethlehem!
- When Jesus Christ returns, the King of kings and Lord of lords will reign over the entire earth. Although Judah will be recognized as His earthly heritage, Jesus will gather the people unto Himself as the King of Israel.

This is astonishing! The prophecies imparted by God through Israel contain great spiritual connotations. However, they are physical promises that contain literal blessings. God promised military dominance, literal recognition of the Jews upon the earth, and a literal dynasty in their kingly line. I cannot emphasize this enough. We must not spiritualize physical promises. Judah received a prophecy that was (and is) being literally fulfilled. God intends to do the same thing with every other prophecy in this chapter, to each individual tribe!

Joseph

With Reuben, the eldest, and the rest of the brothers looking on, Israel finally turns his attention to Joseph, the favorite. As one can imagine, Israel spends more time prophesying over Joseph than any of the other sons. But the reason is not because of Jacob's favoritism, but because of God's intentions in future days.

Genesis 49:22-26 [22]*Joseph is a fruitful bough, even a fruitful bough by a well; whose branches run over the wall:* [23]*The archers have sorely grieved him, and shot at him, and hated him:* [24]*But his bow abode in strength, and the arms of his hands were made strong by the hands of the mighty God of Jacob; (from thence is the shepherd, the stone of Israel:)* [25]*Even by the God of thy father, who shall help thee; and by the Almighty, who shall bless thee with blessings of heaven above, blessings of the deep that lieth under, blessings of the breasts, and of the womb:* [26]*The blessings of thy father have prevailed above the blessings of my progenitors unto the utmost bound of the everlasting hills: they shall be on the head of Joseph, and on the crown of the head of him that was separate from his brethren.*

Jacob begins by recognizing Joseph's fruitfulness. He is a business-generating machine of a man, that has operated in agriculture (Jacob), the business sector (Potiphar), and government (under Pharaoh).

- His branches run over a wall, by a well. He extends his reach beyond his realm, and his fruitfulness is recognized beyond the waters, the well.
- Joseph is disliked. Jealous leaders (the archers) have grieved him. They constricted his productivity, bringing it to a mere trickle. They have shot at him (speaking of the threat of death and war). They hate him for his boldness, confidence, the love of His father, and his authority.
- His bow abode in strength. His arms and hands were made strong by the mighty God of Jacob. He relies on the Shepherd, the Stone of Israel.

- The God of Joseph's father shall help him, the Almighty shall bless him with the blessings from beneath, blessings from above, blessings of the breast and womb.
- Israel closes by stating that the blessings that originated with Abraham and Isaac have come upon him. ***This covenant blessing is bestowed upon one son out of all the tribes; the tribe of Joseph!*** Not only has Joseph been blessed with the double-portion birthright blessing of material goods (stripped from Reuben); he now has the spiritual blessing of Abraham, Isaac and Israel given to him as well, in the presence of all his brothers!

Please note that while God has blessed Judah in a tremendous way, the greatest blessing (besides gaining the primary honor and promise of the Messiah) has been bestowed upon Joseph. If these prophecies are written for the last days, and will be revealed in the final moments of God's time-clock, who could this be?

- Joseph will be a people that is fruitful in business like no other.
- He will be strongly disliked to the extent that he will be considered to be arrogant and prideful. At times his productivity will falter, and many nations will oppose him.
- But Joseph's strength will be rooted in one principle. It will be his trust in Almighty God. Furthermore, Joseph will rely upon the Shepherd, Jesus Christ. Ephesians 2:20 and 1 Peter 2:6-7 both state that Jesus Christ is the Cornerstone. Hebrews 13:20, 1 Peter 2:25, and 1 Peter 5:4 recognize Jesus Christ as the Shepherd.
- The God of Joseph's father (Israel) shall help him. God will give him immeasurable wealth.
- Joseph will have the full covenant blessing given to him that was bestowed upon Abraham, Isaac and Israel. His land will be a reflection of this blessing more than any other nation on earth.

With that, Jacob gave closing instructions to his sons and yielded his spirit to God. Joseph led the family back to Canaan where they buried Israel beside Abraham and Isaac, in the land God had promised to them as an inheritance. The sons of Israel were on their way to becoming a nation, but many things had to be be fulfilled before they emerged as a national entity from Egypt.

SUMMARY OF POINTS COVERED SO FAR

God has promised Abraham that his seed shall be as the sand of the sea and the dust of the earth. This must be fulfilled both literally and spiritually.

God has promised Abraham and Sarah that they will both be the parents of "nations" (not singular, plural). Therefore, Abraham and Sarah's literal seed cannot be restricted to the Jewish people.

Abraham's blessing carries on to Isaac, his son, and wife Rebekah. Isaac and Rebekah have twins, Jacob and Esau. The covenant promise continues unto Jacob, but not Esau. Esau sells his birthright to his brother and is then tricked out of the prophetic blessing bestowed by his father by the laying on of hands.

Jacob has a meeting with God in Bethel while fleeing his brother's wrath. He vows a vow before God. Then he moves on, working for Laban his future father-in-law. He acquires wives, goods and livestock. God blesses him.

Jacob fathers 12 sons and one daughter through four different women. These are the start of the "Tribes of Israel."

Jacob's name is changed to Israel. He is promised the same blessings conferred upon his grandfather Abraham, that a nation and a company of nations shall come from him.

Reuben, Jacob's oldest son, sleeps with his father's concubine. Because of this, Jacob revokes the birthright blessing from the oldest (Reuben) and is now free to bestow this blessing of material prosperity on any son he chooses.

Jacob's son, Joseph, is sold into Egypt. However, God protects and directs him, allowing him to prosper and be the agent by which his entire family would be protected from tremendous famine.

Jacob's family is reunited in Egypt through Joseph's intervention with Pharaoh. They now prosper in the time of famine. Jacob (Israel) adopts Joseph's two sons, naming his name of Israel upon them. They now become eligible to receive of Israel's covenant blessing and benefits.

Jacob blesses his sons through the laying on of hands, just as his father did to he and Esau. During this blessing, which shall occur in the last days, Reuben the firstborn is stripped of his birthright, and Judah receives the blessing of the sceptre and the blessing of receiving the greatest acknowledgement and honor of the tribes. Joseph (and subsequently his two sons Ephraim and Manasseh) receive the birthright blessing which was revoked from Reuben. Joseph also receives the covenant blessing that was prophesied over Abraham, Isaac and Israel.

The prophecies to Abraham, Isaac and Israel (Jacob) still remain to be fulfilled. There is now an entire chapter and a half of further prophecy (Genesis 48 and 49), specifically broken out to each son (or his seed). All of this is adding up. Still we ask, who or where is the seed that is as the sand of the sea? Where are the peoples who will fill multiple nations? How does the United States of America tie into all of this? We find prophetic answers to these and other questions as we move on.

CHAPTER 5

From Tribes To Nations

Four Hundred Thirty Years. That is a rough estimate of the time between the Covenant blessings to Abraham in Genesis 15, and the first chapter of Exodus. Abraham's grandson Israel (formerly known as Jacob) is dead, buried with his fathers Abraham and Isaac. Joseph is entombed in Egypt, awaiting God's command for the tribes of Israel to move his body to the land of God's promise. Several generations have come and gone, but God still has a covenant people. God was meticulous in His cultivation of this people, and His prophecies would take hundreds of years at times to be fulfilled. This did not mean He had forgotten. He was simply waiting for the perfect timing for the next stage of His fulfillment over His tribes.

Tribes? Did I say tribes? Yes! During this protracted time, the sons of Israel have multiplied! Exodus 1:7 says that the land of Goshen was filled with them! All the "Reubens" have been producing little Reubenites, and so on with all of Israel's descendents. God's prophecies to Abraham, Isaac and Israel that they would be fruitful and would multiply have begun to be fulfilled. Various Bible commentaries tell us that the tribes of Israel have grown from a cluster of 70 people that entered Egypt to a force numbering between 2 and 3 million. In fact, they have multiplied to such a degree that the Egyptians have become afraid of them and forced the Israelites to become their slaves. It is time for the Lord to release them into a land of their own, as he had promised to Abraham (Genesis 15:13-16).

The tribes of Israel have also become physically diverse. Consider this. Every one of the sons (and grandsons) of Israel were his direct descendents. However, Jacob had married two wives, and was also given two handmaids to bear children on his wives' behalf. Joseph had married an Egyptian woman, and had borne Ephraim and Manasseh by her. So while the tribes were united in heritage and covenant, they were also a blended nation in their physical characteristics, attitudes and mannerisms. This would impact their futures as God directed them forward.

The Sons of Israel According to Mother

Leah	Bilhah	Zilpah	Rachel	Asenath
Reuben Simeon Levi Judah Issachar Zebulun	Dan Naphtali	Gad Asher	Joseph Benjamin	Manasseh Ephraim
				Sons of Joseph, Adopted by Israel

But now it was time to move! Egypt was no longer home, and God had promised Abraham a land. In this segment of study we will examine several facets:

- The Israelites will move out of Egypt and ratify the covenant with Almighty God as a nation.
- They will take possession of the land God promised to Abraham, Isaac and Israel.
- The prophetic blessings will spread out, attached to the tribes to which they were given. Some will be more notable than others.
- The Israelites will establish kings to rule over them.
- They will divide into two separate kingdoms, two nations.
- They will be taken captive because of their idolatry.
- Some will return to the promised land. However, the greater portion of Israel will spread outward beyond the land of Promise to fulfill God's last-day prophecies.

Since the Old Testament is in itself the story of the houses of Israel and Judah we will, at this point, break away from a step by step analysis of each chapter or book, and move rather quickly through several books of the Bible to get to our goal.

Exodus 1 *[1]Now these are the names of the children of Israel, which came into Egypt; every man and his household came with Jacob. [2]Reuben, Simeon, Levi, and Judah, [3]Issachar, Zebulun, and Benjamin, [4]Dan, and Naphtali, Gad, and Asher. [5]And all the souls that came out of the loins of Jacob were seventy souls: for Joseph was in Egypt already. [6]And Joseph died, and all his brethren, and all that generation. [7]And the children of Israel were fruitful, and increased abundantly, and multiplied, and waxed exceeding mighty; and the land was filled with them.*

[8]Now there arose up a new king over Egypt, which knew not Joseph. [9]And he said unto his people, Behold, the people of the children of Israel are more and mightier than we: [10]Come on, let us deal wisely with them; lest they multiply, and it come to pass, that, when there falleth out any war, they join also unto our enemies, and fight against us, and so get them up out of the land. [11]Therefore they did set over them taskmasters to afflict them with their burdens. And they built for Pharaoh treasure cities, Pithom and Raamses. [12]But the more they afflicted them, the more they multiplied and grew. And they were grieved because of the children of Israel. [13]And the Egyptians made the children of Israel to serve with rigour: [14]And they made their lives bitter with hard bondage, in mortar, and in brick, and in all manner of service in the field: all their service, wherein they made them serve, was with rigour.

[15]And the king of Egypt spake to the Hebrew midwives, of which the name of the one was Shiphrah, and the name of the other Puah: [16]And he said, When ye do the office of a midwife to the Hebrew women, and see them upon the stools; if it be a son, then ye shall kill him: but if it be a daughter, then she shall live. [17]But the midwives feared God, and did not as the king of Egypt commanded them, but saved the men children alive. [18]And the king of Egypt called for the midwives, and said unto them, Why have ye done this thing, and have saved the men children alive? [19]And the midwives said unto Pharaoh, Because the Hebrew women are not as the Egyptian women; for they are lively, and are delivered ere the midwives come in unto them. [20]Therefore God dealt well with the midwives: and the people multiplied, and waxed very mighty. [21]And it came to pass, because the midwives feared God, that he made them houses. [22]And Pharaoh

charged all his people, saying, Every son that is born ye shall cast into the river, and every daughter ye shall save alive.

Let us note a few significant details in this chapter of Exodus.

- The tribes of Israel were growing. Verse 7 says they were exceedingly mighty and the land was filled with them.
- Verse 9 states that the Israelites actually outnumbered the Egyptians! Verse 20 says as they were persecuted, they multiplied even further. In fact, Exodus 12:37-38 tells us that 600,000 men left Israel on foot. This does not account for women, children, those on horseback or other animals, or of the mixed multitude that is also mentioned. Some estimates place Israel's population at this point to be at least 3 million people.
- The Israelites had become skilled builders. Verse 11 lists them as the builders of the royal cities of Pithon and Rameses.
- Pharaoh came to regard the children of Israel as such a threat that he enslaved them. The special blessings that had been given by God were regarded by the ungodly as cause for persecution, tyranny, and affliction.
- Finally, Pharaoh commanded the midwives that assisted the Israelite women in birth to kill all male children born to the tribes. Ethnic cleansing was first used against God's covenant people.
- However, the midwives disobeyed Pharaoh because they also feared Almighty God. God blessed this act of civil disobedience against a tyrannical government. The midwives were blessed with special birthing centers of their own, because they honored God instead of Pharaoh.

The Cry For Liberty

Chapter 2 of Exodus tells of the story of God's great leader, Moses. Moses should have been slain at birth, but God divinely spared him through the intervention of Pharaoh's daughter. Born into the tribe of Levi, but raised in the king's court, Moses was nursed and instructed in his early years by a nanny that was actually his own birth mother. He had the best of both worlds. He was an Israelite by heritage and at heart, but had the best of Egyptian training scholastically, militarily, and royally. Josephus the Jewish historian tells us that Moses became a conquering general in the Egyptian army, and perhaps was being groomed to take the place of Pharaoh himself. He was sovereignly ordained to lead.

However, when Moses was grown he chose to return to the heritage of his fathers Abraham, Isaac and Israel. *His overtures to lead the tribes were rejected on one hand by the tribes themselves, and Pharaoh became enraged at his actions on the other.* Moses had to flee for his life, and spent between 40-60 years living in the wilderness. The oppression of God's people became even greater; they had refused God's leader. Finally, their cries turned into desperate screams for liberty. Like their fathers before them, they began to pray and call out upon Almighty God. This cry was unique in human history, and it would define the tribes of Israel wherever they would live from this time forward. It was not right for God's people to be enslaved, but to be a free people under God.

God divinely called Moses through a series of miracles found in **Exodus 3** and **4**. Moses had been preserved by God and divinely set apart as a ready-made leader for a ready-made nation. But Moses had been negligent in his duties as an Israelite. Two sons had been born to him while in the wilderness, and neither had been circumcised. God had commanded Abraham (Genesis 17:10) that every covenant son of Israel must be circumcised, and so it had been throughout all the generations to follow.

Exodus 4:24-26 [24]*And it came to pass by the way in the inn, that the LORD met him, and sought to kill him.* [25]*Then Zipporah took a sharp stone, and cut off the foreskin of her son, and cast it at his feet, and said, Surely a bloody husband art thou to me.* [26]*So he let him go: then she said, A bloody husband thou art, because of the circumcision.*

Moses had not circumcised his sons. The reasons are unknown and we can only speculate, but God would not let Moses forsake His commands. He had chosen Moses; now it was time for Moses to choose him. This continued the pattern God had established with the generations before. Every generation of Israel had a responsibility to choose God for themselves, in order to abide under His covenant blessing. God would have killed Moses, if he had failed to obey Him. Fortunately Zipporah, his wife, took responsibility where Moses had failed. Moses' sons were circumcised and Moses lived.

After the plagues of God came upon Egypt, Pharaoh became willing to let the Israelites go. They came out of Egypt and through the Red Sea, to the Mountain of the Lord, Mount Sinai. It was there that God enacted His covenant for the first time with a nation. However, there were other issues God dealt with along the way that were to become significant among the tribes in the years ahead.

Government Of The People, By The People, And For The People

Exodus 18:13-26 [13]*And it came to pass on the morrow, that Moses sat to judge the people: and the people stood by Moses from the morning unto the evening.* [14]*And when Moses' father in law saw all that he did to the people, he said, What is this thing that thou doest to the people? why sittest thou thyself alone, and all the people stand by thee from morning unto even?* [15]*And Moses said unto his father in law, Because the people come unto me to inquire of God:* [16]*When they have a matter, they come unto me; and I judge between one and another, and I do make them know the statutes of God, and his laws.* [17]*And Moses' father in law said unto him, The thing that thou doest is not good.* [18]*Thou wilt surely wear away, both thou, and this people that is with thee: for this thing is too heavy for thee; thou art not able to perform it thyself alone.* [19]*Hearken now unto my voice, I will give thee counsel, and God shall be with thee: Be thou for the people to God-ward, that thou mayest bring the causes unto God:* [20]*And thou shalt teach them ordinances and laws, and shalt show them the way wherein they must walk, and the work that they must do.* [21]*Moreover thou shalt provide out of all the people able men, such as fear God, men of truth, hating covetousness; and place such over them, to be rulers of thousands, and rulers of hundreds, rulers of fifties, and rulers of tens:* [22]*And let them judge the people at all seasons: and it shall be, that every great matter they shall bring unto thee, but every small matter they shall judge: so shall it be easier for thyself, and they shall bear the burden with thee.* [23]*If thou shalt do this thing, and God command thee so, then thou shalt be able to endure, and all this people shall also go to their place in peace.* [24]*So Moses hearkened to the voice of his father in law, and did all that he had said.* [25]*And Moses chose able men out of all Israel, and made them heads over the people, rulers of thousands, rulers of hundreds, rulers of fifties, and rulers of tens.* [26]*And they judged the people at all seasons: the hard causes they brought unto Moses, but every small matter they judged themselves.*

In the wilderness Moses' father-in-law, Jethro, observed the fact that Moses was wearing down over time, dealing with insignificant matters. He was definitely God's leader, but something had to be done. Based on Jethro's counsel, Moses established a governmental structure that was endorsed by God.

- The people had to have a common moral framework, the laws and statutes of Almighty God. This would give them the foundation for their society and every vestige of morality.
- Every governmental ruler had to know the laws and statutes of God, to know how to enact justice properly.
- Governmental officials had to meet God's moral criteria. They had to be able men (men of skill and ability in their various fields); they were required to fear God, hate covetousness, and be men of unbending truth.
- Issues would be solved whenever possible at the local level. If they could not be resolved at the lower level, the issue would escalate to a higher level such as a court of appeals, or an issue that moves from local to state levels today.

These men were then set in authority under Moses, over groups of 10, 50, 100 and 1,000 people. This was the first nationally established, representative government that was drawn from the people themselves instead of a certain sect of nobility. Varying forms of this government would follow the tribes throughout their generations as a hallmark from this time forward. The government was secure under God. Not only was Moses a godly leader; he now had help in every strata of society.

God Makes His Covenant With The Nation

Exodus 19:3-8 [3]*And Moses went up unto God, and the LORD called unto him out of the mountain, saying, Thus shalt thou say to the house of Jacob, and tell the children of Israel;* [4]*Ye have seen what I did unto the Egyptians, and how I bare you on eagles' wings, and brought you unto myself.* [5]*Now therefore, if ye will obey my voice indeed, and keep my covenant, then ye shall be a peculiar treasure unto me above all people: for all the earth is mine:* [6]*And ye shall be unto me a kingdom of priests, and an holy nation. These are the words which thou shalt speak unto the children* *of Israel. [7]And Moses came and called for the elders of the people, and laid before their faces all these words which the LORD commanded him. [8]And all the people answered together, and said, All that the LORD hath spoken we will do. And Moses returned the words of the people unto the LORD.*

God knows how to build a nation. Every person within the nation must be conformed to God's moral standards and live by the same social structure. This maintains cohesion, identity and peace within the people. Under Moses' leadership, God called the tribes of Israel to Himself at Mount Sinai, and gave them His law. The ceremonial customs and religious codes were ultimately fulfilled in the atonement of Jesus Christ for the sins of humankind. But the social laws of God's covenant people still exist to this day.

God called to His people at the Mountain. Now, it was up to them to respond. When they committed to do the Words of the Lord, they became God's chosen people. At this point, they were the only nation on earth that would be blessed by God. Their success was now based on their adherence to God's covenant as a nation. While they had chosen God as their Sovereign, He had chosen them first.

The laws God gave to them are enduringly simple, and yet powerful. Today they are known as the Ten Commandments.

The Ten Commandments

Exodus 20:1-17 *[1]And God spake all these words, saying, [2]I am the LORD thy God, which have brought thee out of the land of Egypt, out of the house of bondage. [3]Thou shalt have no other gods before me. [4]Thou shalt not make unto thee any graven image, or any likeness of any thing that is in heaven above, or that is in the earth beneath, or that is in the water under the earth: [5]Thou shalt not bow down thyself to them, nor serve them: for I the LORD thy God am a jealous God, visiting the iniquity of the fathers upon the children unto the third and fourth generation of them that hate me; [6]And showing mercy unto thousands of them that love me, and keep my commandments. [7]Thou shalt not take the name of the LORD thy God in vain; for the LORD will not hold him guiltless that taketh his name in vain. [8]Remember the sabbath day, to keep it holy. [9]Six days shalt thou labour, and do all thy work: [10]But the seventh day is the sabbath of the LORD thy God: in it thou shalt not do any work, thou, nor thy son, nor thy daughter, thy manservant, nor thy maidservant, nor thy cattle, nor thy* *stranger that is within thy gates:* [11]*For in six days the LORD made heaven and earth, the sea, and all that in them is, and rested the seventh day: wherefore the LORD blessed the sabbath day, and hallowed it.*

[12]*Honour thy father and thy mother: that thy days may be long upon the land which the LORD thy God giveth thee.* [13]*Thou shalt not kill.* [14]*Thou shalt not commit adultery.* [15]*Thou shalt not steal.* [16]*Thou shalt not bear false witness against thy neighbour.* [17]*Thou shalt not covet thy neighbour's house, thou shalt not covet thy neighbour's wife, nor his manservant, nor his maidservant, nor his ox, nor his ass, nor any thing that is thy neighbour's.*

These ten commandments were written by God's hand, and provided the framework for the nation, business, family and personal conduct. The commandments were the foundation for representative government to judge the people, enact complimentary law, and execute fair and impartial rulings at every level. God's covenant people were not under the authority of a king, but under the leadership of the King of Heaven. They submitted to His law, and every individual in society was subservient to it from the pauper to the king on the throne. The decalogue, or ten commandments were the cornerstone of God's covenant people.

Moses ruled the Israelites for the next 40 years, guiding them through the wilderness. Under God's divine inspiration he wrote most of the Pentateuch, the first five books of the Old Testament, providing the civil code for government. Moses also reconnected the people to their heritage repeatedly, warning them to remember the Lord at every turn. His closing prophecy to each individual tribe in **Deuteronomy 33** is a perfect compliment to Israel's prophecies over the tribes in **Genesis 49**.

Not only did Moses give the Law to the Israelites, He also gave them the tabernacle. The law was their civil code for societal government. But the tabernacle was their place for instruction and worship. A nation under God's covenant needed a spiritual foundation and constant spiritual teaching to know how to live before Almighty God.

God's Blessing Upon Levi

Numbers 18:1-8 [1]*And the LORD said unto Aaron, Thou and thy sons and thy father's house with thee shall bear the iniquity of the sanctuary: and thou and thy sons with thee shall bear the iniquity of your priesthood.*

[2]And thy brethren also of the tribe of Levi, the tribe of thy father, bring thou with thee, that they may be joined unto thee, and minister unto thee: but thou and thy sons with thee shall minister before the tabernacle of witness. [3]And they shall keep thy charge, and the charge of all the tabernacle: only they shall not come nigh the vessels of the sanctuary and the altar, that neither they, nor ye also, die. [4]And they shall be joined unto thee, and keep the charge of the tabernacle of the congregation, for all the service of the tabernacle: and a stranger shall not come nigh unto you. [5]And ye shall keep the charge of the sanctuary, and the charge of the altar: that there be no wrath any more upon the children of Israel. [6]And I, behold, I have taken your brethren the Levites from among the children of Israel: to you they are given as a gift for the LORD, to do the service of the tabernacle of the congregation. [7]Therefore thou and thy sons with thee shall keep your priest's office for every thing of the altar, and within the veil; and ye shall serve: I have given your priest's office unto you as a service of gift: and the stranger that cometh nigh shall be put to death.

[8]And the LORD spake unto Aaron, Behold, I also have given thee the charge of mine heave offerings of all the hallowed things of the children of Israel; unto thee have I given them by reason of the anointing, and to thy sons, by an ordinance for ever.

Moses was from the tribe of Levi, and God had allowed Moses to designate his brother, Aaron, to be the high priest of Israel. The brothers operated in complete unity, one enacting national government, and the other overseeing spiritual issues. The tribe of Levi had been known as a clan of hotheaded, impetuous people. Israel's prophecy to them in Genesis 49:7 was more of a curse than a blessing. But Levi was zealous for the Lord. They loved God and passionately hated evil. Because of Moses' zeal for God, Levi received God's blessing.

Jacob's prophecy to Levi was that they would be a scattered people. They would function as a tribe, but would be divided out into various clans. Now God turned this into a favor, something special. In Numbers 18 God designated the tribe of Levi to be His ministers. They would not receive any tribal property as a united inheritance, but they would be chosen by God to be His ministers instead. (Numbers 18:20) Only this tribe would work in the Tabernacle, and later the Temple. Aaron's seed would bring forth the priests, but the Levites (as they became known) would carry the furnishings and the Tabernacle tent itself. This was a great honor! God chose only one tribe for this purpose.

When Israel reached the land God had promised to them, the Tabernacle was erected for the last time. Eventually it was replaced by Solomon's temple. The Levites were "scattered." They had no fixed "land" given to them as a tribal inheritance. Instead, their clans were intermingled with the other 12 tribes. They became the teachers, the rabbis, and the schoolmasters, to teach them the ways of God and ensure they were well versed in the law that would guarantee God's blessing.

More will be revealed about each tribe in the future. However, this event caused the tribes to become known as the "twelve tribes of Israel." In reality, there were thirteen, due to Jacob's adoption of Ephraim and Manasseh. But Levi was scattered, even though they were fiercely nationalistic and retained their tribal identity as a people.

Another Promise Fulfilled

God has now led His covenant people out of Egypt and into the wilderness. They have a leader, a law and a governmental structure. Now it is time for a land.

Joshua 1:1-9 *[1]Now after the death of Moses the servant of the LORD it came to pass, that the LORD spake unto Joshua the son of Nun, Moses' minister, saying, [2]Moses my servant is dead; now therefore arise, go over this Jordan, thou, and all this people, unto the land which I do give to them, even to the children of Israel. [3]Every place that the sole of your foot shall tread upon, that have I given unto you, as I said unto Moses. [4]From the wilderness and this Lebanon even unto the great river, the river Euphrates, all the land of the Hittites, and unto the great sea toward the going down of the sun, shall be your coast. [5]There shall not any man be able to stand before thee all the days of thy life: as I was with Moses, so I will be with thee: I will not fail thee, nor forsake thee. [6]Be strong and of a good courage: for unto this people shalt thou divide for an inheritance the land, which I sware unto their fathers to give them. [7]Only be thou strong and very courageous, that thou mayest observe to do according to all the law, which Moses my servant commanded thee: turn not from it to the right hand or to the left, that thou mayest prosper whithersoever thou goest. [8]This book of the law shall not depart out of thy mouth; but thou shalt meditate therein day and night, that thou mayest observe to do according to all that is written therein: for then thou shalt make thy way prosperous, and then thou shalt* *have good success. [9]Have not I commanded thee? Be strong and of a good courage; be not afraid, neither be thou dismayed: for the LORD thy God is with thee whithersoever thou goest.*

Let's make note of a few things revealed in this passage in Joshua 1.

- Moses, God's servant and leader, is dead. Joshua has been designated by God Almighty as their new leader.
- Although it is not mentioned here, Aaron is also dead along with the majority of the generation that was enslaved in Egypt (Numbers 20:28; Numbers 14:22-23; Deuteronomy 1:35-36).
- God commands Joshua to lead the Israelites forward into the land where Abraham, Isaac and Jacob lived. This will be their property.
- God has promised them this land, not man. It will be eternally theirs.
- Their blessing is contingent on their obedience to God's law. Prosperity only comes when they serve God.
- It is time for the covenant people to possess their first land.

The book of Joshua is the book of conquest. The Israelites did possess the land of Israel, and have laid claim to it ever since. They are the oldest people group that has a claim to that property. Joshua led them through victories and defeats, where they learned critical lessons from God Himself. Finally, he disbursed the land to the twelve tribes and gave the Levites various cities of refuge among the people. God's promise to bless Abraham's seed with the land he traversed has been fulfilled.

Judges And Ruth

After Joshua's death, the Iraelites went through a series of judges that ruled the land. The blessing upon the land was based on whether they followed God's covenant laws or abandoned them to live immoral and self-indulgent lives. The punishments of God were inflicted upon His people through natural disasters and also through destruction brought by maurauding nations that attacked and occupied the nation. When God's people returned to God, He always gave them outstanding leadership and the power to reclaim what belonged to them. Although the tribes would endure hardship, and even at times be in conflict with each other, they were still known as "Israelites" or "Hebrews." They would also retain their unique tribal identities as "states" or mini-nations within the greater realm. The book of Judges tells these stories.

The story of Ruth is also set in this timeframe. It tells of one family from the tribe of Judah that had migrated to Moab during a time of famine. When they returned, only the women came home. One of these was a Moabitess that had godly character, named Ruth. Once again God grafted in an "outsider" that had great faith in God's covenant promises. Ruth's story would figure prominently in coming generations.

Samuel

Samuel was the last judge of Israel. He was from the tribe of Levi, and his family was embedded among the tribe of Judah (as the levites were scattered among the tribes). His mother, Hannah, had been barren, and made a vow before God that her son would be dedicated to him if she were given a child. God heard her prayer, and Samuel was born. Hannah brought him to Eli, the high priest, at the Tabernacle in Shiloh, while still a young boy. Eli raised him in the presence of the tabernacle, and God began to speak to Samuel at a young age. He was known as a prophet, a seer and the things he shared from God were highly accurate. Because of this, he became Israel's last judge.

1 Samuel 8:1-8 [1]*And it came to pass, when Samuel was old, that he made his sons judges over Israel.* [2]*Now the name of his firstborn was Joel; and the name of his second, Abiah: they were judges in Beersheba.* [3]*And his sons walked not in his ways, but turned aside after lucre, and took bribes, and perverted judgment.*

[4]*Then all the elders of Israel gathered themselves together, and came to Samuel unto Ramah,* [5]*And said unto him, Behold, thou art old, and thy sons walk not in thy ways: now make us a king to judge us like all the nations.* [6]*But the thing displeased Samuel, when they said, Give us a king to judge us. And Samuel prayed unto the LORD.* [7]*And the LORD said unto Samuel, Hearken unto the voice of the people in all that they say unto thee: for they have not rejected thee, but they have rejected me, that I should not reign over them.* [8]*According to all the works which they have done since*

the day that I brought them up out of Egypt even unto this day, wherewith they have forsaken me, and served other gods, so do they also unto thee.

As Samuel aged, he set his sons into judicial leadership over the nation as well. However. they were not of the same moral caliber as Samuel, and the people knew it. The elders of Israel gathered together and petitioned Samuel for a change in government. They could have continued to operate with small, limited government that was comprised of godly men, but they had been looking at the other nations around them. They wanted a king instead; someone that would create a dynasty of leadership that was separated from the common life. And God granted their request.

Saul

Samuel anointed Saul (from the tribe of Benjamin) to be the first king of Israel at God's direction. (1 Samuel 9 & 10) Many have puzzled over this action because God clearly specified that the kings of Israel would come from the tribe of Judah (Genesis 49:10). We must remember that God would often test his people before bringing them into a realm of blessing and peace. Abraham first bore Ishmael, not Isaac. Isaac's eldest son, Esau, was not destined to inherit the covenant blessing. Instead; it went to Jacob. Saul was tall and good looking. 1 Samuel 10:23 says that Saul stood head and shoulders above the rest. He *looked* good! God was trying to teach the tribes to look to Him, and not to judge things by appearances or the way other nations lived. They wouldn't listen. God's true kingly line would come out of Judah as He had promised. First, there would be a time of testing, under Saul.

Saul served God for a few years, and then forsook Him completely to follow his own self-will. God knew the structure of government did not need changing. It was the heart of man that made the difference. But God had plans for the kingdom and for the kings. While Saul was yet reigning, God sent Samuel to anoint another young man to be the next king of Israel.

David

1 Samuel 16:1-13 [1]*And the LORD said unto Samuel, How long wilt thou mourn for Saul, seeing I have rejected him from reigning over Israel?*

fill thine horn with oil, and go, I will send thee to Jesse the Bethlehemite: for I have provided me a king among his sons. [2]*And Samuel said, How can I go? if Saul hear it, he will kill me. And the LORD said, Take an heifer with thee, and say, I am come to sacrifice to the LORD.* [3]*And call Jesse to the sacrifice, and I will show thee what thou shalt do: and thou shalt anoint unto me him whom I name unto thee.* [4]*And Samuel did that which the LORD spake, and came to Bethlehem. And the elders of the town trembled at his coming, and said, Comest thou peaceably?* [5]*And he said, Peaceably: I am come to sacrifice unto the LORD: sanctify yourselves, and come with me to the sacrifice. And he sanctified Jesse and his sons, and called them to the sacrifice.*

[6]*And it came to pass, when they were come, that he looked on Eliab, and said, Surely the LORD'S anointed is before him.* [7]*But the LORD said unto Samuel, Look not on his countenance, or on the height of his stature; because I have refused him: for the LORD seeth not as man seeth; for man looketh on the outward appearance, but the LORD looketh on the heart.* [8]*Then Jesse called Abinadab, and made him pass before Samuel. And he said, Neither hath the LORD chosen this.* [9]*Then Jesse made Shammah to pass by. And he said, Neither hath the LORD chosen this.* [10]*Again, Jesse made seven of his sons to pass before Samuel. And Samuel said unto Jesse, The LORD hath not chosen these.* [11]*And Samuel said unto Jesse, Are here all thy children? And he said, There remaineth yet the youngest, and, behold, he keepeth the sheep. And Samuel said unto Jesse, Send and fetch him: for we will not sit down till he come hither.* [12]*And he sent, and brought him in. Now he was ruddy, and withal of a beautiful countenance, and goodly to look to. And the LORD said, Arise, anoint him: for this is he.* [13]*Then Samuel took the horn of oil, and anointed him in the midst of his brethren: and the Spirit of the LORD came upon David from that day forward. So Samuel rose up, and went to Ramah.*

The story of king David is a rags-to-riches blessing from God Himself. David was from the tribe of Judah and was the youngest son of many. God selected him to be king because of his heart and moral character. David endured several years of hardship before he ascended to the throne (in 2 Samuel). And God was so blessed by his integrity and commitment to God that He gave David a covenant promise.

2 Samuel 7:1-17 [1]*And it came to pass, when the king sat in his house, and the LORD had given him rest round about from all his enemies;* [2]*That the king said unto Nathan the prophet, See now, I dwell in an house of* *cedar, but the ark of God dwelleth within curtains. [3]And Nathan said to the king, Go, do all that is in thine heart; for the LORD is with thee.*

[4]And it came to pass that night, that the word of the LORD came unto Nathan, saying, [5]Go and tell my servant David, Thus saith the LORD, Shalt thou build me an house for me to dwell in? [6]Whereas I have not dwelt in any house since the time that I brought up the children of Israel out of Egypt, even to this day, but have walked in a tent and in a tabernacle. [7]In all the places wherein I have walked with all the children of Israel spake I a word with any of the tribes of Israel, whom I commanded to feed my people Israel, saying, Why build ye not me an house of cedar? [8]Now therefore so shalt thou say unto my servant David, Thus saith the LORD of hosts, I took thee from the sheepcote, from following the sheep, to be ruler over my people, over Israel: [9]And I was with thee whithersoever thou wentest, and have cut off all thine enemies out of thy sight, and have made thee a great name, like unto the name of the great men that are in the earth. [10]Moreover I will appoint a place for my people Israel, and will plant them, that they may dwell in a place of their own, and move no more; neither shall the children of wickedness afflict them any more, as beforetime, [11]And as since the time that I commanded judges to be over my people Israel, and have caused thee to rest from all thine enemies. Also the LORD telleth thee that he will make thee an house. [12]And when thy days be fulfilled, and thou shalt sleep with thy fathers, I will set up thy seed after thee, which shall proceed out of thy bowels, and I will establish his kingdom. [13]He shall build an house for my name, and I will stablish the throne of his kingdom for ever. [14]I will be his father, and he shall be my son. If he commit iniquity, I will chasten him with the rod of men, and with the stripes of the children of men: [15]But my mercy shall not depart away from him, as I took it from Saul, whom I put away before thee. [16]And thine house and thy kingdom shall be established for ever before thee: thy throne shall be established for ever. [17]According to all these words, and according to all this vision, so did Nathan speak unto David.

This is a fantastic prophecy, on the scale of those given to Abraham, Isaac and Israel! It had begun when David desired to build God a house, a temple. God had foreordained that purpose for David's son, Solomon. But God wanted David to receive a prophecy from Him that would again be a portion of His eternal covenant, to be fulfilled specifically within a small portion of Israel (that being David's seed).

- **First**, God said that He had watched over David from the earliest time of his sheep-herding days until he sat upon the throne of the Kingdom. In other words, this was God's sovereign hand. David, from the tribe of Judah, was destined to reign upon the throne. This was the beginning of the fulfillment of Israel's prophecy in Genesis 49:10.
- **Second**, God told David that there would be a place He (God) would give to Israel. This place would be a future land. King David and the tribes of Israel were living in the land of Israel when God gave this prophecy to David! Apparently this would be in the future and would fulfill earlier prophecies to a greater extent!
- This land would be for God's covenant people. It would be a place where they could gather, live in peace, and be free from the affliction of their global neighbors.
- **Third**, God told David that his son would build Him a temple. This would satisfy David's heart and bring God into the center of the culture once again.
- **Fourth**, God would ensure that David's future seed would reign over Israel forever! God was so delighted with David that He made a covenant with him, a covenant of royalty. David's seed would reign upon the throne over the tribes of Israel. God specified that this would be forever!

Was God Lying?

You may think this writer has completely forgotten about the original premise of this work. However, that is not true. We are still on the path of determining whether the United States of America is in the Bible and the role she is to play in God's sight. However, in order to get to that place, we must emphasize a few points once again.

First, God does not lie. When He makes a promise in Scripture, we can always rely on Him to fulfill it, even though it may take several hundred years.

Second, God's promises are not merely spiritual, but literal. Although Jesus Christ was from David's seed and is the only Messiah, God promised a physical seed to reign upon a physical throne. This promise and others can not be spiritualized. It would be dangerous to try and do so.

Third, God's fulfillment is always the greatest at the end. God had already given the tribes of Israel the land He had promised to Abraham, Isaac and Jacob. But He was expanding upon that promise and telling David that there would be more land, and a land of peace that would be occupied by Israel in the last days.

The Blessings And Curses Divided By Tribe

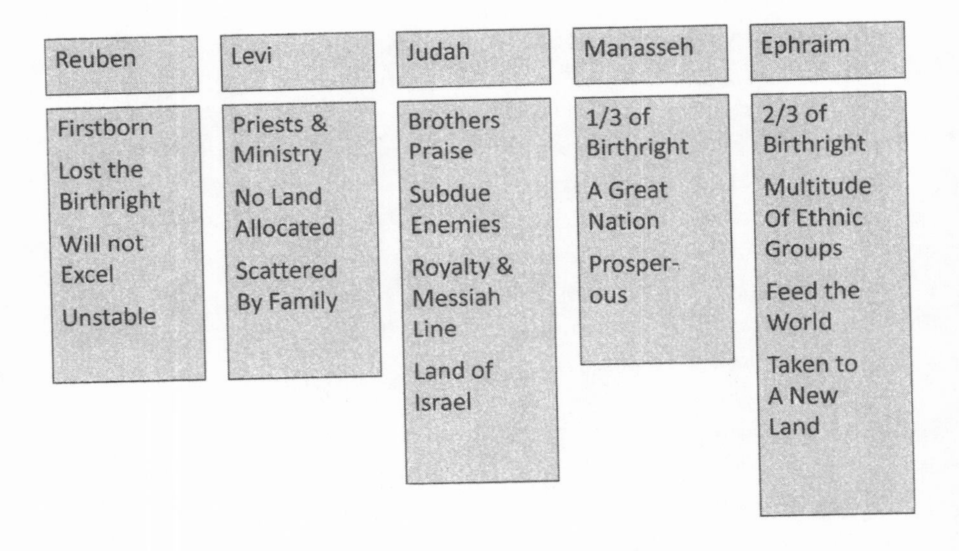

By now it's evident that God is beginning to differentiate between various tribes, by imparting specific blessings or curses upon the unique groups.

- **Reuben** has lost the birthright, the blessing of material goods, and has been told that he will not excel in the last days.
- **Levi** has been divided into clans, and judged for their anger (as has Simeon). God did approve of Levi's zeal toward Him, and sent Levi's clans throughout the rest of the tribes, so that they

became known as the 12 tribes of Israel instead of being 13 in reality.

- **Judah** has risen to the top of the heap. He will be honored above the other tribes, especially by the tribes themselves. He will retain military strength, and carry the royal lineage and the seed of the Messiah. Judah will also retain possession of the land God promised to Abraham, no matter where the tribes scatter. It is his.
- **Manasseh** (Joseph's eldest son) will become a great, prosperous national empire. He inherits 1/3 of the birthright, which means that he will become rich by God's hand. When Manasseh entered the promised land, his land was bisected by the Jordan River. Their nation would be bisected by water in future days as they continued to grow after they were scattered from Canaan.
- **Ephraim** (Joseph's youngest son, the founder of the 13th tribe) received 2/3 of the birthright blessing. His seed would be blessed materially more than any other nation in the world. Ephraim would form a multi-ethnic nation that would feed the world and live in a new land (more on those prophecies later).

God's covenant was designed to cover the entire earth with its influence. These blessings and curses were already in operation in the tribes under David's rule, but they would become more obvious within the next 2 generations.

Solomon

At the time of David's death, there was controversy over who would ascend to the throne. According to 1 Chronicles 3:1-9 David fathered 19 sons and one daughter, besides the sons of his concubines. Amnon, his firsborn, was the assumptive heir, but he had sexually violated his half-sister Tamar. One of his half-brothers, Absolom, then killed Amnon and was subsequently killed himself during an attempted coup. With the firstborn son dead, the heir to the throne was anyone's guess.

David may have been a man after God's own heart (Acts 13:22), but he was also a great sinner. He committed adultery with Bathsheba, and then had her husband murdered. After David married her, God sent Nathan, the prophet, to judge the king, and David repented.

However, God said that the sword would enter David's house, and the strife and killing among his sons were proof positive that what we sow, we also reap.

But God still loved David . . . and Bathsheba. She was David's favorite wife, and bore him four children. Solomon was the eldest living of the four, and in the closing moments of his earthly life, David ordered Nathan, the prophet, and Zadok, the priest, to annoint Solomon to be king over Israel (1 Kings 1). Solomon then had to deal with insurrection among his own brothers, and killed Adonijah who wanted the throne for himself. The kingdom would remain united, at least under Solomon.

Solomon asked God for a wise and understanding heart, so that he could govern the people and continue to bless the kingdom as David, his father, had done. God honored Solomon, and gave him a reign of prosperity and peace. Solomon was the quintessential renaissance man, an author, musician, king, builder, and leader of the nation. He oversaw the building of God's temple in Jerusalem as well as his own palace. It was said to be breathtaking. But Solomon also continued to walk in the sins of his father David, and it would displease the Lord.

God Judges Solomon

1 Kings 11:1-13 *[1]But king Solomon loved many strange women, together with the daughter of Pharaoh, women of the Moabites, Ammonites, Edomites, Zidonians, and Hittites; [2]Of the nations concerning which the LORD said unto the children of Israel, Ye shall not go in to them, neither shall they come in unto you: for surely they will turn away your heart after their gods: Solomon clave unto these in love. [3]And he had seven hundred wives, princesses, and three hundred concubines: and his wives turned away his heart. [4]For it came to pass, when Solomon was old, that his wives turned away his heart after other gods: and his heart was not perfect with the LORD his God, as was the heart of David his father. [5]For Solomon went after Ashtoreth the goddess of the Zidonians, and after Milcom the abomination of the Ammonites. [6]And Solomon did evil in the sight of the LORD, and went not fully after the LORD, as did David his father. [7]Then did Solomon build an high place for Chemosh, the abomination of Moab, in the hill that is before Jerusalem, and for Molech, the abomination of the* *children of Ammon. [8]And likewise did he for all his strange wives, which burnt incense and sacrificed unto their gods.*

[9]And the LORD was angry with Solomon, because his heart was turned from the LORD God of Israel, which had appeared unto him twice, [10]And had commanded him concerning this thing, that he should not go after other gods: but he kept not that which the LORD commanded. [11]Wherefore the LORD said unto Solomon, Forasmuch as this is done of thee, and thou hast not kept my covenant and my statutes, which I have commanded thee, I will surely rend the kingdom from thee, and will give it to thy servant. [12]Notwithstanding in thy days I will not do it for David thy father's sake: but I will rend it out of the hand of thy son. [13]Howbeit I will not rend away all the kingdom; but will give one tribe to thy son for David my servant's sake, and for Jerusalem's sake which I have chosen.

We are told that Solomon loved many strange women. What an understatement! He had 700 wives and 300 concubines. It was customary to take wives from other kings when political alliances were made, but Solomon carred it to an extreme.

- When Solomon was old, his heart turned away from God and looked to idols.
- Solomon decided to adopt a multicultural approach to worship, embracing Ashtoreth and Milcam, as well as Chemosh and Molech. These were demonic deities whose worship rituals involved blood sacrifice up to and including human sacrifice.
- God became angry with Solomon, because he specifically warned Solomon.
- So God imposed judgment upon Solomon. Although God had promised David that his seed would rule on the throne forever, God would now restrict the scope of their authority.
- God would remove 10 tribes out of Solomon's hand. He would be left with 2 tribes to rule (and the Levites that lived among them). One tribe would be because of His promise to David, and one tribe would remain because of God's love for Jerusalem.
- This would not be done in Solomon's reign. Instead, the dividing of the tribes would occur after Solomon's death, when his son is to take the throne.

God Prepares Two Kingdoms

Solomon was a master builder, and employed many highly skilled leaders in his kingdom. One of these was a man named Jeroboam. He was faithful to Solomon, was a military tactician and warrior, and apparently was also found faithful before Almighty God. One day as Jeroboam was on business, he was met by Ahijah, the prophet of God.

1 Kings 11:29-37 [29]*And it came to pass at that time when Jeroboam went out of Jerusalem, that the prophet Ahijah the Shilonite found him in the way; and he had clad himself with a new garment; and they two were alone in the field:* [30]*And Ahijah caught the new garment that was on him, and rent it in twelve pieces:* [31]*And he said to Jeroboam, Take thee ten pieces: for thus saith the LORD, the God of Israel, Behold, I will rend the kingdom out of the hand of Solomon, and will give ten tribes to thee:* [32]*(But he shall have one tribe for my servant David's sake, and for Jerusalem's sake, the city which I have chosen out of all the tribes of Israel:)* [33]*Because that they have forsaken me, and have worshipped Ashtoreth the goddess of the Zidonians, Chemosh the god of the Moabites, and Milcom the god of the children of Ammon, and have not walked in my ways, to do that which is right in mine eyes, and to keep my statutes and my judgments, as did David his father.* [34]*Howbeit I will not take the whole kingdom out of his hand: but I will make him prince all the days of his life for David my servant's sake, whom I chose, because he kept my commandments and my statutes:* [35]*But I will take the kingdom out of his son's hand, and will give it unto thee, even ten tribes.* [36]*And unto his son will I give one tribe, that David my servant may have a light alway before me in Jerusalem, the city which I have chosen me to put my name there.* [37]*And I will take thee, and thou shalt reign according to all that thy soul desireth, and shalt be king over Israel.*

- Ahijah met Jeroboam in the field and began to prophesy over him.
- He divided a garment into 12 pieces, and set aside 10 pieces for Jeroboam to take to himself. These represented the 10 tribes that would be removed from Solomon's leadership. Two pieces (or tribes) would remain under his realm.
- Ahijah reiterated again that the reason for this division was because of sin and idolatry.

- Then, once again Ahijah restated the prophecy. Ten tribes would be torn from Solomon's dynasty and given to Jeroboam to rule. Two tribes would remain in Solomon's hands. Once again God has confirmed His prophetic Word in the mouth of two or three witnesses!

Apparently, this was quite exciting to Jeroboam, and he had to share the news. Word came to Solomon that Jeroboam had been anointed to be king, and this came as a threat to him. Jeroboam had to flee for his life, and lived in exile in Egypt until Solomon's death.

The Tea Party Of 975 B.C.

Despite the fact that Solomon had many wives, his son did not have to fight his way to the throne. Rehoboam was his designated heir, and he ascended to the throne seemingly without any problem. But Jeroboam had returned from Egypt.

1 Kings 12:1-15 *[1]And Rehoboam went to Shechem: for all Israel were come to Shechem to make him king. [2]And it came to pass, when Jeroboam the son of Nebat, who was yet in Egypt, heard of it, (for he was fled from the presence of king Solomon, and Jeroboam dwelt in Egypt;) [3]That they sent and called him. And Jeroboam and all the congregation of Israel came, and spake unto Rehoboam, saying, [4]Thy father made our yoke grievous: now therefore make thou the grievous service of thy father, and his heavy yoke which he put upon us, lighter, and we will serve thee. [5]And he said unto them, Depart yet for three days, then come again to me. And the people departed. [6]And king Rehoboam consulted with the old men, that stood before Solomon his father while he yet lived, and said, How do ye advise that I may answer this people? [7]And they spake unto him, saying, If thou wilt be a servant unto this people this day, and wilt serve them, and answer them, and speak good words to them, then they will be thy servants for ever. [8]But he forsook the counsel of the old men, which they had given him, and consulted with the young men that were grown up with him, and which stood before him: [9]And he said unto them, What counsel give ye that we may answer this people, who have spoken to me, saying, Make the yoke which thy father did put upon us lighter? [10]And the young men that were grown up with him spake unto him, saying, Thus shalt thou speak unto this people that spake unto thee,* *saying, Thy father made our yoke heavy, but make thou it lighter unto us; thus shalt thou say unto them, My little finger shall be thicker than my father's loins.* [11]*And now whereas my father did lade you with a heavy yoke, I will add to your yoke: my father hath chastised you with whips, but I will chastise you with scorpions.* [12]*So Jeroboam and all the people came to Rehoboam the third day, as the king had appointed, saying, Come to me again the third day.* [13]*And the king answered the people roughly, and forsook the old men's counsel that they gave him;* [14]*And spake to them after the counsel of the young men, saying, My father made your yoke heavy, and I will add to your yoke: my father also chastised you with whips, but I will chastise you with scorpions.* [15]*Wherefore the king hearkened not unto the people; for the cause was from the LORD, that he might perform his saying, which the LORD spake by Ahijah the Shilonite unto Jeroboam the son of Nebat.*

During Solomon's reign, heavy taxation had been imposed upon the people, to build Solomon's projects. The temple had been built largely with funds donated by King David, but the fortifications to Jerusalem and other cities, and Solomon's palaces had been built with taxes. Solomon had also strengthened the military and the land had enjoyed peace, but the burden of taxation was too much.

The tribes of Israel actually recruited Jeroaboam, asking him to return from Egypt to be their spokesman. Solomon's son, Rehoboam, was on the throne, but Jeroboam had their hearts. Israel's petition was simple: lower our tax burden and we will serve you as our king.

Rehoboam consulted with the elders, the old rulers and counsellors. They urged him to lower taxes and listen to the people. Then he consulted with the young, progressive leaders. Their counsel? Ignore the people. Set the agenda. In fact, they counselled Rehoboam to raise taxes and increase the burden! Rehoboam listened to their counsel, and was rude and tyrannical in his response.

1 Kings 12:16-20 [16]*So when all Israel saw that the king hearkened not unto them, the people answered the king, saying, What portion have we in David? neither have we inheritance in the son of Jesse: to your tents, O Israel: now see to thine own house, David. So Israel departed unto their tents.* [17]*But as for the children of Israel which dwelt in the cities of Judah, Rehoboam reigned over them.* [18]*Then king Rehoboam sent Adoram, who was over the tribute; and all Israel stoned him with stones, that he died.*

Therefore king Rehoboam made speed to get him up to his chariot, to flee to Jerusalem. [19]So Israel rebelled against the house of David unto this day. [20]And it came to pass, when all Israel heard that Jeroboam was come again, that they sent and called him unto the congregation, and made him king over all Israel: there was none that followed the house of David, but the tribe of Judah only.

When Israel saw that Rehoboam would not listen to their requests, they revolted. There would be no taxation without appropriate representation! (This began a pattern that would continue forward in years to come.) The ten tribes immediately separated from Judah, and appointed Jeroboam as their king. This ten-tribed nation would also be called Israel, or more accurately, the House of Israel.

God Steps Into The Battle

1 Kings 12:21-24 *[21]And when Rehoboam was come to Jerusalem, he assembled all the house of Judah, with the tribe of Benjamin, an hundred and fourscore thousand chosen men, which were warriors, to fight against the house of Israel, to bring the kingdom again to Rehoboam the son of Solomon. [22]But the word of God came unto Shemaiah the man of God, saying, [23]Speak unto Rehoboam, the son of Solomon, king of Judah, and unto all the house of Judah and Benjamin, and to the remnant of the people, saying, [24]Thus saith the LORD, Ye shall not go up, nor fight against your brethren the children of Israel: return every man to his house; for this thing is from me. They hearkened therefore to the word of the LORD, and returned to depart, according to the word of the LORD.*

King Rehoboam decided he disliked this rebellion against the crown. Quickly he organized an army from the two remaining tribes in his realm (Judah and Benjamin), and prepared to attack the newly formed union of Israel. However, one of God's prophets spoke up and commanded Rehoboam to stand down. This separation between the tribes was not from satan, nor was it a work of the flesh. It was sovereignly ordained by God. This command from God Himself stopped Judah and Benjamin in their tracks. They returned to their homes.

The United Kingdom of Israel was now divided into two separate nations.

- Both nations are still children of Israel; they are related to each other.
- Both nations have claim to Abraham's covenant blessing!
- Both nations have been commanded to follow Almighty God as their leader, to receive His favor.
- Both nations will be called Israel, which will be confusing at times.
- And God now has two nations He is overseeing in the earth, not just one!

In Genesis 35, God had promised Jacob that "a nation and a company of nations" would be of him (his seed). This was far more significant than the tribes dwelling together as one united kingdom. God had foretold the day when His covenant people would be divided, and would be in multiple nations of the world. But there was more yet to come.

The Houses Of Israel And Judah

Jeroboam now ruled over a new nation that quickly became known as the "House of Israel." It was called Israel more frequently than its sister nation. In fact, the House of Israel would be mentioned more in Scripture than any other.

Rehoboam (Solomon's son) still reigned over two tribes, the tribes of Benjamin and Judah. The tribe of Levi remained scattered throughout the twelve tribes, and many of them migrated back toward the two-tribe kingdom as the ten tribes quickly forsook the Lord. This kingdom became known as the "House of Judah." They were referred to as "Jews," even though there were those from the tribes of Benjamin and Levi in their midst.

The Tribes Divided

House of Israel Ephraim	House of Judah Judah
Reuben Simeon Levi (Partial) Issachar Zebulun Gad Asher Dan Naphtali Manasseh (Joseph) Ephraim (Joseph)	Judah Benjamin Levi (Partial)

Judah became the leader of the House of Judah. They were the predominant tribe. Ephraim became the leader of the House of Israel. God had foretold in Genesis 48 of his emerging greatness, and it began with his leadership in the ten-tribe nation.

The House of Judah's capital city remained Jerusalem. The people of the land were called Jews, Judahites, or by their tribal names (e.g., Benjamin or Levi) Occasionally, they were also called Israelites. The House of Israel's capital became Samaria, in the northern part of the land. They were called Israelites, or names associated with their tribes as well. They were never called Jews! As they fell away from serving God, and were disbanded, they were later referred to as the dispersed, or scattered tribes, or were called Gentiles.

The Scattering Foretold

At this point, all the tribes of Israel followed the Lord. This meant their males were circumcised, they observed the feasts ordained by Almighty God, and they traveled to the temple to offer sacrifice on a periodic basis. This concerned king Jeroboam of the House of Israel. He feared losing the people (1 Kings 12:25-33) due to their connection to the temple in Jerusalem. Instead of trusting God and following Him, Jeroboam had two idols made. They were golden calves, actually young, horned bulls. He placed one in Bethel, and one in Dan. As king, he encouraged the people to forsake the worship of Almighty God, and regular pilgrimages to the temple in Jerusalem. Instead, they would worship the works of their hands and commerce, the golden bulls set up in the high places. This enraged Almighty God. He had given the House of Israel to Jeroboam to lead.

1 Kings 14:1-15 [1]*At that time Abijah the son of Jeroboam fell sick.* [2]*And Jeroboam said to his wife, Arise, I pray thee, and disguise thyself, that thou be not known to be the wife of Jeroboam; and get thee to Shiloh: behold, there is Ahijah the prophet, which told me that I should be king over this people.* [3]*And take with thee ten loaves, and cracknels, and a cruse of honey, and go to him: he shall tell thee what shall become of the child.* [4]*And Jeroboam's wife did so, and arose, and went to Shiloh, and came to the house of Ahijah. But Ahijah could not see; for his eyes were set by reason of his age.* [5]*And the LORD said unto Ahijah, Behold, the wife of Jeroboam cometh to ask a thing of thee for her son; for he is sick: thus and thus shalt thou say unto her: for it shall be, when she cometh in, that she shall feign herself to be another woman.* [6]*And it was so, when Ahijah heard the sound of her feet, as she came in at the door, that he said, Come in, thou wife of Jeroboam; why feignest thou thyself to be another? for I am sent to thee with heavy tidings.*

[7]*Go, tell Jeroboam, Thus saith the LORD God of Israel, Forasmuch as I exalted thee from among the people, and made thee prince over my people Israel,* [8]*And rent the kingdom away from the house of David, and gave it thee: and yet thou hast not been as my servant David, who kept my commandments, and who followed me with all his heart, to do that only which was right in mine eyes;* [9]*But hast done evil above all that were before thee: for thou hast gone and made thee other gods, and molten images, to provoke me to anger, and hast cast me behind thy back:* [10]*Therefore, behold, I will bring evil upon the house of Jeroboam, and will cut off from Jeroboam him that pisseth against the wall, and him that is shut up and left in Israel, and will take away the remnant of the house of Jeroboam, as a man taketh away dung, till it be all gone.* [11]*Him that dieth of Jeroboam in the city shall the dogs eat; and him that dieth in the field shall the fowls of the air eat: for the LORD hath spoken it.* [12]*Arise thou therefore, get thee to thine own house: and when thy feet enter into the city, the child shall die.* [13]*And all Israel shall mourn for him, and bury him: for he only of Jeroboam shall come to the grave, because in him there is found some good*

thing toward the LORD God of Israel in the house of Jeroboam. [14]*Moreover the LORD shall raise him up a king over Israel, who shall cut off the house of Jeroboam that day: but what? even now.* [15]*For the LORD shall smite Israel, as a reed is shaken in the water, and he shall root up Israel out of this good land, which he gave to their fathers, and shall scatter them beyond the river, because they have made their groves, provoking the LORD to anger.*

God had blessed Jeroboam with a nation, a wife, and a son. But in due time, his son became gravely ill, and Jeroboam feared for his life. Although he was not godly himself, he respected God's prophets. So Jeroboam urged his wife to disguise herself and visit the house of the prophet Ahijah, in Shiloh. Ahijah was now quite old, and his vision had failed. But God revealed the identity of his visitor. God had a prophecy to impart.

- First, God had exalted Jeroboam; it was not his doing.
- God had given the House of Israel to Jeroboam to lead under His all-seeing eye.
- Jeroboam had forsaken God. He had also encouraged idolatry, and had discouraged the people from serving Almighty God.
- God would now destroy Jeroboam's entire family. Every male would die, starting with Jeroboam's son. The remainder would die violent deaths because of their rebellion against God.

But God wasn't done speaking. Ahijah continued. Not only would Jeroboam's family be destroyed, but *God would root up Israel out of this good land* (God's promised land to Abraham), and would scatter them. Why? Because they had forsaken God.

Although the House of Israel was the larger of the two nations, they were still expected to serve Almighty God. God now made this statement very clear. The ten tribes were going to be removed. They would be scattered. They had existed as a sovereign nation for only 17 years, but would be judged for their sins.

The House Of Israel Is Taken Captive

God keeps track of important things. Like time. Obedience and rebellion. Sin. Repentance. One would think the House of Israel would repent after hearing of God's judgment under Jeroboam, but they didn't. In fact, they continued to strengthen their reliance on the golden bulls and other idols, and completely abandoned God. At the appointed time, God acted.

2 Kings 17:5-6 *[5]Then the king of Assyria came up throughout all the land, and went up to Samaria, and besieged it three years. [6]In the ninth year of Hoshea the king of Assyria took Samaria, and carried Israel away into Assyria, and placed them in Halah and in Habor by the river of Gozan, and in the cities of the Medes.*

Two hundred thirty-seven years after God prophesied to Jeroboam, judgment came. Assyria had risen in power, enabled by Almighty God. Their armies plundered Samaria, destroyed the golden bulls, killed thousands, and scattered the House of Israel. Many were carried captive into Assyria. Many more scattered, looking for new places to live.

The House Of Judah Is Taken Captive

The House of Judah served God fitfully during their days as a nation. However, through time they forsook Almighty God as well and served idols and the works of their hands. God's judgment upon them came incrementally, starting with the Assyrians.

2 Kings 18:13 *[13]Now in the fourteenth year of king Hezekiah did Sennacherib king of Assyria come up against all the fenced cities of Judah, and took them.*

Hezekiah was a godly king and interceded for the nation. God did spare some of the cities, and kept the full measure of judgment from occurring. Ultimately, however, it would come because the nation would not fully repent and live by God's covenant law.

2 Chronicles 36:11-21 *[11]Zedekiah was one and twenty years old when he began to reign, and reigned eleven years in Jerusalem. [12]And he did that which was evil in the sight of the LORD his God, and humbled not himself before Jeremiah the prophet speaking from the mouth of the LORD. [13]And he also rebelled against king Nebuchadnezzar, who had made him swear by God: but he stiffened his neck, and hardened his heart from turning unto the LORD God of Israel. [14]Moreover all the chief of the priests, and the people, transgressed very much after all the abominations of the heathen; and polluted the house of the LORD which he had hallowed in Jerusalem. [15]And the LORD God of their fathers sent to them by his messengers, rising up betimes, and sending; because he had compassion on* *his people, and on his dwelling place:* [16]*But they mocked the messengers of God, and despised his words, and misused his prophets, until the wrath of the LORD arose against his people, till there was no remedy.* [17]*Therefore he brought upon them the king of the Chaldees, who slew their young men with the sword in the house of their sanctuary, and had no compassion upon young man or maiden, old man, or him that stooped for age: he gave them all into his hand.* [18]*And all the vessels of the house of God, great and small, and the treasures of the house of the LORD, and the treasures of the king, and of his princes; all these he brought to Babylon.* [19]*And they burnt the house of God, and brake down the wall of Jerusalem, and burnt all the palaces thereof with fire, and destroyed all the goodly vessels thereof.* [20]*And them that had escaped from the sword carried he away to Babylon; where they were servants to him and his sons until the reign of the kingdom of Persia:* [21]*To fulfil the word of the LORD by the mouth of Jeremiah, until the land had enjoyed her sabbaths: for as long as she lay desolate she kept sabbath, to fulfil threescore and ten years.*

The last king of Judah, Zedekiah, was just as rebellious as his predecessors. He refused to serve God and would not obey the words of Jeremiah the prophet. As a result, God sent Nebuchadrezzar, king of Babylon, against Judah. They ransacked Jerusalem, took many captive, put out Zedekiah's eyes, killed his sons, and left the land in ruins for 70 years. God had covenant blessings for His people, but they refused to honor their part of the agreement. God had to punish them, and they died in a strange land for a complete generation, as they considered their sinful ways.

God's Promise To The House Of Judah

Although the Houses of Israel and Judah were sinful, God was still watching over His covenant with Abraham, Isaac and Israel. This becomes apparent when we consider a verse found in the book of Jeremiah. Jeremiah, the prophet, was called by God to do many things, including prophesying to Zedekiah, the king of Judah. Zedekiah's heart was hard, and he repeatedly destroyed Jeremiah's written prophecies, threatening Jeremiah, and finally putting him in the dungeon. While this discouraged the prophet, God spoke to him in that place, and used him for a final, grand mission that exceeds anything you or I could dream. (More on that in a coming chapter.)

As Jerusalem was facing the encroaching threat of war, God gave Jeremiah a promise. It was a promise of hope in the face of disaster.

Jeremiah 29:10 [10]*For thus saith the LORD, That after seventy years be accomplished at Babylon I will visit you, and perform my good word toward you, in causing you to return to this place.*

God told Jeremiah to prophesy over the House of Judah. They would be taken captive. Jerusalem would be destroyed. However, after 70 years in captivity God would release the House of Judah, and they would return to the land God promised to Abraham. It was their possession, and they would live there once again.

After exactly 70 years in captivity God kept His Word. He had prophesied through Isaiah (Isaiah 44:28 through Isaiah 45:1-4) that a ruler named Cyrus would rise up. This ruler would release the House of Judah.

Isaiah 44:28 [28]*That saith of Cyrus, He is my shepherd, and shall perform all my pleasure: even saying to Jerusalem, Thou shalt be built; and to the temple, Thy foundation shall be laid.*

Cyrus! A heathen king, the ruler of the Medes, Persians and king of Babylon. God had raised him up to do God's will. It was time for the House of Judah to return home!

The Jews Return To The Land Of Promise

2 Chronicles 36:22-23 [22]*Now in the first year of Cyrus king of Persia, that the word of the LORD spoken by the mouth of Jeremiah might be accomplished, the LORD stirred up the spirit of Cyrus king of Persia, that he made a proclamation throughout all his kingdom, and put it also in writing, saying,* [23]*Thus saith Cyrus king of Persia, All the kingdoms of the earth hath the LORD God of heaven given me; and he hath charged me to build him an house in Jerusalem, which is in Judah. Who is there among you of all his people? The LORD his God be with him, and let him go up.*

What a fantastic realization! The kings of the heathen are under God's hand, foreordained to operate around God's covenant and Word. When it was time for the Jews to go home, God released them. It was all a part of His covenant plan, and he had leaders prepared among the Jews to facilitate the task as well.

Ezra 1:1-6 [1]*Now in the first year of Cyrus king of Persia, that the word of the LORD by the mouth of Jeremiah might be fulfilled, the LORD stirred* *up the spirit of Cyrus king of Persia, that he made a proclamation throughout all his kingdom, and put it also in writing, saying, [2]Thus saith Cyrus king of Persia, The LORD God of heaven hath given me all the kingdoms of the earth; and he hath charged me to build him an house at Jerusalem, which is in Judah. [3]Who is there among you of all his people? his God be with him, and let him go up to Jerusalem, which is in Judah, and build the house of the LORD God of Israel, (he is the God,) which is in Jerusalem. [4]And whosoever remaineth in any place where he sojourneth, let the men of his place help him with silver, and with gold, and with goods, and with beasts, beside the freewill offering for the house of God that is in Jerusalem.*

[5]Then rose up the chief of the fathers of Judah and Benjamin, and the priests, and the Levites, with all them whose spirit God had raised, to go up to build the house of the LORD which is in Jerusalem. [6]And all they that were about them strengthened their hands with vessels of silver, with gold, with goods, and with beasts, and with precious things, beside all that was willingly offered.

God had prepared Ezra to lead the House of Judah in their return. Ezra's first goal was to rebuild the temple of God as the center of worship. This was a difficult task because occupiers had moved in that were completely against the effort. Furthermore, the people also had to build their own homes, restore their lands, cultivate crops and herds, and reestablish their lives once again. Who would go?

Surprisingly, a great many went. According to Ezra 1:6, they were comprised of members of three tribes: Judah, Benjamin, and Levi. They were all from the House of Judah! God had promised them the land as their inheritance, and He was faithful to His Word, to the smallest detail.

Wait A Minute!

But something is wrong! Didn't God place His covenant blessings and promises upon all the tribes of Israel? Did not God prophesy over each of them individually in Genesis 49, that there would be unique identities for each of them in the last days? If this is the case, we can agree that the House of Judah returned to the promised land. But where is the House of Israel?

There are those that will disagree at this point, noting that there are a few of those within the genealogies listed in Ezra 2 that were part of the 10 tribes. This is true. Apparently, they had joined with the Jews at some point in time, but they are a very small minority of those returning. The ten tribed House of Israel was a much larger people than the House of Judah. The reason some want to point out the very few names that were from the 10 tribes, is because it supports their belief that all of the 12 tribes somehow melded together into one nation again. But neither Bible prophecy nor history supports this claim. It is errant.

Others will argue that the House of Israel remained lost to this day, just scattered like dust in the wind. Many have roved the globe, searching for various, small sects that still keep ancient worship patterns and tribal customs that are "Israelite" in origin. Does this answer the question of their location? Absolutely not. It is true that some pockets of these people exist. But God promised to Abraham a people that would be as great as the sand of the sea and the stars of the heavens. He also promised a people that were blessed materially, had military might, and were recognized the world over for the significance they possessed. This "lost tribes" argument cannot answer that postulation.

Still others will attempt to "spiritualize" the House of Israel. They may argue that while the House of Judah is a literal people, the House of Israel has now been replaced by the global Christian faith they call "the church." They will attempt to explain the fact that Christians are blessed with God's favor, and have God's blessing as a result. They are a large group of people as well, and are known around the world.

Several problems exist with this argument. Among them is the fact that one cannot replace a physical promise with a spiritual outcome. When God promised that Isaac would be born, He meant that a literal, physical son would be born and named Isaac. When God promises to physically heal our diseases, He means just that! If everything becomes spiritualized, then the Jews have no more claim to being Abraham's seed unless they are Christians. However, today they have claim to the land of Israel because of their physical covenant blessings, not because of their spiritual obedience.

When God caused Israel to prophesy over the tribes in Genesis 49 and Moses to prophesy further over them in Deuteronomy 33, those prophecies were to be physically fulfilled in the last days. This cannot be contained within Christianity, because the faith is not broken up into tribal identities. God was careful to proclaim many different times that the seed of the tribes would produce nations, not spiritual faiths. So this argument cannot be valid for these and other reasons.

God has been faithful to the House of Judah. He has returned them to the land of promise. He has seen their repentance, and has continued His covenant blessing on their lives. And yet, the House of Judah is the lesser kingdom.

If God keeps His Word, He must still be at work among the House of Israel, the ten "lost" tribes. And we must dig a little deeper to discover their connection, if any, to the United States of America.

So we ask the question . . .

Where Is The House Of Israel?

CHAPTER 6

Where Is The House Of Israel?

Imagine with me for a moment a scenario in contemporary terms. The nations of Canada and the United States of America have coexisted peacefully, side-by-side for centuries now, and as it says on the peace arch gateway between the two nations in Washington State, they are "children of a common mother," and "brethren dwelling together in unity." What would happen if the United States were attacked by another nation, and scattered throughout the world?

Undoubtedly some U.S. citizens would flee to Canada. Once there, they would take on Canadian citizenship and adopt the customs of their former sister-nation. But what would happen to the vast multitudes that were scattered elsewhere? They would look for each other throughout the world and create new groups. Many of these groups would be subsets of existing nations, or would turn into brand new nations themselves. This people group would be too large to ignore and have too strong a heritage to dismiss. Such is the scenario when the House of Israel went into captivity and was "scattered" by Assyria.

This is what happened to the House of Israel. They were the larger nation and when they were dispersed by Assyria, they set out to find their destiny. Some joined with the House of Judah and identified with them. But the vast majority went into the world, as apostates far away from the God of their covenant. It would take the prophetic Scriptures to properly identify them in the last days, as their behaviors had been predicted by God. Millions of Israelites shifted locations in these years, and it takes historic research to discover their identities and locations today.

The House of Judah was taken captive many years after the House of Israel, but they returned to the land of Israel. They documented their journey home to the land, adhered to their faith in Almighty God and rebuilt their society on God's law. So let's continue our quest that connects America to the Bible by asking a simple question.

Who Are The Jews?

2 Kings 16:1-6 [1]*In the seventeenth year of Pekah the son of Remaliah Ahaz the son of Jotham king of Judah began to reign.* [2]*Twenty years old was Ahaz when he began to reign, and reigned sixteen years in Jerusalem, and did not that which was right in the sight of the LORD his God, like David his father.* [3]*But he walked in the way of the kings of Israel, yea, and made his son to pass through the fire, according to the abominations of the heathen, whom the LORD cast out from before the children of Israel.* [4]*And he sacrificed and burnt incense in the high places, and on the hills, and under every green tree.*

[5]*Then Rezin king of Syria and Pekah son of Remaliah king of Israel came up to Jerusalem to war: and they besieged Ahaz, but could not overcome him.* [6]*At that time Rezin king of Syria recovered Elath to Syria, and drave the Jews from Elath: and the Syrians came to Elath, and dwelt there unto this day.*

Approximately 1,100 years after Abraham's death, the people of Jerusalem were involved in a battle. It is unique in the Bible for a few reasons.

- Ahaz is listed as the king of the House of Judah. However, he is not walking before Almighty God, but living like the kings of Israel. Who is Israel? This is the 10 tribe kingdom of the House of Israel. (Verses 1-4)
- Syria and the House of Israel have temporarily become allies. They decide to go up and make war against Judah! However, Jerusalem is too well fortified and they can not conquer it. (Verse 5)
- So, Syria goes to Elath (Verse 6, and also 2 Kings 14:21-22), and drives the "Jews" out of there. Syria now occupies land formerly controlled by the House of Judah.

You may wonder what is significant about this passage. Did you notice? First, the two nations at war are actually related to each other. They are: The House of Judah, and—the House of Israel! Secondly, this is the first time in Scripture that the word "Jew" is mentioned!

Today the Jews are often referred to in Judeo-Christian circles as "God's chosen people." This term comes from the fact that they are descendents of Abraham, and have recognized the covenant made by Almighty God with Abraham's seed. This is true, but it is not the *whole* truth.

In order to be a Jew by bloodline, one must be either from:

- The House of Judah (the nation); or
- The tribe of Judah (a portion of the nation).

Jew, Or Not Jew?

- Jesus is rightfully called the "Lion of the tribe of Judah." (Revelation 5:5). He was also the "King of the Jews" (Matthew 2:1-2; Matthew 27:37). He was of the house and lineage of David on both Mary and Joseph's family lines.
- The Apostle Paul was a Jew. He was of the tribe of Benjamin (Romans 11:1; Philippians 3:5). Therefore, he was of the House of Judah (which was comprised of some Levites, the tribe of Benjamin and the tribe of Judah).
- In the book of Esther, Mordacai was a Jew, one that descended from Benjamin (Esther 2:5)
- However, the 10-tribe House of Israel is *Non-Jewish*! Ephraim and the other tribes in the House of Israel were *never* part of the House of Judah. They are Israelites, but not Jews!
- All Jews are Israelites, but not all Israelites are Jews. This author, Steven, is a Grant, but not all Grants are Steven!
- Anna the prophetess (Luke 2:36) is specifically listed as being from the tribe of Asher. Asher was part of the House of Israel. Anna is *not* called a Jewess. Why? Because she was *not* one; she was an Israelite from the House of Israel!
- In fact, Abraham was NOT a Jew! This author has heard ministers refer to Abraham as a Jew, but he lived before the time when the House of Judah was created. Judah was Abraham's great-grandson! The term "Jew" is an abbreviated version of

that name. In fact, none of the early covenant men of God were Jews at all!

Therefore, we must conclude that while the Jews are a part of God's covenant people, they are not ALL of God's covenant people! God still has a physical covenant people that is larger than the Jews alone. This does not negate God's promises to the Jews. But we must rightly divide the Word of truth in order to understand who else is included under God's covenant blessing besides the Jews.

Other Observations About The Jews

They own the land. According to Numbers 14:24 and Numbers 13:6 God specified that Judah would occupy the land of Canaan. 1 Kings 14:1-15 stated that God would root the House of Israel out of the land, but the Jews would retain their roots in that region. During the time that Israel was sent to spy out the land, the spy from the tribe of Judah (Caleb) was given a promise that his seed would possess the land. God has kept His word to the Jews, and we must support them in their rightful claim.

In 1948, just hours before the formal presentation of the new nation of Israel to the world, the newly formed Knessett (Israeli Parliament) was still struggling with a key issue. What was it? It was what they would name their new nation. They realized then that they were not from all the tribes of Israel, but were Jews. Therefore, they named their new nation "The Jewish State of Israel." Today we call it "Israel," but that is actually a shortened version of its legal name.

In Jeremiah 24:5-6 God stated that Judah (the Jews) would return to Canaan and possess that land. He gave this promise despite the fact that they had forsaken Him, and were about to be taken captive by Babylon. We see that God kept His promise and Judah is back in the land today.

They keep the language. Another wonderful promise is found in Jeremiah 31:23. [23] *Thus saith the LORD of hosts, the God of Israel; As yet they shall use this speech in the land of Judah and in the cities thereof, when I shall bring again their captivity; The LORD bless thee, O habitation of justice, and mountain of holiness.* The Jews would retain the original Hebrew tongue! After the dispersion of the people of the earth at the tower of Babel, God linked people with their tongues to various lands. Genesis 10:5 says, *"By these were the isles of the Gentiles divided in their lands; every one after his tongue, after their families, in their nations."* Each unique nation had a unique tongue, and it was also linked to their various nations or lands.

When Daniel and other Jews were taken captive by Babylon, some of them were selected to learn the language or tongue of the Chaldeans (Daniel 1:4). It was the "mother tongue of the land." Luke 23:38 states the inscription placed over Jesus' head as He hung on the cross, *"This is the King of the Jews,"* was written in Greek, Latin and Hebrew. Greek was the cultural language of the world, Latin was the language of the over-arching government, and Hebrew was the language of the Jews, of the land.

Today Hebrew is the official language of the Jewish State of Israel, but it was almost a dead language in the 1800's. It was used by the Rabbis and in the synagogues and while some could speak the language, few did. One man, Eliezer Ben-Yehudah, singularly resurrected the language by reinstating the common, spoken language, creating a Hebrew dictionary, and pressing for a resurrected, Jewish nation complete with Hebrew as the spoken language. His work reconnected the land and God's chosen people.

They are a minority. 1 Kings 12:23; 2 Kings 19:30-31 and other passages in the Prophets state that Judah would be a remnant, or few in number. In other words, the Jews would be a minority people upon the face of the earth. Once again, this has been proven to be true as a fulfillment of God's Word.

They will receive the attention. *"Judah, thou art he whom thy brethren shall praise."* (Genesis 49:8) Those words, divinely spoken over Judah by Jacob in prophecy, have proven true as well through the years. The Jews may be a minority people, but they are the tribe or nation that the other brothers praise. While there may be some sibling rivalry from time to time, the Jews have been elevated to a level of acknowledgment above the other tribes, just as God foretold.

They are young . . . and old. As we mentioned in an earlier chapter, God also foretold the following in Genesis 49:8-10:

- Judah would possess military might over their enemies because of God's favor upon them.

- Judah would be a young nation. This was fulfilled in 1948.
- Judah would also be an old lion, an old nation. This is also true because the House of Judah has preexisted all other peoples in that area and have full claim to the land.
- Judah would be the tribe that produced the kings of Israel. We have discussed this already.
- Judah would bring forth the Messiah, the King of kings and the Lord of lords. This is fulfilled in Jesus Christ with His first coming, and will be ratified competely upon his return.

Based on these observations alone, we can safely conclude that the Jews are a *part* of "God's Chosen People." However, the Jews cannot be the House of Israel. They cannot fulfill the vast number of prophecies that were given to the larger kingdom, nor do they fulfill any of the physical requirements. We honor them for their rightful place in God's prophetic Word, but we are still left to search for the Kingdom of the ten tribes, the House of Israel.

Who Is Israel?

The covenant God made with Israel in the Old Testament is spectacular in its size and scope, so much so that most people miss the *physical* impact of God's Word. Today we accept that fact that anybody can enjoy eternal life with God through Jesus Christ and marvel at the *spiritual* impact of the New Covenant. But the massive scale of the New Covenant was built upon the *physical* attributes of the Old Covenant.

Deuteronomy 32:8-9 [8]*When the Most High divided to the nations their inheritance, when he separated the sons of Adam, he set the bounds of the people according to the number of the children of Israel.* [9]*For the LORD'S portion is his people; Jacob is the lot of his inheritance.*

This passage tells us that every nation on earth was allocated a specific inheritance, or land mass, by God Himself. When God predetermined which nation would be in a certain place, God first established how large the nations would be that would spring from the children of Israel. Verse 9 specifies the fact that the Lord's portion is His people; Jacob is the lot (or the sum-total) of His inheritance. In other words, there would be two separate classes of nations established on the earth. They would be: the sons of Adam, and the sons of Israel. The nations of Israel would be the blessed and preferred in land allocation and the heathen would receive the rest.

Numbers 24:5-9 [5]*How goodly are thy tents, O Jacob, and thy tabernacles, O Israel!* [6]*As the valleys are they spread forth, as gardens by the river's side, as the trees of lign aloes which the LORD hath planted, and as cedar trees beside the waters.* [7]*He shall pour the water out of his buckets, and his seed shall be in many waters, and his king shall be higher than Agag, and his kingdom shall be exalted.* [8]*God brought him forth out of Egypt; he hath as it were the strength of an unicorn: he shall eat up the nations his enemies, and shall break their bones, and pierce them through with his arrows.* [9]*He couched, he lay down as a lion, and as a great lion: who shall stir him up? Blessed is he that blesseth thee, and cursed is he that curseth thee.*

The prophet Balaam verified this physical truth when he prophesied over the tribes of Israel. He said that Israel's seed would be in many waters (scattered and established nations in major portions of the world). They would also be exalted. The nations of the world would be blessed or cursed based on how they treated these tribes of Israel!

Keep in mind the fact that this does not nullify the grace of Jesus Christ, nor His salvation provided for all. But it establishes clearly the geographic boundaries of nations as prescribed by God. National boundaries and culture are very important matters to the Almighty.

If Abraham's literal seed are to be as the sand of the sea and the dust of the earth, then the tribes of Israel would receive major land allocations from Almighty God. Since the Jews are a minority in the earth, where are the rest?

Deuteronomy 33:13-17 [13]*And of Joseph he said, Blessed of the LORD be his land, for the precious things of heaven, for the dew, and for the deep that coucheth beneath,* [14]*And for the precious fruits brought forth by the sun, and for the precious things put forth by the moon,* [15]*And for the chief things of the ancient mountains, and for the precious things of the lasting hills,* [16]*And for the precious things of the earth and fulness thereof, and for the good will of him that dwelt in the bush: let the blessing come upon the head of Joseph, and upon the top of the head of him that was separated from his brethren.* [17]*His glory is like the firstling of his bullock, and his horns are like the horns of unicorns: with them he shall push the* *people together to the ends of the earth: and they are the ten thousands of Ephraim, and they are the thousands of Manasseh.*

The House of Israel would be led by Ephraim, Joseph's youngest son. It was Ephraim that received Jacob's right-hand, birthright blessing. He would become wealthy, and the tribal leader over the other tribes in Israel. Judah led the Jews, but Ephraim led Israel.

Notice a couple of traits given by God Himself to Ephraim and to Manasseh as well.

- They are strong, like young bulls. Ephraim, in particular, will be a young nation.
- They have the horns of unicorns. This denotes military might.
- They use their horns, or their size and strength, to push people together. They move people groups out of their traditional places, and move them to other places or lands. They may, in fact, colonize.
- They are the ten thousands of Ephraim, and the thousands of Manasseh. In the last days, the young nation will rise over the older, related nation in status and numbers.

Hosea 1:10 [10]*Yet the number of the children of Israel shall be as the sand of the sea, which cannot be measured nor numbered; and it shall come to pass, that in the place where it was said unto them, Ye are not my people, there it shall be said unto them, Ye are the sons of the living God.*

Some may say that the House of Israel truly was a large nation in the past, but now they are scattered. However, the book of Hosea was a prophecy that pertained to the House of Israel and looked forward into their future as God ordained. This verse contains some powerful observations that must be dealt with if the Bible is to be correctly understood.

- God said that the House of Israel would be large, as the sand of the sea, in future days. In fact, they would be so large that perhaps they would not fit inside of Canaan.
- They would not be known as Israel, or as "the chosen people." They would take on a new identity in the last days. Many of the Old Testament prophets (e.g., Isaiah, Jeremiah, Hosea and

others) stated the fact that the House of Israel would be lost to her heritage.

- They would be called "the sons of the living God." They would be recognized, perhaps as a Christian nation. They might be lost to their Israeli heritage, but they are known to God as His people, and they would be known around the world as a Christian place.

Isaiah 14:1-2 [1]*For the LORD will have mercy on Jacob, and will yet choose Israel, and set them in their own land: and the strangers shall be joined with them, and they shall cleave to the house of Jacob.* [2]*And the people shall take them, and bring them to their place: and the house of Israel shall possess them in the land of the LORD for servants and handmaids: and they shall take them captives, whose captives they were; and they shall rule over their oppressors.*

Another fascinating, future-looking prophecy is found in Isaiah. After the 10 tribes had gone into captivity, God prophesies over them this startling prediction!

- God will still choose Israel. In fact, he will give them their own land. It will not be shared with Judah, nor will it be a land of captivity like Syria or Babylon. They will come together as a nation once again.
- Strangers, or foreigners, will also join to the House of Israel. They will be known as a nation that accepts immigrants from foreign nations.
- Some of these immigrants will be enslaved, so the House of Israel will endure the taint of slavery in the last days.

2 Samuel 7:10 [10]*Moreover I will appoint a place for my people Israel, and will plant them, that they may dwell in a place of their own, and move no more; neither shall the children of wickedness afflict them any more, as beforetime,*

This issue of Israel being given another land, a separate land, was so significant to God that He spoke to King David in 2 Samuel about it. When this was given to David, *all the tribes were living together in the land God had promised to Abraham!* We must understand that God intended to give the House of Israel a new land, a land of peace in the last days. How would this happen?

Zechariah 10:6-12 *[6]And I will strengthen the house of Judah, and I will save the house of Joseph, and I will bring them again to place them; for I have mercy upon them: and they shall be as though I had not cast them off: for I am the LORD their God, and will hear them. [7]And they of Ephraim shall be like a mighty man, and their heart shall rejoice as through wine: yea, their children shall see it, and be glad; their heart shall rejoice in the LORD. [8]I will hiss for them, and gather them; for I have redeemed them: and they shall increase as they have increased. [9]And I will sow them among the people: and they shall remember me in far countries; and they shall live with their children, and turn again. [10]I will bring them again also out of the land of Egypt, and gather them out of Assyria; and I will bring them into the land of Gilead and Lebanon; and place shall not be found for them. [11]And he shall pass through the sea with affliction, and shall smite the waves in the sea, and all the deeps of the river shall dry up: and the pride of Assyria shall be brought down, and the sceptre of Egypt shall depart away. [12]And I will strengthen them in the LORD; and they shall walk up and down in his name, saith the LORD.*

God knew that both the Houses of Judah and Israel would turn their backs on Him, and He would take them into captivity. In His prophecies of judgment over both Kingdoms, God also prophesied hope in the future events. They would be freed from captivity. Judah would return to the land of the Abrahamic covenant. Israel would be taken to a new realm. Zechariah is one of these prophecies. Let's stop here for a moment and analyze this passage verse-by-verse.

- Verse 6—God would strengthen the House of Judah. He would also save the House of Joseph (Israel). He would place them again. (In other words, He would give them land and they would once again become nations in His sight.) God would have mercy on both of them (not just the House of Judah). Both nations would be in God's sight as though He had never cast them off and put them in captivity. God reiterates the fact that He is *their* God (the God of the Covenant), and He will hear *them*.
- Verses 7 and 8—God now turns His attention specifically to Ephraim, leader of the House of Israel. They shall be mighty.

Their children (future generations) will grow in this strength, and they will rejoice in the Lord. God will gather them (the House of Israel). They will progressively grow into the last days, after their captivity and scattering by Assyria.

- Verse 9—The House of Israel will be scattered in far countries, but they will turn to God in those places. They may be scattered by man, but they are known to God.
- Verse 10—They will relocate from Egypt, Assyria and other nations, and consider returning back to the land of Abraham's covenant. But there will not be room for them there! They now must start to move away from that land into the new land God has promised.
- Verse 11—At God's appointed time the House of Israel will leave their bondage and oppression. In order to start their new land, they will pass through the sea with affliction. There will be an ocean of separation between their past and their future.
- Verse 12—In their new land, on the other side of the sea, they shall be strengthened by God, and live in His Name as one nation under God.

Wait A Minute!

"Wait a minute," you may say. *"Do you mean to tell me that God's promised people aren't just the Jews?"*

"That's right."

"And are you trying to tell me that there is more than one chosen nation, blessed by Almighty God," you ask?

"Yes."

"Are you telling me that this other nation is the one that is blessed by God's right hand, so that they will be more wealthy than others?"

"Correct."

"And this new nation that comes out of the House of Israel was foretold by the ancient prophets?"

"Absolutely."

"And this Israelite nation would be lost to their heritage and wouldn't call themselves Israel. But they would be known as a Christian nation instead?"

"I think you are getting it!"
"Then what else can you tell me?"

Other Clues To The House Of Israel

Abortion

Hosea 9:13-14 [13]*Ephraim, as I saw Tyrus, is planted in a pleasant place: but Ephraim shall bring forth his children to the murderer.* [14]*Give them, O LORD: what wilt thou give? give them a miscarrying womb and dry breasts.*

Not everything foretold about the future House of Israel is good. This Scripture states that Ephraim (the leader among the 10 tribes) is planted in a pleasant place. His land is bountiful and may feed other nations. However, he would also bring forth his children to the murderer.

Could this speak of abortion? Absolutely! God foretold a nation that would become decadent and separated from Him. At that time, they would live for themselves and kill their children. They would be judged by natural judgments, a miscarrying womb, and dry breasts.

Food

Isaiah 27:6 [6]*He shall cause them that come of Jacob to take root: Israel shall blossom and bud, and fill the face of the world with fruit.*

This last-days prophecy about Israel speaks of her prosperity. But there is one, primary item for which she would be known. The House of Israel would feed the world! Her land would be so bountiful that she would export her meat, grain and other produce worldwide. Many nations would have the land-mass and capability to accomplish this, but only Israel would be successful in these endeavors.

Missions

Isaiah 49:6 [6]*And he said, It is a light thing that thou shouldest be my servant to raise up the tribes of Jacob, and to restore the preserved of Israel: I will also give thee for a light to the Gentiles, that thou mayest be my salvation unto the end of the earth.*

In the last days the House of Israel (tribes of Jacob) would do two things. First, they would be instrumental in restoring Israel. They would stand with the Jews, perhaps more than any other people, giving them a right and claim to their own land. Second, they would also be given as a "light" to the Gentiles, to be God's salvation unto the end of the earth. This speaks of missions activities, spreading the gospel of Jesus Christ into the whole earth. Through their global dominance as a nation and their Christian values, missionaries would cover the earth to preach the gospel of Jesus Christ.

Language

Isaiah 28:11 *[11]For with stammering lips and another tongue will he speak to this people.*

Just as the House of Judah would retain Hebrew as their national language, so the House of Israel would have their own language. What would it be? It would be a "stammering lip." And today there is a language that is similar to the original Hebrew language of the House of Israel that is a stammering language.

In Hebrew the word "stammering" is "laeg." It means stammering and also foreigner. So this new language given to the 10 tribes would be a foreign language to the Jews, not Hebrew. As the tribes scattered, they retained portions of their language, but it became a foreign tongue. Today that stammering tongue is known as . . . English.

The noted Bible translator, William Tyndale, observed this when he translated the Scriptures. He said, "*The properties of the Hebrew tongue aggreeth a thousand times more with the English than with the Latin. The manner of speaking is in both one, in a thousand places, there needest not but to translate the Hebrew word forward.*"

Another noted translator, Canon Lyson, found 5,000 Hebrew roots in the English language, and other linguists have raised that figure even higher. Welsh is so much like Hebrew that the same syntax may be used for both languages. Ancient Saxon, the language of Isaac's sons, is said to be eighty percent Hebrew. And the oldest poems in Celtic language (found in the "Book of the Dun Cow," published in 1106, A.D.) are very similar to the poetic passages of the Old Testament.

So how can we observe this language connection? Let's contrast a few English words with their Hebrew roots.

- English: Kitten. Hebrew: Quiton (a little one).
- English: Elephant. Hebrew: Eleph (ox).
- English: Pig. Hebrew: Piggul (an abomination).
- English: Crow or Rook. Hebrew: Qraw (to call).
- English: Gull. Hebrew: Gul (to move in a circuit).

There are literally thousands of these connections between Hebrew and English. However, sometimes the letters can be switched or inverted as shown in the following words.

- English: Rabbit. Hebrew: Arnbit (hare).
- English: Snipe. Hebrew: Insop (water fowl).
- English: Squash. Hebrew: Quasha (cucumber).
- English: Buzz. Hebrew: Zebub (fly).

One of the words that became inverted in the migration from Hebrew to English was the word, "stammering." In Hebrew, this word was "laeg." When this word migrated to the Scottish Highlands, they kept the term. The word, "laig" means to stammer, chatter, or talk a great deal.

This same word, "laig," means "weak" in Gaelic. But the Normans and others referred to the inhabitants of Wales, Cornwall and the Scottish Highlands as the "stammerers," or "the weak ones." According to the Department of History at the Univesity of Aberdeen, Scotland, they called them "Gaels." It was a play on words, spoken disdainfully about these "stammering ones," but the name stuck.

In Hebrew, the word for man is "iysh." Because of the correlation between Gaelic and Hebrew, a stammering man would be called "gael-iysh." Today that term has been modified, and we know it as "English." Just as God prophesied through Isaiah, in the last days there would be a stammering language given to His people that would be known by the world. It would be similar to the mother tongue, Hebrew, but it would be its own language. Once again, the 10 tribes would change the world through their language.

They Would Lead The World

Do you remember our studies in a previous chapter about Genesis 48 and 49? God spent the entire chapter establishing the preeminence of Joseph's seed (Ephraim and Manasseh) in chapter 48. In Genesis 49 God blessed Joseph more than any other son, and stated that the entire birthright blessing would come upon him. Joseph's son, Ephraim, would rise to be the top tribe in the House of Israel. He had the right hand blessing, and this would continue into the last days as God said in Genesis.

1 Chronicles 5:1-2 [1]*Now the sons of Reuben the firstborn of Israel, (for he was the firstborn; but, forasmuch as he defiled his father's bed, his birthright was given unto the sons of Joseph the son of Israel: and the genealogy is not to be reckoned after the birthright.* [2]*For Judah prevailed above his brethren, and of him came the chief ruler; but the birthright was Joseph's:)*

God reinforced this promise in 1 Chronicles, when he states that the birthright was taken from Reuben because of his unfaithfulness. Reuben is truly the firstborn son according to age, but the birthright blessing has been passed along to Joseph. This means that his seed will be blessed in the last days, and will be materially rich when contrasted to the rest of the world.

A Superpower

Psalm 60:7 [7] *Gilead is mine, and Manasseh is mine; Ephraim also is the strength of mine head; Judah is my lawgiver;*

Ephraim was known by God as the strength of His head. The word strength denotes military might and force in the original language. This nation would be known as a military superpower in the last days, a force known around the world.

Liberty and Religious Freedom

Exodus 5:1 [1]*And afterward Moses and Aaron went in, and told Pharaoh, Thus saith the LORD God of Israel, Let my people go, that they may hold a feast unto me in the wilderness.*

Israel would be known for its pursuit of liberty and religious freedom. The cry of Moses before Pharaoh would ring other times throughout the centuries as Israel proclaimed their allegiance to Almighty God and to Him alone.

Who Is The House Of Israel?

These are the last days, foretold in the Scriptures. God Himself provided the clues, so we can know His covenant people, the House of Israel, on the earth today. Here are His indicators:

- The House of Israel doesn't necessarily claim to be Israelite. They have forsaken their heritage and background in search of new lands and ways.
- The nation must be large and prosperous, so much so that it is known around the world.
- It is a nation that has moved various people groups out of their realms, to possess the land.
- This nation must be across the seas, separated by oceans from other nations. It will be bounded to a large degree by oceans.
- The House of Israel will take some as slaves, and be forced to deal with this sin.
- They will also abort their children in the last days and face judgment for it.
- This nation will be a young nation in contrast with others. In fact, they will break away from their older siblings to found a new civilization.
- The House of Israel will be a nation that literally feeds the world. Food will be a large factor in their blessing.
- They will also be known as a Christian nation, one that sends and enables missions to spread throughout the world.
- The House of Israel will no longer speak Hebrew. Instead, they will speak a stammering tongue, English!
- They will be a global superpower, with military might and the ability to use it.
- Israel will contain the heartbeat of liberty and religious freedom. They will remain attached, even in their sin, to the God of Abraham, Isaac and Jacob more than to the other idols of the earth.

Can we find such a nation?

Who is the House of Israel?

It is the United States of America!

Now it all makes sense!

What is the reason the people of the USA would stand united with the Jewish State of Israel in the Middle East, despite the fact that other Arab and Middle Eastern nations provide oil and other materials to America? It's simple. The House of Israel (the United States) and the House of Judah (the Jewish State of Israel) are bound together by blood covenant, under Almighty God. They understand each other, and despite their differences and the attempts of many to try and break their bonds, they remain united as nations.

Historic Clues In American History

Genesis 48:16. The names of Abraham, Isaac and Jacob were conferred on Ephraim and Manasseh. Do you remember the quote by Professor Totten? According to his studies and teaching, he stated that Isaac's sons have evolved in history from Isaac's sons, to Isaacsons, to Isacsons, to Sacsons or Sachae, to Saxons. Other notable linguists and theologians have also correlated these facts. These Saxons and their brothers were the founders of this new world.

- Pastor John Robinson and the Mayflower pilgrims, upon arriving in the new world, called this nation "New Israel," as noted in "The Light And The Glory," by Peter Marshall, Jr.
- Only two nations on earth have been established in the name of freedom and religious freedom. They are Israel and the United States of America.
- All 50 states of the United States of America contain words in their preamble expressing praise or reliance upon Almighty God.
- The capstone on the Washington Monument contains the latin words "Laus Deo." Praise to God! This was in reverence to the Judeo-Christian God and His Son, Jesus Christ.
- The national motto of the United States remains "In God We Trust." This is not a "generic" god or a universalist term. This is Almighty God, the God of Abraham, Isaac and Israel.

These, and other numerous references in history, serve to demonstrate the hand of God in returning His House of Israel to the God of their Fathers, in their own land, in the last days.

The Number Thirteen

There were actually thirteen tribes of Israel. We know them as the twelve tribes of Israel, but the tribe of Levi was granted no land allocation in Canaan. They were the tribe that cared for the Tabernacle and Temple during that era, and they lived as teachers and ministers interspersed among the other twelve tribes.

Jacob adopted Joseph's sons, Manasseh and Ephraim, as his own (Genesis 48). This was Joseph's "double portion" blessing, brought forth in his sons. As a result, Manasseh was tribe number 12, and Ephraim was the youngest . . . tribe number 13. Today Manasseh is England and other areas of the British Commonwealth, and Ephraim is their brother nation, the United States of America. Today, the U.S. standard is the bald eagle, king of birds. England's standard is the lion, king of beasts. These were passed down from the original four standards used by the tribes of Israel. They are: the eagle, the lion, the face of a man, and the ox (or bullock). All of these are found in Saxon and other areas of early European history.

The Tribes By Overall Birth Order

1. Reuben
2. Simeon
3. Levi
4. Judah
5. Dan
6. Naphtali
7. Gad
8. Asher
9. Issachar
10. Zebulun
11. Benjamin
12. Manasseh
13. Ephraim

The number thirteen often represents rebellion. The U.S. Founding Fathers rebelled against Europe and crossed the seas to found a new nation. Pastor Robinson's closing message to the Mayflower Pilgrims in 1620 was taken from Genesis 12:1-2, where God commanded Abram to leave his kindred and get to a new land where he would be blessed.

The United States had 13 original colonies when she declared independence from Britain. Her battle cry? "We have no king but King Jesus!"

The Great Seal And The Number Thirteen

The number 13 is impressed into U.S. heritage in many ways. This is particularly notable in the Great Seal of the United States. Work on the Great Seal was commissioned July 4, 1776 by the Continental Congress, and the final seal was completed twelve years later. It was intended to be a significant connection between the future of the nation and its heritage.

In the U.S. seal is a bald eagle.

- He clutches an olive branch bearing 13 leaves in one talon.
- In his other talon are 13 arrows.
- Over his head are 13 stars.
- On the flag on his breast are 13 stripes.
- Over his head are 13 letters, spelling "E Pluribus Unum." This means "One of Many." The House of Israel is gathered once again into their own country.

The reverse side of the seal contains a pyramid.

- This pyramid consists of 13 layers. Thomas Jefferson wanted a picture of Moses leading the Israelites through the Red Sea as a part of the seal, to connect the Colonies to their Israelite roots. However, the pyramid was selected instead, noting the Israelite connection to Egyptian bondage and slavery.
- Above the pyramid is a triangle representing the "eye of Providence." The original description of this eye in 1782 states that "Providence" is the God of Abraham, Isaac and Jacob. It has never been attributed to any other God!
- The 13 letters above the pyramid spell "Annuit Coeptus." This means "God has prospered our undertakings," or beginnings.

The upper portion of the Great seal was to be filled, on both sides, with emanating "radiance." According to Benjamin Franklin, this was to represent the light from the pillar of fire, as God led the Israelites through the wilderness. Once again we can understand the allegiance of our Founding Fathers to their roots as the House of Israel.

Significant Dates and "Thirteens" in American History

- The Civil War began April 13, 1861.
- The Spanish American War ended August 13, 1898.
- The Mexican American War began on May 13, 1846 and ended on September 13, 1847.
- On June 13, 1917 a convoy of ships departed for France. They were 13 days in crossing the Atlantic.
- The last battle of General Pershing was September 13, 1918.
- George Whitfield, the famous missionary evangelist, made 13 trips to the Colonies to preach the gospel.
- The U.S. Constitution was ratified by 13 states.
- The first flag of the United States had 13 stripes and two crosses. Adopted by the Continental Congress in 1775, it flew over General George Washington's headquarters near Boston, Massachussets. This flag was known as the "Grand Union."
    - o The first cross is red, and is vertical and horizontal. It is the cross of Calvary.

  - o The second cross is white, and crosses the flag horizontally under the cross of Calvary. It is the cross that stems from the time when Jacob blessed Manasseh and Ephraim in Genesis 49. It is the cross of Jacob's blessing.
- The second flag of the United States had both 13 stars and 13 stripes.

These numbers correlate directly to the youngest of the 13 tribes, Ephraim. Ephraim was the leader of the House of Israel, and 13 was his number. It still is his today, in the United States of America.

Let's Summarize Things

The dots have been connected. The United States is the House of Israel from the Bible! The reason the United States of America has been blessed is not because it has a great or mighty people, but because God has kept His covenant with Abraham, Isaac and Israel! The House of Israel is not known as an Israelite nation in the last days, as Hosea prophesied. Instead, she is known as a Christian nation.

This also means that you and I must study the Bible differently! We can no longer lump together all of the Bible prophecies and Scriptures, and pass them off on the Jews. Paul told Timothy to rightly divide the Word of Truth. This means we must understand this one fact: there are prophecies in the Bible that pertain to the United States! They will happen in America, not to the Jews in their Jewish State of Israel. This is critical to every Christian!

If Israel is God's time clock, then every believer around the world must know that the USA is the House of Israel. They must understand that current events relate to two specific nations on the earth, not just one. They should watch the signs of the times, as they pertain to the United States AND the Jewish State of Israel. Every American must also be on their guard and must study the Scriptures with fresh understanding.

What Did Jesus Know?

In Matthew 19:28 and Luke 22:29-30, Jesus was recorded making an unusual statement to His disciples. He told them that in the age to come, they would sit upon thrones, reigning with Him. They would judge the twelve tribes of Israel. The term used for "twelve," is literally "the 10 and the 2" tribes. These were not spiritual tribes, but literal Israelites that would be alive in the last days.

John 7:35 [35]*Then said the Jews among themselves, Whither will he go, that we shall not find him? will he go unto the dispersed among the Gentiles, and teach the Gentiles?*

The Jews themselves wondered if Jesus would go to the dispersed, the diaspora, among the Gentiles and teach them. The Jews rejected Christ at this point, but they all knew that the other tribes were outside of the Jewish realm. In order to understand this better, we must understand what the term "gentile" means.

There are four classifications of people in the Bible. They are: Jews, Israelites, Gentiles and Heathen.

- **Jew**—In order to be a Jew, one must be of the tribe of Judah, or of the House of Judah. The House of Judah included people from the tribes of Judah, Benjamin and Levi.
- **Israelite**—Israelite was a generic term for all the tribes of Israel. But it was more specifically used to refer to the 10-tribe nation of the House of Israel. In this sense, one could be an Israelite, but not be a Jew.
- **Gentile**—This word comes from the Greek term ethnos. It refers to ethnic groups that are non-Jewish! Therefore, it was recognized that many of the Gentiles were actually Israelites that had left their heritage and were disconnected from the Jews! This becomes even clearer when the fourth term is defined.
- **Heathen**—This term was reserved only for those that were not of the seed of Israel. All of the seed of Abraham, Isaac and Israel were called either Jew, Israelite or Gentile, or they were known by their tribal names (Paul from the tribe of Benjamin, Anna from the tribe of Asher, etc.).

When we understand this, we now see that many of the Jews in Jesus' day wondered if Jesus was going to minister to their "Israelite-Gentile" brothers!

James 1:1 further magnifies this fact when James, the half-brother of Jesus, writes his letter *"to the twelve tribes which are scattered abroad!"*

This is why so many of the apostles and early church fathers are buried in various places around the globe.

- James' burial site is attributed to Spain. (*The Search For The Twelve Apostles, McBierney*)
- Paul ministered in Spain (Romans 15:24).
- Joseph of Arimathea preached in Britain within two years of Christ's resurrection. (*Saint Paul In Britain, Morgan*)
- Lazarus, Mary and Martha are thought to be buried in France. (*The Origin And Early History Of Christianity In Britain, Gordon*)
- And the prophet Jeremiah? His tomb is in Ireland! (*Judah's Scepter & Joseph's Birthright, Capt*)

The tribes were alive and well in Jesus' time, and they received the gospel with gladness in their day.

Claudia And Pudens

2 Timothy 4:21 is part of a list of early believers in Christ who lived in Rome during that time. Among those listed are two interesting names, and their stories were explored in the book *"Saint Paul In Britain"* by R. W. Morgan. They are Claudia and Pudens. Claudia was the daughter of a British king who had been brought to Rome as a hostage. She eventually married Pudens, a Roman military officer. Both were Christians, and Paul preached in their home while in Rome. Based on ancient church records, it is now believed that Claudia had become a Christian while still in Britain. Who had ministered to her there? Apparently it was Joseph of Arimathea and the Apostle Paul! The apostles had gone to Europe, seeking out the ten tribes, to bring them the gospel of Jesus Christ.

History And The House Of Israel

How does history treat the migration of the House of Israel? There are more references than you might think!

The Jewish historian Flavius Josephus lived around the time of Christ, and wrote extensively about the history of the Israelites. In his writings titled *"The Antiquities Of The Jews,"* Book 11, chapter 5, verse 133, he writes, *"Wherefore there are but 2 tribes in Europe and Asia subject to the Romans, while the ten tribes are beyond the Euphrates till now, and are an immense multitude, and not to be estimated by numbers."* At the time of Christ, the ten tribes had spread out from Northeastern to Northwest Europe, beyond the region Rome ruled. This would have included much of Western and Northwest Europe.

Herodotus was called the "Father of History." He was perhaps the most important historian of the pre-Christian world, living in Asia Minor around 480-430 B.C. He visited Europe and wrote much about a newly arrived people he called "Scythians," or tent-dwelling nomads. In Book IV, paragraph 63, he writes, *"Such are the observances of the Scythians with respect to sacrifice. They never use swine for the purpose, nor indeed it is their wont to breed them in any part of their country."* It is likely these nomads were dispersed Israelites.

Gildas "the Wise," a famous 6th century writer of Britain writes of an interesting epoch in Saxon history. When the Saxons, yet pagan, invaded Celtic England, he wrote that these events occurred, *"to the end that our Lord might in this land try after His accustomed manner these His Israelites, whether they loved Him or not . . ."*

In 1320 A.D. the Scottish Declaration of Independence was signed by Scottish nobles at Arbroath Abbey. It states, in part, *"We know, and from the chronicles and books of the ancients gather, that . . . the nation of the Scots . . . passing from the greater Scythia through the Mediterranean Sea and pillars of Hercules and sojourning in Spain . . . and coming thence One Thousand and two hundred years after the outgoing of the people of Israel . . ."* In short, they attached their heritage directly to the tribes of Israel. They knew they were Israelites.

In 1610, noted English scholar and dean of Canterbury, Dr. John Boys, wrote his *"Exposition Of The Scriptures Used In The Liturgy."* In the introduction he wrote, *"England is swept from Babel, and Hierusalem (Jerusalem) and situated in our owne country."*

In 1723, the noted French minister and Huguenot refugee, Dean Abadie, published his book, *"The Triumph of Providence."* In a chapter titled *"Israel Reappeared amongst the Scythians,"* he wrote, *"Unless the ten tribes of Israel are flown into the air, or sunk into the earth, they must be those ten Gothic tribes that entered Europe in the fifth centure (B.C.) . . . and founded the ten nations of modern Europe."*

In 1761 Alexander Cruden first published *"Cruden's Concordance."* This set the early standard for Hebrew and Greek studies. The original dedication page of the first edition bore the following prayer, "*. . . that it may be said by the present and future ages that King George the Third has been an Hezekiah to our British Israel.*"

More Recent Believers

You may be asking why you have not heard of any type of teaching about this dividing of the Word of God. Part of the answer lies in the watered-down theology and liberalism that is rampant in various seminaries and colleges today. Another part of that reason lies in the overly simplistic and lazy, shallow teaching that comes from most pulpits. However, it has not always been this way. A perfect case-in-point is the historic theologian, Ezra Stiles.

Dr. Stiles was a Congregationalist minister and President of Yale University for more than 20 years. Stiles taught many of these foundations and adhered to them himself, raising up a generation of pastors in the United States that passed that heritage along. Other pastors and leaders that believed these truths numbered into the thousands. Here is a small list of noted adherents from all types of backgrounds and denominations. As you dig through the list, you may be shocked to learn how deeply these truths permeated America's theology in the past.

- Polydore Vergil, the learned Italian historian;
- Martin Lyman Streator (1843-1926), state evangelist and home missionary for the Christian Church, a friend and student to Alexander Campbell;
- Joseph Wild, D. D. (b.1834), pastor of the Union Congregational Church of Brooklyn, NY and the Bond Street Congregational Church of Toronto, whose Sunday sermons were published in Canada's largest newspapers;
- Richard Reader Harris (1847-1909), English barrister, counselor to Queen Victoria, founder of the Pentecostal Prayer League and personal friend of Oswald Chambers;
- Elieser Bassin, Christian Jewish scholar who stated in his book, "the Hebrew Scriptures point to the British Isles as the home of God's first born";

- William H. Poole, D.D., prominent pastor in Detroit who authored "Anglo-Israel or the Saxon Race? Proved to be the Lost Tribes of Israel" (1889), which received widespread favorable reviews throughout the Christian literary world.
- Dr. Mordecai F. Ham (1877-1961) under whose old fashioned Gospel preaching Billy Graham and Grady Wilson were converted to Christ;
- Dr. William M. Groom (1884-1957) who served pastorates in Texas; the popular Lincoln McConnel, D.D., who served the famous People's Church in Atlanta and speaker in large national conferences; great soul-winning evangelists such as Jay C. Kellogg who authored "The United States in Prophecy" (1932) and Henry Wellington Stough D.D. (1870-1939), a young associate of D. L. Moody, personal friend with evangelist Bill Sunday and preaching associate of J. Wilbur Chapman.
- Among the Church of the Brethren would be M.M. Eshelman, prolific author and co-founder of Lordsburg College in California, University of LaVerne and McPherson College in Kansas; of Presbyterian persuasion was Roger Rusk (1906-1994), University of Tennessee professor of physics, expositor of scientific, historical and Biblical studies and brother of Secretary of State, Dean Rusk; prominent clergymen of the Church of England would be Bishop J.H. Titcomb and Dr. Dinsdale T. Young (1861-1938) the master pulpiteer and a host of others too numerous to mention;
- The name of Harry D. Clarke (1888-1957), song writer, Moody Bible College professor, song leader for four years in the Billy Sunday campaigns and founder of the Billy Sunday Memorial Tabernacle in Sioux City, witnessed to this great truth.
- Great Holiness preachers would include Maynard James (1902-1988) a leading figure in the International Holiness Mission of Great Britain, Foreign missions Director, co-founder of Beech Lawn Bible College and co-organizer of the Church of the Nazarene in Britain;
- A.M. Hills (1848-1935) Yale Divinity School graduate, first president of the Texas Holiness University, co-founder of the Southern Nazarene University in Bethany, Oklahoma where he served as professor of theology, Dean of the School of Religion

for years, held evangelistic meetings in Great Britain and America and authorized over thirty volumes in "Defense of the Christian Faith", plus tracts and booklets including, "Christian Education and Anglo-Israel."

- George O. Barnes, pastor and missionary evangelist;
- Luke Rader (1890-1952), author, pioneer radio broadcaster, founder and pastor of the River Lake Gospel Tabernacle of Minneapolis. His nationwide ministry was instrumental in bringing over 60,000 people to a saving knowledge of Jesus Christ. He associated with the most well-known ministers of his day and held one of the most successful campaigns for Dr. Oswald J. Smith at the People's Church in Toronto.
- Dr. John Alexander Dowie (1847-1907), one of the most prominent of the modern divine healing movement, who made many recorded statements such as "Israel today is to be found in the Anglo-Saxon and Scandinavian races."
- Other believers included Dr. John G. Lake, whose powerful ministry shook all of South Africa and F.F. Bosworth (1879-1958), healing evangelist, author of "Christ the Healer," who gave a scholarly masterpiece in his sermon, "The Bible Distinction Between the House of Israel and the House of Judah."
- We must not forget Charles F. Parham (1873-1929) Pentecostal pioneer; George R. Hawtin, acknowledged as a father of the Latter Rain movement; H.A. Maxwell Whyte, Toronto pastor and missionary evangelist; Charles O. Benham (1891-1974), early Assemblies of God evangelist and friend of many Pentecostal leaders; Frank W. Sandford (1862-1948), founder of "The Holy Ghost and Us Bible School." Among his students was A.J. Tomlinson of the Church of God, Cleveland, Tennessee, and Gordon Lindsay whose articles published in the "The Anglo-Saxon World" of Canada in 1940 clearly expressed his belief in this truth along with his father Thomas Lindsay. Also included in this list was personal friend and associate of Smith Wigglesworth and early Pentecostal pioneer W. H. Offiler, whose church in Seattle, Washington set the standard for ministry in the Pacific Northwest.

- The believing Pentecostal ministers of Great Britain are numerous, which include, Principal George Jeffreys (1889-1962) of the Elim Pentecostal Alliance; Stephen Jeffreys, William O. Hutchinson, James Brooke, Albion Gaunt, Daniel and James Williams and many more of the Apostolic Faith movement.

Why Is This So Important?

Let's return for a moment to a quote by Charles Totten, Professor of Military Science and Tactics at Yale University. He said, *"I can never be too thankful to Almighty God that in my youth He used the late Professor Wilson to show to me the difference between the two houses. The very understanding is the key by which almost the entire Bible becomes intelligible, and I cannot state too strongly that the man who has not yet seen that the Israel of the Scriptures is totally distinct from the Jewish people is yet in the very infance, the mere alphabet of Biblical study and that to this day 7/8ths of the Bible is shut to his understanding."*

Now consider for a moment the bold assertion of the noted pastor, the one that we started with in chapter one. He emphatically stated the United States was not mentioned in Scripture. What would he do with this teaching? How would he lead his congregation and significant ministry? If God has placed the United States in the Bible and he has ignored these facts, it may be a case of the blind leading the blind.

However, if the United States of America is the House of Israel in Scriptures, placed on this earth for the last days, then there is much misinterpretation of Scripture today. Every prophecy concerning Ephraim or Israel in the Old and New Testaments no longer applies to the Jews. They are directed toward the United States!

This is serious! Perhaps you have been one that thought everything would happen over in the Middle East while you watched it unfold on tv from the comfort of your recliner. Instead, there are some things that could be happening on your very doorstep. Do you know what they are? Do you know what the Bible says about this? Are you prepared? Today ignorance may be bliss, but tomorrow it may be to your peril.

God Has His Hand on America

God has His hand on the United States of America. It is the only reasonable answer to her blessing, her divine protection and her history. But God also has His hand very deeply in her future. In coming chapters we will delve into what will happen next. The future of Bible prophecy is about to strike very close to home.

CHAPTER 7

The Diaspora

By now you realize the fact that the tribes of Israel have a rich and colorful past. Today the Jews occupy the "Promised Land," in the Jewish State of Israel. The House of Israel has re-gathered in the United States of America, to fulfill God's promises to Abraham, Isaac and Israel. However, they are still two separate nations and will be until Christ returns to reunite them.

Let's recap a few items.

- **First**, there are two separate nations that can claim the name of Israel. One is the Jewish State of Israel. The other is the United States of America. Both of them have historic connections to the twelve tribes.
- **Second**, these tribes were originally united into one united nation. However, during the "tea party" rebellion of 975 B.C. found in 1 Kings (no taxation without representation), the House of Israel, the 10-tribe kingdom, separated from the House of Judah, the 2-tribe kingdom. They have been divided nations ever since that time.
- **Third**, both nations forsook Almighty God, and were punished for their sins. The House of Judah repented, and returned to reclaim Canaan as God promised. The House of Israel was scattered and largely forsook her heritage to embrace the new world.
- **Finally**, God promised both nations would be alive and well *in the last days*. However, there was a time when the tribes would be scattered throughout the earth. Where did they go, and who did they become?

They Knew Then . . .

During the earthly ministry of Jesus, there was much discussion about the tribes. At that time they were called "the diaspora" or the dispersed. They were scattered, but still known.

In John 7:35 the people asked each other if Jesus would go to the dispersed among the Gentiles. The term dispersed comes directly from the Greek word *diaspora*. This means "dispersion" or "Israelites resident in Gentile countries." Please note what this term does **not** mean! It does **not** refer to Jews in Gentile countries, but Israelites! While it is true that there were Jews scattered abroad, the largest scattered group consisted of the 10-tribe House of Israel!

In Matthew 19:28 and Luke 22:29-30, Jesus told his disciples they would judge the twelve tribes in the regeneration. In other words, in the last days all of the tribes would be accounted for. They must have certain identifying factors while they are dispersed, and when they are gathered once again!

James, the half-brother of Jesus Christ, began his epistle in James 1:1, greeting the twelve tribes that are scattered, or dispersed, abroad. In other words, the House of Israel was dispersed during Jesus time, but they were still known as descendents of Israel.

In Revelation 7:4-8 God seals 144,000 Israelites in the last days. This author has heard many erroneously refer to these as 144,000 "Jews," but they are not. God specifically states that they are from *"all the tribes of the children of Israel."* (Verse 4) If God does this in the last days, then the tribes must be in existence and be known to Him at that point.

Sometimes history blurs the lines as nations and cultures change. Take for example, the history of the Mayan empire in the Yucatan peninsula of Mexico. The Mayans built a significant nation that worshipped the serpent god until they were conquered by other invaders. Today, there are still Mayans on the earth, but their culture has changed. They live in a region in Mexico and have also scattered into other lands in the general area.

This is what happened with the House of Israel. They were scattered by Assyria, but God still had a plan. We will discover what He had to say about them in a few moments. History will not call them "Israelites." That must be discerned by study of God's Word as it intersects with history.

Two Important Factors To Consider

There are two important variables to consider before we begin, in earnest.

- **First**, the Israelites were called Israel, Hebrew, Semite, Isaac's sons, and other Hebraic names in their culture. When they scattered, that changed over time. Furthermore, the Bible called them tribes. However, history often referred to them as "clans, bands, nomads, seafarers, trading parties," and other terms.
- **Second**, while some of the Israelites would re-gather and reclaim their heritage, not all of them would do this. This was (and is) the case even among the Jews. The story of Esther and Mordecai is written in the Bible about a young Jewess who saved her people. She lived in Babylon, even though many of the Jews had returned to the land of promise to rebuild Jerusalem and replant their nation. Today there are more Jews that live in the United States alone than live in the Jewish State of Israel. Why? They chose to remain where they were scattered, and create a life there apart from the reunited Jewish State.

So it is with the House of Israel. Many Israelites scattered and built new nations. Some of these nations even established satellite nations of their own. (This is particularly true of Manasseh and Ephraim, who God had foretold would colonize.) When the House of Israel was re-gathered in the United States of America, not all of Israel would join them there. Many had chosen to remain where they were.

It's Big!

Genesis 17:4-6 [4]*As for me, behold, my covenant is with thee, and thou shalt be a father of many nations.* [5]*Neither shall thy name any more be called Abram, but thy name shall be Abraham; for a father of many nations have I made thee.* [6]*And I will make thee exceeding fruitful, and I will make nations of thee, and kings shall come out of thee.*

The real issue we must wrestle with pertains to God's promise to Abraham, found in Genesis 17. When God changed his name to Abraham (father of many nations), God promised Abraham that he would be the father of many nations. Later in the chapter, God also specifies that Sarah will be the mother of many nations. If this is true, then there are nations that have sprung up from the tribes of Israel! God set this plan into motion, many generations ago.

Isaiah 49:22 [22]*Thus saith the Lord GOD, Behold, I will lift up mine hand to the Gentiles, and set up my standard to the people: and they shall bring thy sons in their arms, and thy daughters shall be carried upon their shoulders.*

God further prophesied through Isaiah to Abraham's seed. They would be a people that would receive His standard, His Messiah. You may question this by noting that this prophecy refers to "gentiles." But in Hebrew the word is the same as when God promised Abraham that he would be the father of many *nations*! Although God would scatter Israel, He would redeem them unto Himself even where they were scattered.

Acts 9:15 [15]*But the Lord said unto him, Go thy way: for he is a chosen vessel unto me, to bear my name before the Gentiles, and kings, and the children of Israel:*

The term "Gentile" is the word "gowy" in Hebrew. According to Strong's and other concordances, it means: a race or tribe that is non-Jewish, usually by implication pagan. This term did not fit the House of Judah, but it did fit the scattered House of Israel! This is why the Apostle Paul was called to be the apostle to the Gentiles, most notably the House of Israel. He was calling Abraham's scattered seed back to the God of Abraham, Isaac and Israel through Jesus Christ. The tribes were receptive to the message of the gospel in their respective lands. But there are other identifying markers as well.

Where Did They Scatter?

God did not give us a series of genetic markers to use in tracking the tribes. Instead, He requires us to dig into the markers in the greatest truth of all, His Word. Proverbs 25:2 says, *"[2]It is the glory of God to conceal a thing: but the honour of kings is to search out a matter."*

God has given us characteristics for every tribe in several prophetic passages. These characteristics would be revealed in the last days, the era following Christ's earthly ministry (as we discussed in chapter 2). 2 Corinthians 11:22 is a perfect example of one such text.

2 Corinthians 11:22 [22]*Are they Hebrews? so am I. Are they Israelites? so am I. Are they the seed of Abraham? so am I.*

Did you notice the clue? The apostle Paul referred to himself in three, unique ways. He was a Hebrew, an Israelite, and Abraham's seed. Let's look at just one of these biblical "markers" for a moment.

The term "Hebrew" was the name the Old Testament nation of Israel used for itself, especially in the early years. They were descendents of Eber (or Heber), who had been born to Shem. Shem was one of Noah's sons. So, they became known as Shemites (or Semites). They were also known as Hebrews or Heberites. Their nation may have been known as Heberea, just as the land of the Philistines was called Philistia. So, when the House of Israel was scattered by Assyria, a number of them migrated to a region in Western Europe that became known as "Eberea," or "Iberea." This was one of the places of the Heberites, and became known as a region of Spain. This is why when the apostle Paul speaks of taking a missionary journey to Spain (Romans 15:24), he was going to speak to descendents of Heber, the House of Israel. Their "generic" name was "gentile," but they were the seed of Abraham.

Abraham's Promise Of Nations

Let's take a look at some other Scriptures. They will tell us characteristics of the House of Israel in their many lands today. Some of these nations have established other countries besides (e.g., England, Australia, New Zealand, etc.), so this is not an all-inclusive list. In fact, you may make new discoveries on your own, especially if you refer back to older translations of Scripture.

There are three key passages of Scripture where Almighty God spoke His Word over the tribes to be fulfilled in the last days. They are:

- Genesis 48—the prophecy to Joseph's sons, Manasseh and Ephraim.
- Genesis 49—The prophesy of Israel over his 12 sons.

- Deuteronomy 33—The prophesy of Moses over the tribes of Israel.

We will use these passages as our foundation, and will weave in other verses that illustrate the characteristics of the tribes through their generations.

In The Last Days

Genesis 49:1 *[1]And Jacob called unto his sons, and said, Gather yourselves together, that I may tell you that which shall befall you in the last days.*

Many teachers have avoided this and other passages because they cannot reconcile how prophecies to the individual tribes pertain to the last days. However, now that you understand this, you can also know the characteristics each tribe possesses today! Let's begin with Jacob's prophecy to his firstborn son, Reuben.

Reuben

To identify Reuben in the last days, we will consider passages from Genesis 49, Deuteronomy 33, Judges 5, 1 Chronicles 5, and Ezekiel 38.

- Genesis 49:3. Reuben is identified by several characteristics:
  - he is the firstborn;
  - he is mighty;
  - he is the beginning of Israel's strength;
  - he is dignified;
  - he has all the trappings of power.
- Genesis 49:4. Reuben is judged for his sin. He had slept with his father's concubine and was now going to have the birthright blessing revoked from him. He would also have a curse bestowed upon him because of his sin.
  - he would be as unstable as water;
  - he would not excel;
  - he defiled his father's bed.
- Deuteronomy 33:6. In this Scripture, Moses blesses Reuben with two things:

  - o he shall live and not die;
  - o he shall have many men.
- Judges 5:15. Reuben had mighty divisions of warriors for battle.
- I Chronicles 5:1-4. This gives us information about the lineage of Reuben. Here, Gog is first mentioned in the Bible . . . . as a descendant of Reuben!
- Ezekiel 38:1-3. This passage gives us further information on where Gog, Reuben's descendant, lives.
  - o He lives in the land of Magog;
  - o He is the chief prince of Meshech and Tubal.

Whoever Reuben is today must fulfill *all* of the Scriptures mentioned above. Who is Reuben today? Reuben Is Russia.

Russia

Let's list a few of Russia's characteristics and connect them to the Word of God.

- Russia is an old nation. It was one of the first regions settled after the Israelites were dispersed. The historian Herodutus says that this tribe moved north. It was the *firstborn* of the dispersed tribal nations. Numbers 32 tells us the tribes of Reuben and Gad (as well as part of Manasseh) asked Moses if they could settle on the other side of the Jordan River. They loved their cattle, and wanted to settle in this region because it was good for livestock. Moses consented to their request based on a few conditions. Because of this separation from the other tribes, Reuben did not come as frequently to Jerusalem to worship God. Reuben was one of the very first tribes to be taken captive, and he migrated northward.
- Russia's *military might* is undisputed. They have won countless wars and skirmishes from the days of the Cossacks to the present. Today, they remain a global superpower.
- Russia has started many things. They are the *beginning of strength*. They were the first to develop a space program, the

first to develop ICBM's and the first to implement military technology on a larger scale.

- Russia is *dignified.* The Russian Orthodox church is the epitome of dignity, rivaled only by Rome, but they were slow to embrace Christianity. I learned the following history from a Russian Orthodox priest, several years ago, as he told me about the history of Russian faith. In 957 A.D. Princess Olga became a Christian. She had sent her grandson, Vladimir, to Constantinople to investigate which religion would be the most suitable for his people in Russia. He listened to presentations of representatives of Islam, Judaism and Christianity. But when he saw the liturgy celebrated in the magnificent cathedral of Saint Sophia, the delegation was so moved by the majesty and mystery of the worship, they decided this would be the religion of Russia. Vladimir and his nobles were baptized in 988. This united the land of Russia under the banner of Eastern Orthodox religion, and prevented Islam from dominating the region. Today the church is known for its tradition, pageantry, and great wealth.
- Speaking of dignity, Russian parades are punctuated with military processions, all carefully orchestrated and choreographed. These have been dramatically displayed to the western world, especially since the early days of Communism.
- Russia has the *trappings of power*. It has a large, productive land mass, natural resources in abundance, many people, and great innovation. Russia should excel.
- However, while Russia displays short decades of excellence, overall Russia is *not excelling*. They are struggling. Their economy has failed repeatedly, not because of a lack of crops but because of a lack of ways to bring food to market. Their military spending has eroded their prosperity many different times. Food production continues to be a problem for the nation due to natural disasters and production problems on many of the farms. Russia should be a successful nation, but they are not!
- Russia is as *unstable as water*. They have broken every treaty they have signed. They are master chess players, always looking for ways to manipulate treaties! They are not to be trusted, even

now! They will fight a battle with Israel (Ezekiel 38-39), but shall not excel, shall not overcome. Russia has been judged the loser by God. Why?

- Russia has *defiled his* Heavenly *Father's bed.* First, Russia embraced Christianity based on pageantry and appearances, not primarily because they embraced Jesus Christ. This created a state-church that became rotten and corrupt. In the past century, Russia has embraced communism and renounced Christianity. He shall be cursed for this. Although recent happenings make it appear as though this is turning around, history shows that past Russian governments also relaxed their views on Christianity only to smash it once again when the church came out into the open.
- Russia should have succumbed to disaster many years ago. War, famine and internal strife has killed many Russians. However, Russia has managed to *live and not die*, in accord with Moses' prayer.
- Russia has *many men.* They have the second largest standing army in the world (second only to China). Their men are conscripted into the military upon graduation from school. They are trained to fight. They have many mighty men, with many divisions as in the days of Judges.
- Gog, Reuben's descendent lives in the *land of Magog.* One of the Hebrew meanings of the word "Gog" is "a northern nation." "Magog" is translated as "a barbarous northern region." Magog is a descendent of Japheth, one of Noah's sons (Genesis 10). Japheth is thought to be the father of the oriental peoples today. Much of southern Russia is occupied by the orientals (mongols, etc.). Russia moved to the Siberian Region, near the Black Sea and has gradually occupied more and more territory.
- Gog is the *chief prince of Meshech and Tubal.* In the Hebrew, the word "Meshech" translates into the word "Mosoch" or "Moscow!" "Tubal" could be translated to "Tubalsk," which is one of the former capitols of Russia! Gog is the head of Moscow and Tubalsk! Incidentally, the Hebrew word "Rosh" which is mentioned in some Scriptural translations (in Ezekiel 38) could translate as "Russia."

Are you Russian?

If you are Russian, then you most likely have Israelite blood in your veins. God will eventually judge your nation; unfortunately, it is under a divine curse. We need to understand that God loves people and seeks to save the lost of all nations. But His plan will be executed in His sovereign will over the nations. This is what has made Russia what it is, and what it will be.

Simeon

Jacob continued his prophesies to his sons in Genesis 49:5-7. He addressed the next two brothers together. Their roots are still closely connected as we shall see, but we will address them separately.

- Genesis 49:5. Two characteristics are mentioned here:
    - Simeon and Levi are brothers, coming from the same father and mother.
    - They are warlike. Instruments of war are in their dwellings.
- Genesis 49:6. They are angry men, and stubborn.
    - They can become so angered that they will kill a person.
    - They were so stubborn that they dug up an entire wall.
- Genesis 49:7. Simeon and Levi's anger is cursed. Consequently, they will be divided in Jacob, and scattered in Israel.
- I Kings 19:19. Elisha the prophet was a descendent of a Simeonite named Shaphat. We see here that Elisha was plowing drought hardened land with twelve yoke (24) oxen!
    - Stubbornness is a hallmark of the tribe of Simeon.
- 2 Kings 2:23-25—The Simeonite prophet Elisha was mocked by a group of children for his baldness. He cursed them, and two she bears came out of the woods and tore forty-two children.
    - Although God sanctioned this, again we note the anger of Simeon.
- I Chronicles 12:25. Simeon is known for its mighty men of valor.
- II Chronicles 15:9. Ephraim, Manasseh, Judah, Benjamin and Simeon join together for a battle after seeing the moving of God.

  - o Simeon is not afraid of war.
  - o Simeon also recognizes the hand of God and is respectful toward it.
- II Chronicles 34:6. Manasseh, Ephraim, Simeon and Naphtali are cleansed of idolatry.

Jacob prophesied over Simeon in Genesis 49, but Moses did not address them in Deuteronomy 33. Still, we have a great number of Scriptures that define their characteristics. Who are they? Simeon is Ireland.

Ireland

There are a great many characteristics that link Simeon and Ireland together.

- Ireland and neighboring Scotland are Simeon and Levi. Both are a part of the British Commonwealth today and are still "*brethren.*"
- Ireland has been divided by conflict throughout its life. Even today, they are a fighting people. Famous boxers and fighters have come from Ireland. *Fighting and warfare* are still a part of today's Ireland.
- The word "ire" means "anger" (e.g., irate, irritated, etc.). In the Hebrew, "Irish" means "anger man." Simeon was known for his anger; so are the Irish! The name of their country, Ireland, means "*Anger Land!*"
- The Irish have been punished and scattered for their anger and stubbornness. Many migrated throughout Great Britain, and even more came to the U.S.A. Even before this time, the Irish clung to their various clans, and remained divided even within their own nation and people. Jacob's prophecy of a *scattered people* has been fulfilled in the Irish.
- The Irish are *stubborn*. In Genesis 34, Simeon and Levi massacred an entire town against their fathers' wishes, refusing to comply with his request. That massacre occurred because of a religious conflict. Today, Ireland is divided into northern and

southern regions over yet another religious conflict, because neither side will give in to the other's proposals!

- Ireland is a small nation, but a *mighty* one. In fact, the football team at the University of Notre Dame is named "the fighting Irish," in honor of the Irish man's fighting spirit. Many Irish men have served in world wars and have been renowned fighters on the battlefield.
- Ireland has a tender *heart toward God*. Many Irish preachers have ministered throughout Great Britain. Just as they are not afraid of battle, they also jump into the midst of spiritual warfare to win souls to Christ!
- Hebrew writings allude to the fact that Simeon and Levi were the shepherds of the family. After the tribes dispersed, these two groups left with their flocks, arriving in Scotland and Ireland approximately two years later. Today, the Irish are still fine shepherds. Their Irish linens and fine weaving are also world-renowned. Their family colors are woven together into spectacular garments that tell the stories of their clans.

Are You Irish?

Based on these observations, we could safely conclude that Ireland truly is the tribe of Simeon. To a degree, they are religiously divided between Protestant and Catholic. Yet, they are strong in their national heritage and culture. It is interesting to note that Ireland's culture began to flourish shortly after the fall of the Israelite nation. But there is one curious connection between Ireland and Genesis 38.

Do you recall the story we discussed in a previous chapter, where we wondered why God would allow such a passage to be included in Scripture? It was the story of Judah, going in to sleep with a woman that he presumed to be a prostitute. Only later would he discover that he had slept with his daughter-in-law, Tamar. Judah's son (and her husband) had died, and she was determined to be a part of the covenant people. She wanted her children to be blessed!

When Tamar gave birth to twin sons, the one stuck his hand out of the womb. The midwife tied a scarlet thread around his wrist, but he drew it back again. Then the other son was born first and named

Pharez. Later, his twin brother was born with the scarlet cord around his wrist. He was named Zareh.

Pharez remained in Egypt during that time, and established the tribe of Judah in his later generations. However, at some point Zarah left Egypt (under his descendent, Calcol), and migrated into Western Europe. When the House of Israel scattered, many of the descendents of Simeon encountered a unique group already established in present day Ireland. They were descendents of Judah, from Zarah's line, and were called the "children of the Red Hand." Today these Irish people retain the Red Hand, circled by a scarlet cord in many of their coats of arms. The official symbol of Ulster (Northern Ireland) is a "Red Hand and scarlet cord," superimposed over a six-pointed star of David.

Why did God allow Genesis 38 to be placed in the Scriptures? It was so we could know His divine imprint upon the nations today. Thus, we find another one of Jacob's tribes alive and well in Ireland.

Levi

The story of Levi is the story of a tribe that began with a curse that was changed into a blessing. In Genesis 49, Jacob blasted both Simeon and Levi for their anger and stubbornness. But things had changed in Levi's heart by the time Moses prophesied over them in Deuteronomy 33. Yes, they would be scattered and divided into clans, but the Lord would use this division for His glory in the days to come. Let's look at some characteristics of this tribe that would be revealed as they settled into their own land after the House of Israel was dispersed.

- Genesis 49:5. As in our last study of Simeon, two characteristics are mentioned here:
  - Simeon and Levi are brothers, coming from the same father and mother.
  - They are warlike. Instruments of war are in their dwellings.
- Genesis 49:6. More characteristics of Simeon and Levi.
  - They can become so angered that they will kill a person.
  - They were so stubborn that they dug up an entire wall.

  - Genesis 49:7. Simeon and Levi's anger is cursed. Consequently, they will be divided in Jacob, and scattered in Israel.
- Deuteronomy 33:8. Levi here is blessed with a ministry gift, to minister to the other tribes.
- Deuteronomy 33:9. Levi is known for forsaking their father, mother, sisters, brothers, etc., for the sake of the ministry.
- Deuteronomy 33:10. Levi shall be known as a teacher of the law (or the Word) of God.
  - Deuteronomy 33:11. Moses asks God to: bless Levi's substance; accept the work of Levi's hands; and smite his enemies.
- Numbers 18. God chooses the tribe of Levi to be his ministering tribe. They receive no national allocation. Rather, their group is broken into families and dispersed among the other tribes. However, they still retain a strong sense of tribal identity.
- Numbers 25—Israel turns to idols, but Levi stands for God when others do not.
  - Phinehas, Aaron's son, kills a man and his mistress for violating God's 10 commandments.
  - God blesses Levi because of his zeal, and promises to him God's covenant of peace.
  - Levi is zealous for God in a very bold way.
  - God guarantees Levi an everlasting priesthood before Him because of his zeal.
- I Chronicles 6:1. The Levites are divided up into ministering families with various responsibilities. Some were shepherds over flocks of animals that were to be sacrificed. Others were music ministers. Still others were skilled warriors. These became known as the mighty "temple guards." And, of course, many of the Levites were devoted to teaching the law and offering guidance to the people. Who is Levi today? Levi is Scotland.

Scotland

What characteristics does Scotland display that link them to the tribe of Levi? Consider these.

- Scotland and Ireland are both a part of the British Isles (these Isles could be those which are mentioned in Isaiah 41:1). They are still *brethren*, living under the blanket of the British Commonwealth.
- Like Levi, their patriarch, the Scots are known for their *warlike* spirit. The famed "black watch" was a Scottish group of fighting men. Earlier still, this country was divided up into clans (or families), which occasionally warred against each other and against neighboring countries.
- Scotland's king, Robert the Bruce, led the Scots in a revolt for independence. He was repelled six times. However, the seventh, he and the Scottish armies prevailed. The Scots are both people with *tempers* (like their brother country Ireland) and very *stubborn* people, too! This was aptly depicted in the movie "*Braveheart*," which was a classic about Scotland.
- Jacob also cursed Levi for his temper and said he would be *divided*. Scotland is not a single nation. It is a united nation of separate families, or clans. This is the national dwelling place for the clans of Levi. However, many Scots have also scattered throughout the world. Many more migrated to the U.S.A. where they reside in present day Israel.
- Scotland is known for its *ministers*. Incidentally, the words "Scotland, Scot" and "Scottish" are all derived from the earlier word "Scoloti," which means "nomadic" or "wandering." The Levites wandered from town to town teaching the law to the other tribes. Eventually, they wandered to Scotland and became a nation themselves.
- The word "British" is derived from two Hebrew words. "Beriyth" is the Hebrew word for "covenant," and "iysh" is the Hebrew word for "man." Therefore, Beriyth-Iysh or British means "Covenant Man." This term is connected to the language of the Highlands in its origins. The Scots truly are a covenant people who were the original Levites, the *keepers of God's covenant*.
- The July, 1989 issue of "*Israel My Glory*," a Jewish focused publication, had this to say about the Scots. *"The tiny nation of Scotland has given the world many things; the sport of golf, the bagpipe, the Highland Games, and the poetry of Robert Burns. Unfortunately, one of Scotland's greatest contributions is often*

overlooked. Scotland has probably produced more missionaries, in proportion to her population, than any other country on earth. David Livingstone, the man who blazed a trail through Africa, was a Scot, as was Mary Slessor. The famous runner, Eric Liddel, was the son of Scottish missionaries, and John Paton, also a Scot, loved the heather hills of Scotland almost as much as he did the South Sea island on which he ministered. And Manchuria, considered the farthest outpost of Christian conquest in 1868, was manned by a Scot, William C. Burns." So we see that the Scottish Levites truly were known for forsaking their families for the cause of spreading the news of the covenant, both the old and the new!

- The Stone of Destiny resides in Edinburgh Castle, Scotland at the time of this writing. (More about this in a later chapter.) This stone, known as "Jacob's pillow stone" was shepherded by the Tribe of Levi during their time in the wilderness, as well as within Canaan. How appropriate that it now resides in Scotland.
- Like his brother, Simeon, Levi was also a shepherd. However, he herded the sacrificial animals. The wool gleaned from them was used to make the *brilliantly colorful garments* of the priesthood. Today, Scots are still known for their world renowned colorful plaids and tartans.
- In 1320 A.D. the Scottish Declaration of Independence was signed by Scottish nobles at Arbroath Abbey. It states, in part, *"We know, and from the chronicles and books of the ancients gather, that . . . the nation of the Scots . . . passing from the greater Scythia through the Mediterranean Sea and pillars of Hercules and sojourning in Spain . . . and coming thence One Thousand and two hundred years after the outgoing of the people of Israel . . ."* In short, they attached their heritage directly to the tribes of Israel. They knew they were Israelites.

Are You Scottish?

If you are of Scottish heritage, you probably have Israelite blood in your veins. God turned their curse into a blessing and made them a bold and noble nation that has fought for Christ and liberty throughout history.

Judah

Judah was given tremendous promises in Jacob's prophesies. These were also partly echoed by the prophesies of Moses in Deuteronomy 33. Other characteristics of the tribe of Judah are found in several places throughout the Scriptures. He was a noble tribe and led the House of Judah for centuries. Let's look further at some of the prophecies before we turn our thoughts to their present-day state.

- Genesis 49:8. Judah was given three promises in this passage:
  - his brothers would praise him;
  - his hand would be on the neck of his enemies; and
  - his father's children (e.g., the other tribes) would bow down before him.
- Genesis 49:9. This Scripture shows the tribe of Judah as both:
  - a young lion's cub (a lion's whelp); and
  - an old lion.
- Genesis 49:10. This verse promises Judah that:
  - he will receive the scepter blessing. Out of Judah, kings shall rule the tribes.
  - Shiloh shall also come out of Judah; the Messiah.
- Genesis 49:11-12. These verses provide foreshadows of the Messiah and the things which will be acquainted with his ministry. He will spring forth out of Judah.
  - he entered Jerusalem upon the foal of an ass.
  - his garments being washed in wine is likened as to Christ shedding his blood.
- Deuteronomy 33:7. Moses prays over Judah here, and requests three things of God:
  - first, hear the prayers that Judah prays;
  - second, let him be a self-sufficient people; and
  - third, help him to defeat his enemies.
- Genesis 37:26-28, Joshua 6:18-19. These two passages further illustrate Jewish characteristics, which are irrefutable.
  - Genesis 37—in this passage, Judah sold his brother.
  - Joshua 6—here Achan, a Jew, coveted a garment, money and jewelry.

  - o The Jews like the finer things and often deal in valuables and expensive merchandise around the world.
- Numbers 14:24, Joshua 14:6-12. Caleb, a descendent of Judah, is told by God that his seed shall possess the land of Canaan forever!
- Psalms 60:7. It is interesting to note that in the last days Judah is mentioned as the tribe who will carry on the administration of the law, not Levi!

Judah has both a mighty and a noble heritage. They have been hated throughout the world, partly due to the fact that they rejected Jesus Christ. Christ said their house (the House of Judah) would be left desolate until they would welcome Him. Today the tribe of Judah is known by a shortened version of the tribal name "Jew." They are still a vital part of God's covenant people.

The Jews

There are those that would attempt to push out the Jews, and say they are not part of God's covenant people, based on their behavior. But they are still beloved by God Himself. He prophesied over them, He will redeem them in time to come, and we give them due recognition and honor as a part of the Abrahamic covenant people.

- Judah is truly *praised* today by his brethren! The Jews are venerated and respected by Christians worldwide. Jesus, the Messiah, is the lion of the tribe of Judah (Revelation 5:5). The Jewish people are also respected for their strength of character, their uncanny business sense, and for the historic land which was given them by God forever!
- Judah certainly *dominates her enemies!* Shortly after declaring the formation of a Jewish state (in 1948), the Jewish State of Israel was attacked by five nations, all larger then she. However, the Jews won the war!
- The six-day war was fought with five opposing nations. Not only did the Jews prevail, they succeeded in taking back land promised to Abraham's seed (e.g., Jerusalem and the West Bank).

- After Idi Amin had taken a planeload of Jews hostage, the Jewish army flew commandos hundreds of miles, undetected, to rescue them singlehandedly. This was a miraculous feat that was applauded worldwide.
- The Jews bombed Iraqi nuclear facilities in another amazing feat, slowing Iraqi attempts to develop nuclear warfare capabilities.
- The Jews invaded Lebanon and were immediately attacked with advanced Soviet armaments. Not only did they successfully evade and repel the rebel attack, the Jews seized hundreds of millions of dollars worth of weapons that were stored up for an attack against them!
- Wars were fought in the 1960s, 1970s, and 1980s to defend present day Israel. In all wars, the Jews won conclusively, demonstrating God's support of this prophecy to them in Genesis 49!
- Judah is both a *lion's whelp and an old lion.* Judah lives in the historic land of Israel. It is one of the oldest nations on earth. Furthermore, the Jews possess archaeological items which link them to the land for more than two millennia. No other Middle-Eastern people group can lay claim to the land as far back as the Jews. Consequently, Judah is an "old lion." However, Judah was reestablished in 1948 as well, making it a young nation by today's standards. Thus we see that Judah is both the young and the old lion simultaneously.
- Judah did receive the *scepter blessing*. Kings would come out of this tribe. There is both a literal and a spiritual fulfillment to this prophecy. First, Jesus fulfills the prophecies concerning "Shiloh," the Messiah (in verses 10-12). He is of the house and lineage of David, the one through whom God established a literal royal dynasty. Only Jesus could fulfill all of the prophecies. He is our Shiloh, our peace!
- Judah's *scepter blessing* still carries on in a literal sense, too. In Jeremiah 33:7, God states that David's lineage shall reign over Israel. This is fulfilled within the royal house of England, who claim to be able to trace their lineage back to king David. They claim to be Judahites, a fact that was verified in conversation with their office of heraldry by this author. Since Manasseh and

Ephraim are "Israel" according to God, we see that David's seed truly does rule over Israel today.

- According to Golda Mier, the former Israeli Prime Minister, one of the major debates in the Israeli Knesset (or parliament) in 1948 was, "what shall we name our country?" The recommended names: Judah and Israel. All members of the Knesset were Jews. That land was reestablished as a *homeland for Jews* and for Jews alone. However, since the land was historically known as Israel during Bible times, history and tradition won out over common sense. Thus, it is recognized today that present day Israel truly is the land of Judah. Its formal name is *"The Jewish State Of Israel."*
- Sandra Childress, this writer's sister, was with a tour group through the land of Israel in November, 1991. The tour guide there reiterated the fact that no person could become a citizen of Israel unless they could prove conclusively that they were of the tribe of Judah; they were Jews. God promised this land to Caleb's seed for an everlasting possession. It truly does belong to the Jews according to the Scriptures!
- The Jews are a *self-sufficient* people. In fact, because of international persecution, they are trained to make themselves indispensible to society and self-sufficient as a culture. This is how they survive. They often deal in valuable merchandise, including the realms of clothing, jewelry, and finance. There are higher percentages of Jews in these fields than in any others. Why? Because they are talented in *sales* and the *management of finances.*

Are You A Jew?

If you have Jewish blood, you will be recognized more readily as one of "God's covenant people." The tribe of Judah receives the praise from the other brothers, even to this day. God has given Judah His eternal covenant, and as with every other tribe and nation, He has opened the door so that Jesus Christ may be your Messiah, Savior and King. This will be the struggle of the Jews in the last days, to see and embrace Jesus Christ.

Zebulun

Zebulun? If you are like many people today, you have assumed the Jews comprise all of God's covenant people! Now you know that God's covenant was truly huge, and encompasses more than one nation. The Bible comes alive when we begin to study the lesser-known tribes and their characteristics. There is much to learn about where they scattered, what they did, and who they are today. One of those trailblazing tribes that few understand is Zebulun. We will examine a few passages, because he is not in the spotlight. But the Scriptures say enough for us to understand his place in God's history books.

- Genesis 49:13. Zebulun is prophetically given three characteristics here which clearly distinguish him in the last days:
  - he shall dwell near the sea;
  - he shall be a haven for ships; and
  - his border shall extend north. He shall be a "North man."
- Deuteronomy 33:18-19. Further attributes of both Zebulun and Issachar are:
  - Zebulun shall go out, he shall be a traveler;
  - they shall both call the people to righteousness;
  - they shall both draw abundant treasures out of the seas; and
  - they shall both find treasures hidden in the sand.
- I Chronicles 12:33. This passage mentions that the children of Zebulun were excellent warriors who did not draw back in battle, because they were single-minded; they were not of a double heart.

Did you catch some of those characteristics God would use to *move* His tribes? They are interesting, and may become more obvious when you discover who Zebulun is today. He is Norway.

Norway

Here are some of the features of this nation, and the associated nations around him.

- Zebulun *dwells by the sea.* He originally lived by the sea of Galilee; now he lives by the sea of the Nations (Isaiah 9:1) in the land of Norway.
- The Norwegians are a seafaring people. Their land contains inlets and fjords that are *havens for ships* and these types of industries.
- Zebulun's border was to extend north to Sidon. He was a "*north man.*" This was later changed to the term "Norseman." These are the ancient seafaring Vikings who ventured far and wide.
- The Vikings are said to have discovered the Americas even before Columbus' voyage in 1492. This is entirely possible, since the Scripture says that Zebulun would be *a traveler.*
- Many *revivals* have occurred in Norway. The Anabaptists took root in the 1500's with a mighty revival. The Pentecostal revivals occurred in the 1800's and 1900's. Many Norwegians are ministers of the Gospel.
- Norway is a nation that draws from the *treasures of the sea and sand.* They are excellent fishermen. They are also lovers of sand creatures, shellfish (e.g., crab, shrimp, lobster, clams).
- The men of Zebulun certainly were *single minded* during World War II. Many Norwegians worked with the underground, aiding resistance efforts. They were focused and dedicated, excellent warriors from this nation.
- Zebulun and Issachar were often linked together in Scripture, just as Simeon and Levi were. They lived in close proximity to one another and had the same interests. Today, Norway (Zebulun) and Sweden (Issachar) are still closely linked together in proximity, in overall avocations, and in philosophies. They have had their sibling rivalries, but have still remained connected. Other closely related nations that may spring from this heritage include Lapland, Finland, Iceland and Greenland.

Are You Norwegian?

The Norwegians are noted for their single-mindedness, even in the Bible. Their stolid determination has carved out a society when virtually nothing existed in Northern Europe. But this was also the case when they migrated to North America and settled in the prairies. As seafarers, this tribe undoubtedly helped to move some of the scattered tribes of the House of Israel. So once again we see with Zebulun that even the lesser mentioned tribes play an integral part in God's plans and events in the last days. Norway exists because of the prophetic Word of God. Now, we will turn to Norway's friend and brother nation, Issachar.

Issachar

Moses said very little about Issachar and Zebulun in Deuteronomy, but Jacob spoke of them both in Genesis. There are strong characteristics mentioned, however, and they give us clues to their last-day existence. Here are some of them.

- Genesis 49:14. Issachar is characterized as a strong nation that rests between two burdens.
- Genesis 49:15. Further enlightenment on verse 14 follows:
    - he saw that rest was good;
    - he found a pleasant land;
    - he bowed his shoulder (willingly) to bear (a burden); and
    - he became a servant to tribute (or taxation).
- Deuteronomy 33:18-19. Several characteristics are also mentioned here of both Issachar and Zebulun.
    - Issachar loves to dwell in tents; they remain at home while Zebulun travels about;
    - they shall both call the people to righteousness;
    - they shall both draw abundant treasures out of the seas; and
    - they shall both find treasures hidden in the sand.
- I Chronicles 12:32. Here, the men of Issachar were given an understanding of the times, and had the wisdom of God, to know what to do.

Who is this tribe of Issachar today? It is Sweden.

Sweden

The nation of Sweden and the last-day characteristics God pronounced over Issachar are markedly similar. Consider these.

- Sweden is a strong nation in physical characteristics. Many immigrants from Sweden to other nations settled into hardscrabble lives, building sod huts on the prairies, and working in the logging camps of the forests. They do not shrink from physical labor or "burden bearing."
- However as a nation, Sweden truly is laid down *between two burdens*: socialism and taxation. The September, 1991 issue of the Readers Digest shared an article about "Sweden: The Nation that Tried to Buy Happiness," which examined this fact, concluding that Sweden was hindered by some of the highest taxation in the world and by a socialist government that is not working.
- The Swedes are also a peace-loving people. They have managed to stay out of the last two world wars (*rest is good)*, remaining neutral both times. The Nobel prizes, including the annual peace prize, are awarded from their headquarters in Stockholm, Sweden.
- The land of Sweden is very *pleasant*. It has been blessed with massive reserves of iron ore, timber and water power, more so than other nations.
- Sweden truly is a *servant to tribute* and taxation, and has been so for many decades. In the early 1990's, Sweden's tax rates ran as high as 51 percent! Because of this and other factors, it also bears Europe's highest inflation rate.
- Many *revivals* have also occurred in Sweden. These people are known for their Lutheran roots, which have existed since the latter years of Martin Luther himself. The Pentecostal revivals, which touched Norway in the 1800's and 1900's, also influenced Sweden. Many Swedes are ministers of the Gospel.
- Like Norway, Sweden is also a nation that draws from the *treasures of the sea and sand*. They are excellent fishermen. They are also lovers of sand creatures, shellfish (e.g., crab, shrimp, lobster, clams). Many Swedes migrated to other nations, and remained by the sea because of their love for this lifestyle.
- Zebulun and Issachar were often linked together in Scripture, just as Simeon and Levi were. They lived in close proximity to one another and had the same interests. Today, Norway

(Zebulun) and Sweden (Issachar) are still closely linked together in proximity, in overall avocations, and in philosophies.

Are You Swedish?

If you are a Swede, you probably have Israelite blood in your heritage. The nation of your heritage has been blessed by God. Although Sweden and her northern neighbors were idolatrous, they also chose to embrace Jesus Christ when He was introduced to them. God has watched over Sweden through the years because of His covenant with Abraham, Isaac and Jacob.

Dan

The tribe of Dan displays some very interesting characteristics that are still notable today! He is the only tribe not listed in the book of Revelation, when the other tribes are sealed, and there is a great deal of speculation as to the reason for this. But Dan's history has been long and winding.

- Genesis 49:16. Dan is to be a judge to his people.
- Genesis 49:17-18. Dan will be known as a serpent by the path that strikes out at the horse, causing the rider to fall off. This denotes treachery, warfare.
- Deuteronomy 33:22. Dan is to be a lion's whelp (cub). He shall leap from Bashan.
- Joshua 19:47. Dan's inheritance was small; too small, they thought. So, they attacked a heathen city. Then, they did something that was unique to this tribe; they renamed this city after their patriarch . . . . "Dan." This was to become one of their tribal trademarks (also Judges 18:29).
- Judges 5:17. Dan has taken to traveling by ship. He, like Zebulun, is a traveler, a wanderer.

This tribe of Dan was quick to forsake the Lord, partly due to their sense of adventure. They would mix their culture with others, and would not be as single-hearted toward God. Who is the tribe of Dan today? He is Denmark.

Denmark

Dan's heritage becomes quickly apparent as you examine their history and heraldry.

- The original name of the nation of Denmark is "*Dan's Mark.*" This was recorded as early as 899 A.D., making Dan an ancient nation. Dan was driven out of his land by the Amorites and built ships to travel (Judges 1:34, Judges 5:17). This was the beginning of his trail.
- Dan was to be an *adder by the path*. "Path" in Hebrew means "race, troop" or "caravan." "Adder" means to "bite" or "strike." Dan stuck out at many troops, often blazing the way for his other tribal brethren to follow after and settle European nations.
- Today, the seal of Denmark is *three serpents heads* with lions tails. Dan was to judge his people. He ruled over Norway and Sweden for more than 600 years. He also controlled parts of Ireland, Britain, Scotland, Spain, and present day Belgium during early European history.
- Wherever the Tribe of Dan went, they drove the inhabitants out and *renamed the cities* after their patriarch, Dan (Joshua 19:47; Judges 18:29). However, the Hebrew alphabet contains no vowels. Consequently, the name "Dan" could be spelled several ways; "dan, dun, don, din, den." The Dan-ites were travelers, and were known for their sailing (Judges 5:17). According to Raymond Capt, author of *Judah's Scepter and Joseph's Birthright*, some of the marks Dan may have left throughout Europe are: London, Danube, Dundee, Edinburgh, Dunkirk, Dardannelle (Turks), and Dedans (off the coast of Spain). These are only a few of the marks on Dan's serpentine trail.

Are You A Dane?

As a Dane, you may have Israelite blood in your heritage. Your past ancestors ruled over much of Europe, and were a mighty, seafaring people. Dan's marks are scattered throughout Europe as he moved from Israel. As mentioned, he is not listed among the tribes in Revelation.

What will happen to Dan in the last days? This is an issue open for study, observation and prayer.

Gad

Gad was a tribe that received two unique prophecies, to be fulfilled in the last days. Although not much was said about Gad, he had distinct characteristics, and would play a key role in the days to come.

- Genesis 49:19. This verse states that Gad will be overcome by a troop or a warring party, but he shall finally overcome their attack.
- Deuteronomy 33:20-21. This passage mentions several things of Gad:
  - he is enlarged;
  - he dwells as a lion;
  - he tears the arm with the crown of the head;
  - he provides the first portion for himself; he is self-serving.
- I Chronicles 12:8,14. These two verses portray the Gadites as expert military leaders and fighters. They are hard to defeat.
- Numbers 32:1. Gad (along with Reuben) was known for his cattle. He had good farmland, and was one of the tribes that settled on the far side of the Jordan River. Gad often chose to live more independently, apart from his fellow tribes. Consequently he went into captivity and was scattered by Assyria among the first tribes.

Gad has played an instrumental role among his fellow tribes in days past, and continues to be a dominant nation, even today. Who is Gad? Gad is Germany.

Germany

How do Gad and Germany compare? Consider these thoughts.

- When this author began to study the correlation between last-day prophesies and various nations, he quickly understood the fact that Gad was in fact Germany. However, the Berlin Wall still stood, and the nation was divided because of World War II. During World War II, Germany was *overcome* by the allied forces. The Soviet Union occupied half of Germany and created a separate communist state. This divided the country, and the city of Berlin was also cut in half. However, on November 9, 1989, *Germany had overcome* at the last. The Berlin wall fell and democracy prevailed. Germany was reunited once again. A troop had overcome them, but the wall came down, in accordance with Bible prophecy.

- The Word "Gad" means "troop." This is a Hebrew military term which means "to attack or invade." Germany is a warlike nation that has started two world wars by *invading other countries*. They are brilliant military strategists with notable Generals. During World War II, they were technologically more advanced than the allies, and were defeated by defecting scientists and the work of the underground resistance that destroyed some of their research and manufacturing capabilities.
- Germany truly did tear at the *crown of the head*. Once we understand who the tribes are in prophecy, this Scripture becomes very clear. The tribe of Judah had the scepter blessing. The kings would come from Judah. However, it was prophesied that this tribe, Gad, would attack and tear at the tribe that had the blessing of the crown! What happened in World War II? The Germans (Gadites) killed millions of Jews, fulfilling the last-day prophecies of the Sovereign Lord!
- Germans are an inventive people that have pioneered such things as the telephone and rocket propulsion. They are great *military strategists.*
- German cooking is filled with recipes which contain their favorite meat . . . . *beef.* They are cattlemen. Bratwurst, liverwurst and veal are only some of the German beef dishes which are served around the world today.

Are You German?

If you are a German, you may well have Israelite blood in your veins. Germany may well continue to play a dominant role in last-day prophecy. As a central component of the European Union, Germany may well be a key element in the globalist agenda. But God has used Germany for His plans in these last days.

Asher

When Jacob's wives, Leah and Rachel, were competing for his affections, Rachel was faced with the fact that she was barren. She tried to overcome this in the natural realm, and gave her handmaid, Bilhah, to Jacob as his wife. Leah joined in the fight, too. She gave Jacob Zilpah, her handmaid, as his fourth wife. These two women bore Jacob sons, and Asher was one of Zilpah's offspring. Based on historic study it is thought that Asher was somewhat separated from his brothers. Yes, he was a part of the family, but he tended to do his own thing at times. Let's look at other clues the Bible provides in Genesis and Deuteronomy.

- Genesis 49:20. As one of the "lesser" tribes, Asher will still be distinctive.
  - His bread shall be fat; and
  - he shall yield royal dainties.
- Deuteronomy 33:24-25. Five things are mentioned here of Asher:
  - he will be blessed with children;
  - he will be acceptable to his brethren (he was not notably close to any of them);
  - he will dip his foot in oil;
  - his shoes will be iron and brass; and
  - his strength shall match his days.

Iron and brass. Dipping his foot in oil. He shall yield royal dainties. Who could this be in the world today? Today, many believe Asher is France.

France

How does this information correlate to present day France?

- France is noted for its pastries and cooking (cuisine). French chefs are world-renowned. Asher's bread is the *fattest in the world.*

- France yields *dainties for royalty* the world over. They are an international center for art, clothing fashions, perfume, cosmetics, fine jewelry, cooking, decorating, etc. Queen Elizabeth of Great Britain sent to France for the clothes she wore at her coronation. Many of the crown jewels were created by noted French jewelers. Today, Paris is the capitol of fashion and luxury, superseding noted cities such as Milan, Italy and New York.
- The French have been *blessed with children*. Most of France is Catholic, and in accordance with their religious training, French families are notably large, larger than those in other European countries.
- Asher was probably closest to Manasseh; however, he was not very close to any of his brethren. The same could be said of France today. However, because of France's "dainties," he has become an *accepted* part of the family.
- France has dipped his *foot in oil,* cooking oil, that is! The French are noted Chefs and Vintners. Their culinary expertise and wineries are noted throughout the world.
- Although France is not known for their material wealth, they do possess a fair amount of raw *Iron*. With this, they manufacture automobiles and other goods for distribution throughout Europe.
- The fact that France has survived two occupations during two world wars is an amazing feat. The French Resistance movement was during World War II was filled with amazing men and women of courage. This fact alone helps to cement God's promise of *enduring strength* to Asher.

Are You French?

God's blessing to Asher has preserved France as a nation, and given him a distinctive place in the world. Although France is mostly Roman Catholic in its religion, nationally, many French came to the United States as Huguenots. They sought freedom to worship God in spirit and in truth. Again we see God's hand over a nation and a people, one that is of the seed of Abraham, Isaac and Israel.

Naphtali

Naphtali was one of the sons born to Jacob through Bilhah, Rachel's handmaid. Like Dan, his brother, Naphtali liked to travel and venture out. The prophecies concerning him in Genesis and Deuteronomy may not seem significant, but they are.

- Genesis 49:21. Two things are mentioned of Naphtali:
  - he is like a hind let loose; and
  - he gives goodly words.
- Deuteronomy 33:23. Naphtali was blessed with the blessing of the Lord in this passage. Also,
  - he was to possess the west and the south (the southwest).
- I Kings 7:14. Hiram, the famous gold and brassworker of Solomon's temple, was from the tribe of Naphtali. This trade was passed down from his father.
- II Kings 15:29. Naphtali is taken captive by the Syrians. This caused the first exodus of this tribe (approximately 760 B.C.).

Because little is said about Naphtali, we also must look for clues in the stories of the Kings. Who is Naphtali today? He is Spain.

Spain

The early migration of the House of Israel was assisted by their adventurous brother, Naphtali. Let's examine the clues together.

- Spaniards are known for their love of the dance. They are light on their feet (*like a deer*). They are graceful, expressive people that enjoy Flamenco music (that includes quick guitar strumming and light dance work).
- Spanish is known as one of the *primary "romance" languages* by linguists worldwide. Spanish is a fluid, "soft-sounding" language. It is not guttural, like German or Russian. Many love songs and ballads have been composed by Spaniards. Many classical and popular music stars with Spanish heritage can be listed in every generation. Why? It is a part of their culture and heritage as prophesied by God Himself.

- Spain truly did *possess the west and the south.* They first arrived in Spain, taking dominion there in the southwest portion of Europe. However, during the 1400's, 1500's, 1600's and 1700's, Spain was the primary explorer of South and Central America as they spread further to the south and west. Their influence in that region, as well as in the Southwestern United States, caused this area to become known as "Latin America."
- The Spanish are known for their fine *gold, silver and brass work.* Great cathedrals and castles exist in present day Spain which exhibit their fine work in this field. The Spaniards took thousands of tons of Gold and Silver out of South and Central America, to further develop their trade in this field.
- The area of present day Spain was settled shortly after the tribe of Naphtali was dispersed by Syria in *760 B.C.* According to the *U.S. Library of Congress*, this region was called "Iberia" as a group of Saxons began to move into the region around that same time period. These "Iberians" could well have been from the tribe of Naphtali. A study of Hebrew culture and language bears this out further. The Israelites were also known as "Hebrews" during this time (Genesis 14:13, Exodus 2:13, I Samuel 4:6, etc.). The Palestinians were known as the "Philistines." Just as the Philistines' land was known as "Philistia" (Psalms 87:4, Psalms 108:9), it is possible that the land of the Hebrews was known as "Heberia." Thus, when the tribe of Naphthali moved into the area of Spain, it became known as the land of Heberia . . . . or "Iberia." Today the marks of Iberia are still present. In fact, the nation airline of Spain is called Iberia Air.

Are You Spanish?

Because of Spain's aggressive and sometimes brutal policies toward nations they conquered, there are those that are hostile toward the Spanish heritage. However, God blessed Spain and gave them the south and the west. This causes us to see the fact that God was working in the establishment of nations, and in last day expansion. Naphtali is present day Spain, one of God's tribes on the earth today.

Benjamin

At this point, we will deviate momentarily from following the list of prophetic blessings as they are listed in Genesis 49. We will return to the blessing over Joseph in a little while. However, we will now turn to consider the blessing Israel placed upon his youngest son, Benjamin. Manasseh and Ephraim were younger in age, but they were technically Joseph's sons, whom Israel adopted. Benjamin was Jacob's youngest, and had been his cherished son during the time that he thought Joseph to be dead. Rachel died giving birth to Benjamin and had named him Benoni, which means "son of my sorrow." Israel overruled, and renamed his son "the son of the right hand." Benjamin. Let's delve into the prophecies over his life in the last days.

- Genesis 49:27. This prophecy tells us that:
    - o Benjamin shall ravin (or stalk) like a wolf;
    - o he shall devour prey in the morning and divide spoil at night.
- Deuteronomy 33:12. Further characteristics of Benjamin are illustrated here.
    - o he shall dwell in safety, protected by God;
    - o the Lord shall cover him; and
    - o he shall dwell between God's shoulders.
- Genesis 45:22. In this Scripture, Benjamin is given a great amount of money. Finances have flowed into this tribe.
- I Samuel 14:4, 13. Saul, the first king of Israel was of the tribe of Benjamin. In this passage, his son, Jonathan, demonstrates two characteristics of the Benjaminite men:
    - o he is at home on the mountains and rocks (their country was mountainous); and
    - o he is a mighty warrior (the Benjaminites were known to be mighty in battle).
- Psalms 68:27. This passage refers to Benjamin as a little country.
- Romans 11:1. Paul the apostle refers to himself as a Benjaminite.

The tribes of Benjamin and Levi (to a great extent) joined together with Judah, to form the House of Judah. Consequently, many Benjaminites became known as Jews. However, some retained their tribal identity and branched off to find new lands after the time of their captivity. Where did these people go, and where do they reside today? In Switzerland.

Switzerland

Today, the Swiss dwell between God's shoulders, as He prophesied. How so? Let's take a look at the Scriptures and characteristics, blended together.

- Benjamin means *few in number and ignoble*. The end of the book of Judges tells their story, how that they refused to conform to the tribal moral standards and embraced homosexuality. The other tribes attacked them and forced them to embrace God's moral code once again.
- Today, the Swiss are fewer than many nations of the world. They also live by their own rules, refusing to disclose bank accounts, etc. to the rest of humanity. They are somewhat ignoble in this sense.
- The Swiss live on the *prey of the world*. Their banks and bank accounts flourish on secret funds, huge gold deposits and Arab oil monies. Benjamin does ravin like a wolf and divide the spoil. During World War II, the Swiss acted as a banking enterprise for the Germans and the Allies, concealing many of these facts until long after the war was finished. They act for their own self-interests, and enjoy the spoils of others.
- Switzerland has been *protected* for centuries. They repelled attacks by France, Austria and Germany. Even Hitler backed down and did not attack this tiny nation; so fierce was their resistance! Every home is armed with military-style weapons, and every man is trained to defend their nation. They have lived in peace through the last two world wars.
- Benjamin rests amid the Alps. This is one of God's "*shoulders*" in the world today. King Saul, the first king of Israel, was from the tribe of Benjamin. His son, Jonathan, conquered the

Philistines by assaulting their mountain fortress (1 Samuel 14). Just as Jonathan was adept at mountain climbing in his day, today's Swiss climb their Alps.

- The Benjaminites were mighty in battle and were expert marksmen with bow and arrow. This has carried on as well. William Tell, the man sentenced to shoot an apple from his son's head with a bow and arrow, was Swiss. Hitler feared Switzerland's 500,000 marksmen during WWII. Today their army, although small, is still known for its *marksmanship*. Today, every man above the age of 20 is required to keep and maintain a loaded, fully-automatic assault weapon in his house at all times for the protection of the country. Consequently, the crime rate in Switzerland is very low.

Are You Swiss?

Benjamin, the little country, truly does exist. It is Switzerland. Like their fellow "Jews," this tribe excels at money management, banking, and protecting financial assets for the world. They have been able to remain neutral in delicate financial and political climates. Because of this one characteristic, this "smallest tribe" was also instrumental in the spread of Christianity as it rekindled throughout Europe in the 1500's. How? Switzerland provided safe haven for Bible translators and those persecuted by the Roman Catholic Church. This place of refuge stirred the fire of God once again among God's people.

How Can You Be Sure?

For years, these truths have been studied using the Bible and God-given characteristics as their foundation. However, this writer was stunned in 2000 A.D. when he read about the early findings of a research project conducted in Western Europe. According to Reuters News Service (and taken from the scientific journal *"Proceedings of Royal Society B"* as presented at Oxford and Edinburgh Universities) DNA samples were taken from a broad spectrum of Western Europeans, to determine what genetic, historic links could be found.

According to their findings, eighty percent of Western Europeans came from 10 men that had their origins in the Middle East! These ten men had DNA patterns that showed they came from the Middle East. Who were these ten men? Could they have been the sons of Jacob, the patriarchs of the House of Israel? This author certainly notes a connection! In these days of advancing genetic research, perhaps even DNA evidence will reveal God's mighty hand.

Since that initial finding in 2000 A.D., more research has been conducted by Professor Mark Jobling and Dr. Patricia Balaresque on British subjects in particular. Their research leads to very similar conclusions. While their viewpoint is definitely secular, it is startling in its similarities to the Bible and what we present to you today.

Joseph—Father of Manasseh And Ephraim

We have one son left to address. His name is Joseph. As we stated in a previous chapter, the birthright blessing was supposed to go to Reuben. He was the firstborn son. However, he defiled his father's bed, and Jacob revoked this blessing. Reuben was cursed instead. Now, the birthright, the blessing of material wealth, went to Jacob's eldest son given to him by his favorite wife, Rachel. It was given to Joseph.

Since Joseph was the father of both Manasseh and Ephraim, these prophecies would apply to the lineages of both sons. However, Ephraim was to be blessed above all of the others, even above Manasseh (Genesis 48:19). Because of this, these prophecies would certainly be weighted in his favor. Let us, then, examine Joseph's prophecies with these facts in mind.

- Genesis 49:22. Joseph is described with three key phrases, which will typify his lineage:
    - he is a fruitful bough;
    - he is a bough by a well; and
    - his branches run over the wall . . . . they extend outward.
- Genesis 49:23. This passage describes a prophetic affliction, since Joseph's brothers never shot at him with bow and arrow. Consequently, this must apply to Manasseh and Ephraim's seed.
    - archers have sorely (or severely) grieved him;
    - they shot at him and hated him.

- Genesis 49:24. This speaks of future deliverance of these two nations from a tremendous attack.
  - o Joseph's bow abode in strength;
  - o his arms were made strong by the hands of the mighty God of Jacob;
  - o the shepherd stone, the stone of Jacob resides with Joseph's seed.
- Genesis 49:25. This verse indicates that:
  - o God will help Joseph's seed;
  - o God will bless his seed with the blessings of heaven (proper balance of sunshine, moisture, fair winds, etc., necessary for growing crops);
  - o God will give Joseph's seed great blessings under ground (mining, minerals, rocks, natural resources, etc.);
  - o God will bless Joseph's seed as they multiply. He shall also bless their cattle, etc. and multiply them.
  - o In Summary: JOSEPH'S SEED IS TO INHERIT THE BIRTHRIGHT BLESSING!
- Genesis 49:26. Jacob states here that the blessings that he has received from the Lord have exceeded all of the blessings given to his forefathers, Abraham and Isaac. The words "everlasting hills" translate into the words "to whom it is due." Simply put, this blessing was the blessing which the firstborn, Reuben, was to receive. However, because of Reuben's sin, he lost the birthright blessing. Israel now bestows those blessings upon Joseph's seed!
- Genesis 48:22. Israel, speaking to Joseph, gives him an additional prize. It is a material blessing that he won in battle. This would not be included in the division of his property; it was to go to Joseph and his seed alone.
- Genesis 50:16-21. After Israel, Joseph's fathers', death his brothers were afraid that Joseph would retaliate against them for their selling Joseph into slavery. So they approached Joseph and asked forgiveness. Joseph immediately forgave them. Furthermore, he nourished them, spoke kindly to all of them and comforted them. This is a characteristic of Joseph's seed.
- Genesis 41:56-57. Joseph was placed in a position of authority and distribution by Pharaoh. He literally fed the world! This

characteristic also carried over into Joseph's seed. Ephraim became the leader of Israel, the ten tribe nation later on.

- Deuteronomy 33: 13-16. In this passage, Moses adds to the blessing of Joseph's seed, Manasseh and Ephraim.
    - he blesses their land and the heavens above them;
    - he promises them dew upon their crops;
    - he blesses them with an abundance of natural resources and minerals;
    - they are blessed with fruit; even tropical fruit (things brought forth by the sun);
    - they are blessed with an abundance of root crops and vegetables (things brought forth by the moon);
    - he bestows chief things from ancient mountains and precious things from lasting hills;
    - he further bestows all of the abundance of the earth;
    - and finally, Moses also blesses Joseph's seed with the favor of Him (denoting God) who dwelt in the bush (this speaks of Moses' encounter with God at the burning bush). Joseph's seed specifically receives an extra portion of the favor of God!
    - This favor is to rest on Joseph's seed, the one who was separated from his brothers.
- Deuteronomy 33:17. Moses further describes the characteristics of Joseph's seed.
    - they are a strong people, like a young bullock or ox.
    - they are mighty in battle. Their horns are like the horns of a unicorn.
    - they push the people together to the ends of the earth.
    - Ephraim will have tens of thousands in his country (denoting tens of millions);
    - Manasseh shall have thousands (denoting millions) in his nation!
- I Chronicles 5:1-2. This passage specifically mentions that Israel's birthright became Joseph's!

If you merely scan these pages, you may be amazed by the amount of attention God pays to Joseph! God spoke over Joseph and his sons more than he spoke over the tribe of Judah. Therefore, any prophetic utterance of this magnitude must have a major impact on the world in the last days. Who is Joseph? Who are His sons in the world today? Manasseh is England, and Ephraim is the United States of America.

England And The United States Of America

Before we consider each nation individually, let's look at them together. Joseph's sons, Manasseh and Ephraim, were children of a common mother. Because of God's prophetic blessings, and because of their natural characteristics, they share many common features.

- Both England and the U.S.A. are *fruitful countries*. They abound with natural resources. The U.S.A. is more plenteous; this nation is Ephraim the younger.
- England and the U.S.A. have a great amount of water surrounding their countries; they are fruitful *boughs by the well.*
- England and the U.S. have ventured all *across the world*. England's earlier conquests and establishments are well documented. The United States has also established military presence in many countries that are sovereign, with more than 900 military bases presently in existence. Many outside nations have relied on the U.S.A. for their very lives.
- The enemy has severely grieved both the United States and England during several world wars. However, *archers* and arrows could be terms for armaments such as missiles. If this is true, the greater fulfillment of this and subsequent scriptures could be forthcoming (See Ezekiel 38, 39 for more information), possibly in our generation.
- When attacks do come against the U.S. and/or England, they will only be defeated as these two nations call upon the Name of the Lord and *repent* (II Chronicles 7:14, Joel 2).
- The *stone* that is mentioned in Genesis 49:24 carries a special significance. However, we will reserve it for a later study.
- The *great blessings* of material resources and abundant crops can truly be found in both the United States and England. England's influence has also extended to nations such as Australia and Canada, which are strong areas with vast reserves of natural

resources. To further confirm the England/U.S. connection, consider the inscriptions on the Peace Arch. The Peace Arch straddles the U.S./Canada border between Washington State and British Columbia. The inscriptions state, "children of a common mother," and "brethren dwelling together in unity."

These great blessings are only found in Israel's seed, in the lands of Ephraim and Manasseh!

- In Genesis 50, Joseph was depicted as a *forgiving* man. This is also a characteristic of England and the United States. After both WWI and WWII, they behaved in this same exact manner, helping their former enemies rebuild and become reestablished on the world scene. (Incidentally, the enemies that we fought against in those wars were "brother" nations!)
- The U.S.A. and England have truly been the *"administrators" and "helpers" to the world!* The United States supports the U.N. almost singlehandedly, and both the U.S. and Great Britain have shipped hundreds of thousands of tons of food and grain to disaster ridden areas of Africa, Europe, South and Central America . . . even the Soviet Union!
- Both England and the U.S.A. are like the *young, strong bullock* and the *powerful unicorn*. They have truly pushed peoples together to the ends of the earth, colonizing new nations and raising up entire countries! The United States is the melting pot of the world, drawing nationalities from all lands.
- Manasseh was the older brother; Ephraim was the younger. However, Ephraim outgrew Manasseh and was blessed more abundantly as well. Similarly, England was an older nation when the United States was born. It is the younger of the two. And on the world scene, *the United States has eclipsed its older brother* (and it's tributaries) in every way. Truly, we see Israel's prophecy fulfilled within our nation, one nation under God!

These two superpowers in the world are blessed because of God. First, they received the greatest blessing of material goods. Second, they retained the name and identity of "Israel." If there is any doubt that the Manasseh and Ephraim of the Old Testament are present day England

and the United States, we present further proofs, beginning with their prophetically significant adoption.

The Adoption

Let's recap the momentous events found at the adoption of these two boys by Israel, found in Genesis 48. We will focus mainly on verses 5-6, and 13-20.

Genesis 48:5-6 [5]*And now thy two sons, Ephraim and Manasseh, which were born unto thee in the land of Egypt before I came unto thee into Egypt, are mine; as Reuben and Simeon, they shall be mine.* [6]*And thy issue, which thou begettest after them, shall be thine, and shall be called after the name of their brethren in their inheritance.*

- Verse 5. After Israel reminded Joseph of the covenant God made with the family, he adopted Manasseh and Ephraim as his own sons. *"As Reuben and Simeon, they shall be mine."* These two sons would be adopted.
- Verse 6. Israel then specified to Joseph that any children that would be born to Joseph and Asenath after this time would fall under Joseph's blessing. But Manasseh and Ephraim would be known as sons, tribes, and later as nations of Israel.

Genesis 48:13-20 [13]*And Joseph took them both, Ephraim in his right hand toward Israel's left hand, and Manasseh in his left hand toward Israel's right hand, and brought them near unto him.* [14]*And Israel stretched out his right hand, and laid it upon Ephraim's head, who was the younger, and his left hand upon Manasseh's head, guiding his hands wittingly; for Manasseh was the firstborn.* [15]*And he blessed Joseph, and said, God, before whom my fathers Abraham and Isaac did walk, the God which fed me all my life long unto this day,* [16]*The Angel which redeemed me from all evil, bless the lads; and let my name be named on them, and the name of my fathers Abraham and Isaac; and let them grow into a multitude in the midst of the earth.* [17]*And when Joseph saw that his father laid his right hand upon the head of Ephraim, it displeased him: and he held up his father's hand, to remove it from Ephraim's head unto Manasseh's head.* [18]*And Joseph said unto his father, Not so, my father: for this is the firstborn; put thy right hand upon his head.* [19]*And his father refused, and said, I know it, my son,*

I know it: he also shall become a people, and he also shall be great: but truly his younger brother shall be greater than he, and his seed shall become a multitude of nations. [20]And he blessed them that day, saying, In thee shall Israel bless, saying, God make thee as Ephraim and as Manasseh: and he set Ephraim before Manasseh.

- Verse 13. Joseph guided his sons toward Israel, his father. He led Manasseh forward with his left hand, toward Israel's right hand. He brought Ephraim forward with his right hand, toward Israel's left hand.
- Verse 14. However, when Israel reached out to bless Joseph's sons, he crossed his hands! Israel laid his hands on Manasseh and Ephraim, with the right hand resting on Ephraim's head! This was important, because the "right hand blessing" was the more powerful of the two. This was the foundation of "Jacob's cross of blessing."
- Verses 15-16. Israel blessed Joseph's sons. First, he called upon the God of Abraham and Isaac, and acknowledged God's guidance on his own life Then he asked God to bless the two boys. After this came an unusual request. Israel, or Jacob, asked that God place his name, the name of Israel, upon them, and them only. He further asked that the names of Abraham and Isaac be attributed to them as well. He closed his prayer to Heaven by asking God to cause these two boys' seeds to grow into a multitude in the midst of the earth! It was a magnificent, prophetic moment.
- Verses 17-18. But there was a problem! Joseph had noticed the fact that his father, Israel, had crossed his hands. He placed the primary hand of blessing (the right hand) upon Ephraim, the youngest son. So, Joseph held up his father's hands. He explained to his near-blind father that the eldest son, Manasseh, is on the other side. Joseph wants Jacob's right hand to be laid upon Manasseh.
- Verse 19. Israel responded. He knew exactly what he was doing, and it was a prophetic moment before God. Just as God had promised the blessing of Isaac instead of Ishmael, and allowed Jacob to be blessed instead of Esau, this was one of

those sovereign times. Once again, Israel spoke prophetically. Manasseh's seed would be great, and he would be a people, but Ephraim's seed would be something unique. His seed would be a multitude, a melting pot, of nations.

- Verse 20. This blessing would be so significant that Israel would look to Manasseh and Ephraim as the standard for physical wealth and blessing. Israel then closed this prophetic time by setting Ephraim, the younger, ahead of Manasseh, the older. Ephraim's blessing was sealed for the last days.

This Cannot Be Ignored

Many Bible scholars have chosen to avoid or ignore this passage because it is controversial. They relegate *all* physical blessings to the Jews, and avoid the other tribes, despite the fact that God Himself recognizes all of them throughout the Scriptures. ***This approach to Scripture is completely wrong.*** God's blessing is upon the Jews, but not *just* the Jews. It is upon the other tribes, especially upon Ephraim in the last days.

Several things are significant about this chapter.

- Both Manasseh and Ephraim shall have true claim to the term "Israelite." Many of the other tribes would retain their own identities (such as Dan, Judah, etc.). However, these two tribes would be true Israelites.
- Ephraim, the youngest (and the thirteenth) tribe, would far surpass Manasseh, his brother. Since these two boys also received the birthright blessing which was passed on to Joseph in Chapter 49, they would outshine every other tribe (except for Judah, who was honored with the Scepter blessing).

When these prophecies are considered in their proper perspective, it is no wonder why God has blessed England and the United States of America. They have been great, not because of their own strength, intellect or wisdom, but because of the covenant God made with Abraham, Isaac and Israel. Now, let's look at some of the individual characteristics of these two great lands.

England

Within two years of Christ's ascension, the gospel of Jesus Christ was preached in Britain. Early land records record the establishment of a church by Joseph of Arimithea, and the apostles visited the land. The tribes had scattered here, and God was reclaiming them as His own. Here are some other Scriptures that pertain to Britain and her characteristics.

- Psalms 60:7. God refers to Manasseh as one of His countries. He loves Britain.
- Psalms 80:2. In this passage, it is mentioned that Ephraim, Benjamin and Manasseh have great strength, to win battles and save other peoples.
- The word "British" means "*covenant man.*" It is translated from two Hebrew words, "Brith" (meaning "covenant") and "Ish ("man"). England is truly an Israelite nation.
- England's national coat of arms is bears the *unicorn and the lion.* In Deuteronomy 33:17, the unicorn is attributed to Joseph.
- The *lion* is the symbol of Judah. England is ruled by a dynasty of kings and queens that claim to have descended from king David. They claim to be Judahites. In England, the lion and the unicorn are united. In Jeremiah 33:7, God told the prophet Jeremiah that the lineage of David would rule over the House of Israel, not the House of Judah. This was accomplished within a generation of this prophecy. Today, king David's seed yet rules over Britain.
- In England's Westminster Abbey, there is a special chair, that is used only for coronation ceremonies, whenever a new king or queen is crowned. The following information is provided by the curator of the Abbey. In the base of this chair is a stone. It is called Lia-fail, "the stone of destiny," or "Jacobs pillow stone." It is believed to be the stone which Jacob used as his pillow at Bethel, and the one referred to in Genesis 49:24 as the *stone of Israel.* The stone usually resides in Scotland, guarded by the descendents of the tribe of Levi as in generations past, but it is used to crown the offspring of David as they ascend to the throne.

- Canada is a key offshoot of England. It is a nation that still honors the queen and allies itself with it's parent nation. There is a beautiful garden and an archway that has been built directly on the U.S./Canadian border in Washington State. On the arch are two inscriptions. One says "children of a common mother." The second says "brethren dwelling together in unity." This is literally true.
- England has been a mighty nation that has won countless battles. Coupled with the strength of its brother nation, Ephraim, the might of present day Israel is notable.
- In 1611, the King James Version of the Bible was translated under the commandment of England's King James. It has been the best-selling book in all history, and still competes with modern translations for the #1 book annually purchased and read around the world. The Wesleys held great Methodist revivals in England. John Knox, the great Scotsman, William Booth, the founder of the Salvation Army, Charles Spurgeon and other famous men of God also preached there.
- England's *flag*, known today as the "Union Jack," consists of two crosses. The vertical and horizontal cross is red, representing the cross of Calvary. The second is a white, diagonal cross, representing Israel's cross of blessing (when he crossed his hands to bless Manasseh and Ephraim!).

Are You British?

If you are British or even reside in one of her subject territories, you probably have Israelite blood in your veins. The early tribe of Manasseh was segmented by water. The Jordan River divided the tribal inheritance of Manasseh. Even today, Manasseh's lands are segmented by water.

God has continued to use Britain to be a blessing around the world. Because of persecution, her people even founded the colonies that would become the United States of America. Ephraim, the younger brother, needed to grow, and when the fullness of time was come, grow he did.

The United States of America

When God foresaw the United States of America, He had something different in mind. We will deal with that momentarily. However, let's start by looking at some of the last day characteristics God would implant within Ephraim.

- Psalms 60:7. Ephraim is referred to as the strength of God's head. Ephraim is a superpower!
- Amos 6:1. Zion, Samaria (Ephraim's old capital city) and Israel are mentioned as being one and the same. Because of this, many of the prophecies pertaining to Zion may well refer to the United States. Samaria was also the capital for the 10-tribe House of Israel. Although the tribes were autonomous, they looked to Ephraim for leadership and direction.
- Numbers 13:8. Joshua, one of the key leaders of Israel, was of the tribe of Ephraim. (His best friend was Caleb, from the tribe of Judah.) As long as this tribe sought the Lord, God gave them great wisdom and leadership abilities. In fact, God selected Joshua, an Ephraimite, to lead the conquest of the land of Canaan.
- Joshua 17:7-8. This passage illustrates just how close Ephraim and Manasseh were. They often shared cities, etc.
- The names of Abraham, Isaac and Israel were conferred on Ephraim and Manasseh (Genesis 48:6). They truly have carried on these names in the U.S. and England! In fact, the present term "*Anglo Saxon*" is an evolving term. The original word "Saxon" is believed to have evolved from the term "Isaac's Sons," to "Isaacsons," to "Isacson," to "Sacson," to "Saxon."
- Pastor John Robinson and the Mayflower pilgrims called our nation "*New Israel.*" This was mentioned in the notes of Governor William Bradford as well as Pastor Robinson's own writings.
- The Scripture (Genesis 48:19) indicates that the younger brother will become greater than the elder. The U.S. broke away from England and Europe and has become a *greater nation* although it is *much younger*. (NOTE: Ephraim was the youngest of all of the thirteen tribes.)

- Ephraim was the thirteenth tribe. The number *13* has often been attributed to rebellion. The U.S. Founding Fathers rebelled against tyranny and crossed the seas to start a new nation. Pastor Robinson's message to the Mayflower pilgrims before they departed for the new land was taken from Genesis 12:1-2! In this passage, God told Abram to leave his kindred and go to a new land that was promised by God Himself.
- The first form of government in the U.S. was comprised of *13* colonies. The U.S. standard is *the bald eagle*, king of birds. England's standard is the lion, king of beasts. These two standards were passed down from the original four standards used by the tribes of Israel. These were: the eagle, the lion, the face of a man and the ox (or bullock). The unicorn was also occasionally used.
- *The number thirteen* is impressed into the United States' heritage. A list of significant dates, events and symbols were shared in the previous chapter. You may want to look at them in greater detail.

Why America?

United States citizens are as proud of their nation as any other citizen might be of their land. They sing songs, asking God to bless America, and declaring the words, *"my country 'tis of Thee, sweet land of liberty, of Thee we sing."* These words connect the United States directly to God. But is God connected to this nation?

A Place Of Christian Liberty

To understand this, we must delve into the Scriptures once again.

Exodus 2:23-25 [23]*And it came to pass in process of time, that the king of Egypt died: and the children of Israel sighed by reason of the bondage, and they cried, and their cry came up unto God by reason of the bondage.* [24]*And God heard their groaning, and God remembered his covenant with Abraham, with Isaac, and with Jacob.* [25]*And God looked upon the children of Israel, and God had respect unto them.*

When Israel was in bondage, in Egypt, they were under the tyrannical hand of Pharaoh. Their rights were taken from them, and they were subjected to hard labor. Their children, especially their baby sons, were to be slaughtered and they lived like cattle. But they cried to the Lord and God sent them a deliverer: Moses.

Exodus 8:1 [1]*And the LORD spake unto Moses, Go unto Pharaoh, and say unto him, Thus saith the LORD, Let my people go, that they may serve me.*

Throughout the early chapters of Exodus, Moses echoed God's Words. He repeatedly told Pharaoh that God's people were to be freed, liberated to serve Almighty God! Pharaoh did not submit, and God judged Him. God also liberated His people and took them to the land He had promised to Abraham. This was the first nation established to serve Almighty God and Him alone, but it was not to be the last.

In November, 1620, a group of pilgrims gathered aboard the ship *"The Mayflower,"* and drew up the first governmental document in the new colonies. It was called the Mayflower compact.

THE MAYFLOWER COMPACT

In the name of God, Amen. We whose names are under-written, the loyal subjects of our dread sovereign Lord, King James, by the grace of God, of Great Britain, France, and Ireland King, Defender of the Faith, etc.

Having undertaken, for the glory of God, and advancement of the Christian faith, and honor of our King and Country, a voyage to plant the first colony in the northern parts of Virginia, do by these presents solemnly and mutually, in the presence of God, and one of another, covenant and combine our selves together into a civil body politic, for our better ordering and preservation and furtherance of the ends aforesaid; and by virtue hereof to enact, constitute, and frame such just and equal laws, ordinances, acts, constitutions and offices, from time to time, as shall be thought most meet and convenient for the general good of the Colony, unto which we promise all due submission and obedience. In witness whereof we have hereunder subscribed our names at Cape Cod, the eleventh of November, in the year of the reign of our sovereign lord, King James, of England, France, and Ireland, the eighteenth, and of Scotland the fifty-fourth. Anno Dom. 1620.

The forty-one signatures added to the document formed the first governmental agreement. This agreement founded the United States of America, and plainly stated that it was to be founded for the glory of God, and the advancement of the Christian faith. The Magna Carta had recognized God's rights, and other nations were striving for them. America was different. The colonies were established to be independent from man and dependent upon God.

This spirit of Christian liberty found its way into the Declaration of Independence in 1776 and also into the United States Constitution ratified in 1788. The world was in darkness, but God's Spirit had established a nation with the reunited tribes of Israel. It was unlike Greece, Rome, or even its predecessor nations with the scattered tribes. It was to be one nation, under God, indivisible, with liberty and justice for all.

A Gathering Place For Israel

God also had another reason for establishing the United States of America. The ancient prophecies had foretold a gathering of the House of Israel. They had been scattered for centuries. One could move to Germany, but never be German. You could live in Britain and not be British. Now it was time for the tribes to gather.

Psalm 33:12 [12] *Blessed is the nation whose God is the LORD; and the people whom he hath chosen for his own inheritance.*

God had chosen a people for His own inheritance. They were the tribes of Israel. It was the people of these tribes that came to the colonies, and later to the United States of America. Even though there would be many heathen (and some brought to the new land as slaves), the vast majority of those that heard the call in their spirit to come to this land, came from the House of Israel. Germany, Scandinavia, Spain, the British Isles, France. They came in search of freedom under Jesus Christ.

Hosea 1:10 [10] *Yet the number of the children of Israel shall be as the sand of the sea, which cannot be measured nor numbered; and it shall come to pass, that in the place where it was said unto them, Ye are not my people, there it shall be said unto them, Ye are the sons of the living God.*

God had foretold a future nation. This nation would be gathered from the House of Israel, but would not be known as God's people (e.g., Israelites). But this large, growing nation would be known as the sons of the living God. They would be known as a Christian nation in the last days. There is only one nation on earth that can fulfill this prophecy. The United States of America!

Amos 6:1 [1]*Woe to them that are at ease in Zion, and trust in the mountain of Samaria, which are named chief of the nations, to whom the house of Israel came!*

This nation would be established by Ephraim. Keep in mind the fact that Samaria was Ephraim's capital city, and it led the rest of the 10 tribes. The House of Israel would come to this nation, established by Ephraim in the last days. It would also be known as Zion, the blessed of God.

Ezekiel 37:15-17 [15]*The word of the LORD came again unto me, saying,* [16]*Moreover, thou son of man, take thee one stick, and write upon it, For Judah, and for the children of Israel his companions: then take another stick, and write upon it, For Joseph, the stick of Ephraim, and for all the house of Israel his companions:* [17]*And join them one to another into one stick; and they shall become one in thine hand.*

Did you notice the magnificent truth shared in this passage? God has a "stick," a rod of authority given to the tribe of Judah. He loves Judah and has a land for them. This was provided in 1948, when the Jewish State of Israel came into being. However, God also has another "stick," another rod of authority. It is for Ephraim and for all of Israel that is his companions. Who is this? This is the House of Israel, found today in the United States of America! Today, the United States is in God's hand!

Let me reiterate this fact. Not all of Israel gathered in the U.S.A., but the United States is the gathering place for the House of Israel. Israel prophesied that Ephraim's seed would be a multitude of nations (Genesis 48:19). America is a melting pot, gathered from many nations. God always keeps His Word.

How Did America Get Her Name?

Another interesting clue is found in the history of how America received its name. The most popular lie taught in public school, is the one about America being named after the Italian explorer, Amerigo Vespucci. Others attribute the name America to a version of the name of Richard Ameryke. He was the supporter and financier of the explorer, John Cabot. However, both of these thoughts are untrue.

The earliest map with the word "America" named on it was created by a German geographer and cartographer named Martin Waldsemuller.

There are very few Waldsemuller maps in existence today, they are extremely valuable, and reside in museums.

Waldsemuller's work was studied by Louis Miskovsky, professor of Slavic languages and linguistic history at Oberlin College, in Oberlin, Ohio. A fluent linguist with knowledge of 17 languages, Miskovsky discovered Waldsemuller's own writings on the subject. America was not named after Ameryke or Vespucci. So where did the name originate?

The North-men, or Norsemen were among the first known to have explored ancient America. Their word for the country was, "Ommerike." "Omme" meant "out there, ultimate," or "final." The term "rike" was spelled many different ways, but it was the equivalent to the German word, "reich." It meant "kingdom."

Using his knowledge of linguistics, Professor Miskovsky was able to correlate this term to an ancient Gothic phrase. It was the term "Amalric." It was the same as the German term "Himmel reich" in meaning. What did this mean? "Amal" meant "heaven," and "reich" meant "kingdom." The kingdom of heaven. America! This was what Martin Waldsemuller called this nation when he made his first maps of this new land. It was the ultimate kingdom for the tribes of Israel in the last days.

Are You An American?

If you have come into the United States of America today, you have been grafted into the House of Israel. For many of us, we have a literal Israelite heritage. Other nations, tribes and tongues have also been grafted into this nation. God accepted the heathen such as Tamar, Ruth, Rahab and others throughout the centuries. The House of Israel is standing tall in the world today as a melting pot of nations.

As we see by this in-depth analysis, the facts present a challenging truth: <u>the United States of America is the Israel of Bible prophecy</u>! The last evidence, coupled with the prophecies bestowed upon Joseph, Ephraim's father, point conclusively to the establishment of a mighty latter day nation that would be instrumental in the fulfillment of Bible prophecy. This is none other than the U.S.A.

Let's be clear once again. Our national heritage will never be good enough to cause us to attain heaven. We must all come by way of the Cross, through the shed blood of Jesus Christ. However, when it comes to the dividing of the Word of God, with regard to Bible prophecy, these issues have a huge impact on how Scripture is both taught and understood.

Consider with me, if you will, what would happen if we thought that the "Israel" that is mentioned prophetically in some of the prophets (Jeremiah, Ezekiel, Joel, Amos, Hosea, etc.) was the United States of America, instead of the present nation where Judah resides. What would we believe?

These are questions that must be answered! Are there more clues? Did God give us even more information, so that we might know how His Eternal Word is to play out in the end of days? Yes! Some of His clues are written in the stones. It's time to discover them as we move on.

CHAPTER 8

The Stone And The Scepter

God likes rocks. He speaks through them in the Bible. Abraham built an altar of stones before God on Moriah. Moses built a stone altar in the wilderness and Elijah the prophet built another one atop Mount Carmel when he confronted the prophets of baal. As Israel passed through the Jordan River on dry ground God told Joshua to take 12 stones from the center of the riverbed, and build a lasting memorial where they camped that night. The stones were to speak to the generations to come.

Jesus was once criticized by the Pharisees as the people praised Jesus Christ as the Messiah. The religious rulers wanted the people to be silenced. They hated the fact that Jesus was receiving praise as God from the crowds. Jesus responded with a curious statement, telling them that the very stones would cry out if His people were silent. It was no mistake when the Apostle Paul referred to stones as he taught the New Testament church in Corinth. In fact, he referred to one stone in particular. It was a stone whose story meandered throughout much of the Old Testament. It played a significant role in the Houses of Israel and Judah and is still important as a significant witness, even today. We pick up the trail of this stone in 1 Corinthians 10.

1 Corinthians 10:1-4 *1Moreover, brethren, I would not that ye should be ignorant, how that all our fathers were under the cloud, and all passed through the sea; 2And were all baptized unto Moses in the cloud and in the sea; 3And did all eat the same spiritual meat; 4And did all drink the same spiritual drink: for they drank of that spiritual Rock that followed them: and that Rock was Christ.*

The Apostle was telling the early church about something they must understand. They were not to be ignorant (literally "agnostics") about this issue in Israel's history. The Tribes of Israel had travelled through the wilderness as they departed from Egypt, moving into the promised, covenant land. While they were traveling, they had three distinct experiences Paul mentioned. They traveled under the cloud, they were baptized in the sea, and they drank of a rock!

Let's look a little deeper at what this represents.

The cloud. The Israelites were led by the cloud. They only moved when it moved, and when it stayed in a certain place, they stayed there too. The cloud gave them light at night. It was their "night light" in the wilderness. It protected them from the heat during the day (Exodus 13:21-22). The cloud stood between the Israelites and their Egyptian enemies at the Red Sea (Exodus 14:19-20). The Israelites were "baptized" in the cloud according to 1 Corinthians. It typified the Holy Spirit.

The sea. The Israelites were baptized unto Moses in the Red Sea. The cloud covered them and the water was on every side. They were immersed. Moses was a physical representation of Almighty God, the lawgiver and judge of Israel. The crossing of the Red Sea permanently separated Israel from Egypt's bondage and began their new life under God. After the Red Sea came the giving of the Law in the Wilderness. This event represented Israel's commitment to Almighty God.

The rock. 1 Corinthians 10 is already quite clear in stating that the Rock was Jesus Christ. If this is the case, then Paul was illustrating the fact that the great strength of the Tribes of Israel was in their covenant with Almighty God. They would succeed when they embraced the values, morals and government under Almighty God, embraced Jesus Christ as their national faith, and followed the Holy Spirit in their lives. The covenant God made with Israel in Exodus 20 was unchanging and eternal. It was to be embraced by every generation following Moses. This principle is still the same today.

A Traveling Rock?

There is a curious statement made by Paul about the rock in 1 Corinthians 10:4. He said the rock followed them! What does this mean? Did Israel have an idol that they carried, or was there something significant about a certain stone? Let's find out. To do this, we return once again to the book of beginnings, the book of Genesis.

Genesis 28:10-22 [10]*And Jacob went out from Beersheba, and went toward Haran.* [11]*And he lighted upon a certain place, and tarried there all night, because the sun was set; and he took of the stones of that place, and put them for his pillows, and lay down in that place to sleep.* [12]*And he dreamed, and behold a ladder set up on the earth, and the top of it reached to heaven: and behold the angels of God ascending and descending on it.* [13]*And, behold, the LORD stood above it, and said, I am the LORD God of Abraham thy father, and the God of Isaac: the land whereon thou liest, to thee will I give it, and to thy seed;* [14]*And thy seed shall be as the dust of the earth, and thou shalt spread abroad to the west, and to the east, and to the north, and to the south: and in thee and in thy seed shall all the families of the earth be blessed.* [15]*And, behold, I am with thee, and will keep thee in all places whither thou goest, and will bring thee again into this land; for I will not leave thee, until I have done that which I have spoken to thee of.* [16]*And Jacob awaked out of his sleep, and he said, Surely the LORD is in this place; and I knew it not.* [17]*And he was afraid, and said, How dreadful is this place! this is none other but the house of God, and this is the gate of heaven.* [18]*And Jacob rose up early in the morning, and took the stone that he had put for his pillows, and set it up for a pillar, and poured oil upon the top of it.* [19]*And he called the name of that place Bethel: but the name of that city was called Luz at the first.* [20]*And Jacob vowed a vow, saying, If God will be with me, and will keep me in this way that I go, and will give me bread to eat, and raiment to put on,* [21]*So that I come again to my father's house in peace; then shall the LORD be my God:* [22]*And this stone, which I have set for a pillar, shall be God's house: and of all that thou shalt give me I will surely give the tenth unto thee.*

We discussed this time in Jacob's life in an early chapter, but now we will look at it with fresh eyes. This time we are looking for a rock, God's rock, that He will use as a marker of His covenant with Israel.

Jacob has left his family after being blessed by his father Isaac, and is heading for his in-laws home in Haran. Along the way, he lay down for the night, and built up an elevated "bed" for himself. He took one of the stones and used it for a pillow, or bolster, over which he could lay his coat. As he fell asleep, he began to dream.

The Covenant In A Dream

The dream has become known as "Jacob's Ladder." Jacob saw God standing at the top of the ladder, in Heaven, and the angels ascended up and down, from heaven to earth. God reiterated His covenant with Abraham and Isaac in the words that followed.

- I am the Lord, God of Abraham your father, and the God of Isaac.
- The land where you are sleeping will be given to you and your seed.
- Your seed shall be as the dust of the earth.
- You shall spread abroad, north, south, east and west.
- In you and in your seed all the families of the earth shall be blessed!

The promise to Jacob was unconditional, and magnificent! However, it was also awesome. Jacob awoke shaking and moved with fear. He took his pillow stone and set it up as a memorial pillar. He anointed it with oil and called the name of the place "Beth-El," which means, house of God. He then vowed his life to God and asked for God's blessing. If God would keep him, he would return to this land, and he would also call this stone the house of God.

The God Of The Stone

Many years pass, and Jacob's life is blessed. He marries and bears many sons. His herds are blessed, he lives with the woman of his dreams, and the early stages of God's promises given in the dream have been fulfilled. Now it is time for God to speak once again.

Genesis 31:13 *I am the God of Bethel, where thou anointedst the pillar, and where thou vowedst a vow unto me: now arise, get thee out from this land, and return unto the land of thy kindred.*

Did you catch it? God identified Himself to Jacob as the God of Beth-El; the God of the stone! Jacob undoubtedly recognized the voice of God, and remembered the covenant. He returned to the land, facing his own failures and sins along the way. Eventually he reconciled with his brother and lived at peace in the land of the covenant. As a nomadic shepherd, Jacob and his family would move occasionally in search of pasture. Beth-El, the stone, was his center point at this time, but he didn't remain there. However, to God it was more significant than that.

Genesis 35:1-4 [1]*And God said unto Jacob, Arise, go up to Bethel, and dwell there: and make there an altar unto God, that appeared unto thee when thou fleddest from the face of Esau thy brother.* [2]*Then Jacob said unto his household, and to all that were with him, Put away the strange gods that are among you, and be clean, and change your garments:* [3]*And let us arise, and go up to Bethel; and I will make there an altar unto God, who answered me in the day of my distress, and was with me in the way which I went.* [4]*And they gave unto Jacob all the strange gods which were in their hand, and all their earrings which were in their ears; and Jacob hid them under the oak which was by Shechem.*

When God wanted to make a significant statement to Jacob, He would take him back to the stone. This time was no different. Jacob was stirred. He commanded his family to give him all of their teraphim, their household idols. They also had to release all of their earrings. These were signs of slavery and attachment to other cultures and religions. They also had to change into fresh, clean garments. They were going to the House of God.

After arriving, Jacob built an altar (verse 7), and called it "El-Bethel," which means "The God of Bethel." His entire life was now devoted to Almighty God.

Genesis 35:9-15 [9]*And God appeared unto Jacob again, when he came out of Padanaram, and blessed him.* [10]*And God said unto him, Thy name is Jacob: thy name shall not be called any more Jacob, but Israel shall be thy name: and he called his name Israel.* [11]*And God said unto him, I am God Almighty: be fruitful and multiply; a nation and a company of nations shall be of thee, and kings shall come out of thy loins;* [12]*And the land which I gave Abraham and Isaac, to thee I will give it, and to thy seed after thee will I give the land.* [13]*And God went up from him in the place where he talked with him.* [14]*And Jacob set up a pillar in the place where he talked with him, even a pillar of stone: and he poured a drink offering thereon, and he poured oil thereon.* [15]*And Jacob called the name of the place where God spake with him, Bethel.*

God then gave Jacob a promise that would eclipse his generations. But first, God changed Jacob's name.

- Your name is Jacob! This means supplanter, con-artist, heel-catcher. It tells the world you are to be distrusted, avoided, and feared.

- Your name is now Israel. You are a prince with God! You will be respected and accepted as royalty in my sight, and in future generations, in the sight of the world.

But God doesn't stop there!

- He commands Israel to be fruitful and multiply. The spirit of Israel, the covenant people, will be a large multitude.
- A nation (a singular, solitary nation)
- And a company of nations (specifically an assemblage of nations) will arise out of Israel.
- Kings shall come out of Israel's loins!
- Furthermore, the land God has given to Abraham and Isaac is now promised to Israel forever.

This is such a significant promise given to Israel that he is stirred. He must do something to let God know that He will commit his life to this covenant relationship.

- In verse 14, Israel takes a stone from that place and sets it up as a pillar, a covenant marker.
- He anoints the stone with the most precious commodity in a desert land, water.
- He also anoints this pillar stone with oil, denoting its status as a sacred object before Almighty God.
- This object is a testimony, a witness between God and Israel, of the covenant promise God has made to Israel.
- Jacob's pillow stone has now become the pillar of the covenant.

Water In The Desert

Exodus 17:1-7 [1]*And all the congregation of the children of Israel journeyed from the wilderness of Sin, after their journeys, according to the commandment of the LORD, and pitched in Rephidim: and there was no water for the people to drink.* [2]*Wherefore the people did chide with Moses, and said, Give us water that we may drink. And Moses said unto them,*

Why chide ye with me? wherefore do ye tempt the LORD? [3]And the people thirsted there for water; and the people murmured against Moses, and said, Wherefore is this that thou hast brought us up out of Egypt, to kill us and our children and our cattle with thirst? [4]And Moses cried unto the LORD, saying, What shall I do unto this people? they be almost ready to stone me. [5]And the LORD said unto Moses, Go on before the people, and take with thee of the elders of Israel; and thy rod, wherewith thou smotest the river, take in thine hand, and go. [6]Behold, I will stand before thee there upon the rock in Horeb; and thou shalt smite the rock, and there shall come water out of it, that the people may drink. And Moses did so in the sight of the elders of Israel. [7]And he called the name of the place Massah, and Meribah, because of the chiding of the children of Israel, and because they tempted the LORD, saying, Is the LORD among us, or not?

No mention of the covenant pillar is made for several generations. Then, they are expelled from Egypt and Moses leads them out into the Wilderness at God's direction. As they pitch camp in Rephidim, they encounter a problem. They have no water.

As Moses cried out to the Lord, God gave Moses a strange command. Moses is to smite "the rock" with his rod, and water will come out so that the multitude of approximately 3 million people may drink! Moses does this, and water gushes out! God has preserved His people once again!

The word for rock in Exodus 17 can be translated as a "cliff" or a "boulder." But in Deuteronomy 8:15, Moses referred back to the same event with a different phrase.

Deuteronomy 8:15 *Who led thee through that great and terrible wilderness, wherein were fiery serpents, and scorpions, and drought, where there was no water; who brought thee forth water out of the rock of flint;*

Moses said that God brought forth water out of "the rock of flint." The word "flint" speaks of hardness, a very hard stone. But it also means something else. It is taken from the Hebrew word, *chalam*, which means to be plump, or to dream. In other words, Moses was reminding the tribes of Israel about the time when God brought forth water out of the stone of dreams! Jacob's dream!

Could it be, that this stone that produced the miracle of water was Jacob's pillow stone, the stone of the covenant? If so, there must be another confirmation.

The Second Miracle

Later in Israel's journeys through the wilderness, the tribes were faced yet again with the prospect of no water. True to form, they began to complain once again against Moses, Aaron and God. God told Moses to obtain water from the rock once again, but this time he was supposed to speak to it. But Moses disobeyed God.

Numbers 20:1-11 *1Then came the children of Israel, even the whole congregation, into the desert of Zin in the first month: and the people abode in Kadesh; and Miriam died there, and was buried there. 2And there was no water for the congregation: and they gathered themselves together against Moses and against Aaron. 3And the people chode with Moses, and spake, saying, Would God that we had died when our brethren died before the LORD! 4And why have ye brought up the congregation of the LORD into this wilderness, that we and our cattle should die there? 5And wherefore have ye made us to come up out of Egypt, to bring us in unto this evil place? it is no place of seed, or of figs, or of vines, or of pomegranates; neither is there any water to drink. 6And Moses and Aaron went from the presence of the assembly unto the door of the tabernacle of the congregation, and they fell upon their faces: and the glory of the LORD appeared unto them. 7And the LORD spake unto Moses, saying, 8Take the rod, and gather thou the assembly together, thou, and Aaron thy brother, and speak ye unto the rock before their eyes; and it shall give forth his water, and thou shalt bring forth to them water out of the rock: so thou shalt give the congregation and their beasts drink. 9And Moses took the rod from before the LORD, as he commanded him. 10And Moses and Aaron gathered the congregation together before the rock, and he said unto them, Hear now, ye rebels; must we fetch you water out of this rock? 11And Moses lifted up his hand, and with his rod he smote the rock twice: and the water came out abundantly, and the congregation drank, and their beasts also.*

Moses struck the rock with his rod, as he had done before in Rephidim. The water poured out and the people drank freely. God was not happy with Moses because of his behavior that day. He had something further to say.

Numbers 20:12-13 [12]*And the LORD spake unto Moses and Aaron, Because ye believed me not, to sanctify me in the eyes of the children of Israel, therefore ye shall not bring this congregation into the land which I* *have given them. [13]This is the water of Meribah; because the children of Israel strove with the LORD, and he was sanctified in them.*

Numbers 27:14, Deuteronomy 1:37 and Deuteronomy 4:21 tell us also that the Lord was angry with Moses over this action. He disobeyed God and struck the rock instead of speaking to it. Now Joshua would lead Israel into the Promised Land, not Moses. Why was God so angry about Moses striking a rock?

Clues To The Rock

- According to 1 Corinthians 10:4, there was a rock that was to be a type of Christ. Christ was only smitten one time. Moses struck this rock twice, and made it an imperfect type. God was displeased.
- 1 Corinthians 10:4 also says that the rock in the wilderness followed them. In other words, God provided water out of the same rock in Kadesh as He had done so in Rephidim. This rock could be moved.
- Moses called the water that poured forth the *waters of Meribah* in both locations. What was their common trait? The Israelites complained in both locations, and God poured forth water out of the same rock!
- In Deuteronomy 8:15, Moses called the rock the "flinty rock," or the "rock of dreams." This rock that followed them was the stone of the covenant, Jacob's pillow stone!

Jesus Christ, The Solid Rock

Throughout Scripture, the rock is mentioned many times as a type, a physical representation, of the Messiah, Jesus Christ.

- Deuteronomy 32:18, 30-31. This passage speaks of a "rock" forming mankind. There is no other rock except God Himself which could have formed us from the dust of the earth!
- Daniel 2:34, 44. This passage speaks of the everlasting Kingdom as a "stone, not made with hands." This will be none other than Jesus' eternal Kingdom which shall be set up at the end of God's redemptive week.

- Psalms 118:22-23. This passage speaks of the stone which the builders rejected becoming the head stone of the corner. This is none other than Jesus! In fact, he identified Himself with this Scripture in Matthew 21: 42-44, Mark 12:10, and Luke 20:17-18.
- Isaiah 28:16. God speaks here of a tried and precious corner stone which he lays for a foundation.
- Ephesians 2:19-21. Here, Jesus is mentioned as being the "chief corner stone" of the church.
- I Peter 2:5-8. Peter tells us in this passage that the church is "lively stones," built on the foundation of Jesus the cornerstone. He further states that Jesus is a rock of stumbling and offense to those who do not understand, but He is a precious stone to those who believe (just as the literal rock brought skepticism from outsiders, but provided water to the believers).

The rock that followed them, the pillar of the covenant, was supposed to be a perfect representation of Jesus Christ as Messiah. This is why God was so displeased with Moses when he struck the stone the second time.

Now Jesus has come, and we can see more clearly the types and shadows God intended for us to see. They become all the more clear as we follow the pathway of the literal stone after the time in the Wilderness.

Where Did The Rock Go From There?

After the tribes of Israel came into the land of the covenant, Joshua gathered them together one last time. He called the tribes to Shechem; there the sons of Levi had set up the Tabernacle. It was a holy place and a holy day. There, Joshua gave his farewell address, reminding the Tribes of Israel of God's faithfulness to them as they defeated their enemies and possessed the land God had promised. He called them to serve the Lord, and they agreed to follow Almighty God alone. Joshua wrote the covenant in the book of the Law of God. But Joshua needed a solemn witness to this act. What would he choose?

Joshua 24:25-27 [25]*So Joshua made a covenant with the people that day, and set them a statute and an ordinance in Shechem.* [26]*And Joshua* *wrote these words in the book of the law of God, and took a great stone, and set it up there under an oak, that was by the sanctuary of the LORD.* [27]*And Joshua said unto all the people, Behold, this stone shall be a witness unto us; for it hath heard all the words of the LORD which he spake unto us: it shall be therefore a witness unto you, lest ye deny your God.*

Joshua chose a stone. It was a great, or a significant, old stone (as the original language says). He set this stone up next to God's holy sanctuary, the Tabernacle, in a public site. He told the people that this stone was a witness to God's Word, and to the words of the Tribes. It was the stone of the covenant.

The Stone Of Judges And Kings

From this point, little is said about the covenant stone, but it played a significant role when it was used. In fact, we know it was used as a witness stone in the coronation of at least one of Israel's judges.

Judges 9:6 [6]*And all the men of Shechem gathered together, and all the house of Millo, and went, and made Abimelech king, by the plain of the pillar that was in Shechem.*

When Abimelech was made judge (or crowned king as some versions say), it was done in Shechem.

What was in Shechem? The Tabernacle.

What was beside the Tabernacle? An old oak tree. (The word "plain" is mistranslated, and is literally "oak or other strong tree" in the original Hebrew.)

What was under the oak tree, beside the Tabernacle? The covenant pillar stone!

Apparently this became a regular event. The stone was used by the kings at least twice in later years for coronation events or covenants.

2 Kings 11:12-14 and 2 Chronicles 23:11-13 tell of a much later coronation, the crowning of King Joash. Joash had been rescued from slaughter as an infant, and at the age of 7 was revealed as the royal child. Jehoiada, the High Priest, and his sons oversaw the crowning event on the porch of Solomon's Temple.

2 Kings 11:12-14 [12]*And he brought forth the king's son, and put the crown upon him, and gave him the testimony; and they made him king, and anointed him; and they clapped their hands, and said, God save the king.* [13]*And when Athaliah heard the noise of the guard and of the* *people, she came to the people into the temple of the LORD.* [14]*And when she looked, behold, the king stood by a pillar, as the manner was, and the princes and the trumpeters by the king, and all the people of the land rejoiced, and blew with trumpets: and Athaliah rent her clothes, and cried, Treason, Treason.*

2 Chronicles 23:11-13 [11]*Then they brought out the king's son, and put upon him the crown, and gave him the testimony, and made him king. And Jehoiada and his sons anointed him, and said, God save the king.* [12]*Now when Athaliah heard the noise of the people running and praising the king, she came to the people into the house of the LORD:* [13]*And she looked, and, behold, the king stood at his pillar at the entering in, and the princes and the trumpets by the king: and all the people of the land rejoiced, and sounded with trumpets, also the singers with instruments of music, and such as taught to sing praise. Then Athaliah rent her clothes, and said, Treason, Treason.*

Did you notice the statement in 2 Chronicles? It said that the newly-crowned king was standing by his pillar! This was not one of the great, bronze pillars erected in front of Solomon's temple. It was the pillar of the kings, where those who were crowned would stand and pay their vows to God. The covenant pillar witnessed the event. He was the king of God's covenant people.

This is further validated by information from the *Jewish Virtual Library*. The following material is taken directly from them. *"The tribes of Israel were noted for their lack of decorative, ornate pillars in their culture. Pillars were functional, monolithic items that were used to support ceilings, emphasize ornate doors, or take the place of doorposts. However, there is an exception to this rule. The pillar mentioned in 2 Kings 11:14 is specifically a stand-alone pillar. It is not connected with any other structure. It is designed to attract attention and to serve as a place around which a crowd could gather."*

Later, King Josiah stood beside the pillar, and renewed the covenant before the Lord, along with the House of Judah.

2 Kings 23:3 [3]*And the king stood by a pillar, and made a covenant before the LORD, to walk after the LORD, and to keep his commandments and his testimonies and his statutes with all their heart and all their soul, to perform the words of this covenant that were written in this book. And all the people stood to the covenant.*

This was the pattern of the kings. The covenant pillar had become the pillar of the kings.

- When the kings were crowned, the people would cry out, "God save the king!"
- The king would use the pillar as a witness to their vows before Almighty God. They would acknowledge that they ruled only because of God's covenant and blessings upon their lineage.
- The people would rejoice before the pillar, knowing that the Priests and Levites had guarded it from the earliest days of the Tabernacle. It was the Priests that would crown the kings before the pillar.

But after King Josiah's reign, no mention of Jacob's pillar is made again in the Bible. Where did it go? What became of it? For answers, we begin by looking at a couple of seemingly unrelated passages of Scripture.

The House Of Judah Is About To Fall

The year was 590 B.C., and the House of Judah was under siege. The 10-tribe kingdom of the House of Israel had long been scattered for their wickedness, and now it was time for the 2-tribe kingdom of the House of Judah to be judged. The prophets had warned them repeatedly, but to no avail. The kings and the people had chosen the progressive path, worshipping idols and behaving like the nations around them. Almighty God was supposed to be their only Head, but he was honored only symbolically.

The Kingdom of Babylon was headed toward Jerusalem, to destroy it. King Zedekiah sat upon the throne, rebellious, defiant, and foolish. God had sent a prophet to Zedekiah, one of the highest caliber. He was Jeremiah. Jeremiah was related to the high priests, and also had connections to the kings of Judah. Nobody would listen to the words of the Lord that he spoke. His friend and servant, Baruch, had delivered messages directly to the king, only to see them cut into pieces before his face, and then burned.

Finally, Jeremiah was put in prison. The king had heard enough of his old fashioned pleading. Jeremiah sat in the dungeon, alone. It was there that God spoke to him yet again.

Jeremiah's Prophecy

Jeremiah 33:1-3 [1]*Moreover the word of the LORD came unto Jeremiah the second time, while he was yet shut up in the court of the prison, saying,* [2]*Thus saith the LORD the maker thereof, the LORD that formed it, to establish it; the LORD is his name;* [3]*Call unto me, and I will answer thee, and show thee great and mighty things, which thou knowest not.*

God wasn't limited by Jeremiah's current situation, or by his location. Jeremiah had been faithful to God and God still had an assignment for Jeremiah to complete. God would speak to Jeremiah in that dungeon and give him a magnificent revelation that few recognize, even today.

Jeremiah 33:14-17 [14]*Behold, the days come, saith the LORD, that I will perform that good thing which I have promised unto the house of Israel and to the house of Judah.* [15]*In those days, and at that time, will I cause the Branch of righteousness to grow up unto David; and he shall execute judgment and righteousness in the land.* [16]*In those days shall Judah be saved, and Jerusalem shall dwell safely: and this is the name wherewith she shall be called, The LORD our righteousness.* [17]*For thus saith the LORD; David shall never want a man to sit upon the throne of the house of Israel.*

In the middle of judgment and destruction, God gave Jeremiah a message of hope for Israel. It was a huge promise, and it included the House of Judah and the House of Israel in its scope. The House of Israel had been scattered by Assyria but God still had His hand on their lives. The House of Judah was about to be taken captive by Babylon. What would happen next?

- At some future time, God would perform the good thing He promised to both the House of Israel and the House of Judah.
- The Branch of righteousness would grow up and execute judgment and righteousness in the land.
- Judah would be saved and Jerusalem would dwell safely. It would be known as the righteous city of God.
- Finally, David's seed would continue to rule. They would sit upon the throne of the House of Israel.

Four Promises

At first glance, these four promises may not seem like much, but they are huge!

- **First**, God would continue to watch over both the House of Judah and the House of Israel! The House of Judah would return to the land, but God would oversee the future of the House of Israel in the land to which He was leading them.
- **Second**, the Branch of righteousness would come. This is a term used for the Messiah. Jeremiah received this promise that Jesus Christ would truly come. He excuted judgment and righteousness and He did so in the land of the covenant to Abraham, Isaac and Israel, just as God had foretold!
- **Third**, ultimately Judah would be saved. This was God's promise. Although the House of Judah has forsaken Jesus Christ, they will ultimately be redeemed. Jerusalem shall dwell safely because God has ordained it to be so.
- **Fourth**, the seed of king David would continue to rule! How could this be? War with Babylon was looming. King Zedekiah was the seed royal, and he would likely be taken captive or killed, as would his sons. How could this be?

When God makes a promise, He keeps His Word. We have witnessed His fulfillment of the first two promises. What about the others?

The House Of Judah Falls To Babylon

Jeremiah 39:1-9 [1]*In the ninth year of Zedekiah king of Judah, in the tenth month, came Nebuchadrezzar king of Babylon and all his army against Jerusalem, and they besieged it.* [2]*And in the eleventh year of Zedekiah, in the fourth month, the ninth day of the month, the city was broken up.* [3]*And all the princes of the king of Babylon came in, and sat in the middle gate, even Nergalsharezer, Samgarnebo, Sarsechim, Rabsaris, Nergalsharezer, Rabmag, with all the residue of the princes of the king of Babylon.* [4]*And it came to pass, that when Zedekiah the king of Judah saw them, and all the men of war, then they fled, and went forth out of the city* *by night, by the way of the king's garden, by the gate betwixt the two walls: and he went out the way of the plain.* [5]*But the Chaldeans' army pursued after them, and overtook Zedekiah in the plains of Jericho: and when they had taken him, they brought him up to Nebuchadnezzar king of Babylon to Riblah in the land of Hamath, where he gave judgment upon him.* [6]*Then the king of Babylon slew the sons of Zedekiah in Riblah before his eyes: also the king of Babylon slew all the nobles of Judah.* [7]*Moreover he put out Zedekiah's eyes, and bound him with chains, to carry him to Babylon.* [8]*And the Chaldeans burned the king's house, and the houses of the people, with fire, and brake down the walls of Jerusalem.* [9]*Then Nebuzaradan the captain of the guard carried away captive into Babylon the remnant of the people that remained in the city, and those that fell away, that fell to him, with the rest of the people that remained.* [10]*But Nebuzaradan the captain of the guard left of the poor of the people, which had nothing, in the land of Judah, and gave them vineyards and fields at the same time.* [11]*Now Nebuchadrezzar king of Babylon gave charge concerning Jeremiah to Nebuzaradan the captain of the guard, saying,* [12]*Take him, and look well to him, and do him no harm; but do unto him even as he shall say unto thee.*

Before God could fulfill His promise of blessing to the House of Judah, He had to judge them for their sins. Jeremiah had counseled King Zedekiah to surrender to Babylon, but as usual, he wouldn't listen to wise counsel in the voice of God's prophet. Instead, he fled in the dark of night taking his sons and a group of Jewish nobles.

The Babylonian army hunted Zedekiah down, finding him in the plain of Jericho. This was the region between Jericho and the Jordan river. They returned with him to King Nebuchadrezzar of Babylon. There, Zedekiah suffered a fate worse than death. He watched as his sons were killed before his very eyes. Then Nebuchadrezzar put out King Zedekiah's eyes, and took him as a hostage, in chains, to parade about his capitol city.

The Babylonians burned Jerusalem, taking all valuables from the Temple and the King's house, before completely destroying them both. They also took slaves from among the Jewish people, leaving all of the poor and needy to fend for themselves. However, they showed favor to one man in particular. His name was Jeremiah, the prophet. They had heard of his counsel and rewarded him with his life. He remained in Jerusalem when others were killed or carried away. Apparently though,

God's prophecy to Jeremiah had failed. After all, Zedekiah was the royal seed, and his sons had been killed. There was no one left to carry on the family lineage . . . or was there?

The Refugee Party

Needless to say, Jerusalem was no longer a good place to live. The palace and temple were burned, the walls were torn down and the gates were gone. It was a city of vagrants, thieves and destitute people. In the middle of this scenario a group of Jews decided to leave Jerusalem and venture out on their own.

Jeremiah 43:5-7 *[5]But Johanan the son of Kareah, and all the captains of the forces, took all the remnant of Judah, that were returned from all nations, whither they had been driven, to dwell in the land of Judah; [6]Even men, and women, and children, and the king's daughters, and every person that Nebuzaradan the captain of the guard had left with Gedaliah the son of Ahikam the son of Shaphan, and Jeremiah the prophet, and Baruch the son of Neriah. [7]So they came into the land of Egypt: for they obeyed not the voice of the LORD: thus came they even to Tahpanhes.*

The leader of this group forced some of the remnant to accompany them. The refugee party included a few notable names. Among them were:

- Jeremiah, the prophet
- Baruch, his faithful scribe and the king's daughters!

King's daughters? Yes! Apparently King Zedekiah had young daughters that had not been taken as slaves, nor killed with their brothers. Jeremiah was their custodian, and these young women were now on the road traveling with a group of Jews. Where did they go?

They went to Tahpanhes. This outpost was situated in Egypt, on the Titanic branch of the Nile River. Today, it sits next to the Suez Canal. It was rediscovered in 1886 by Professor William Flinders Petrie, and to this day the locals know this city by the Egyptian description that has endured since the time of Jeremiah. It was called "the castle of the Jew's daughter." (Memoir of the Egypt Exploration Fund, 1888.) Zedekiah's daughters had escaped the carnage of Jerusalem, and were now in Egypt with Jeremiah. But they were not Zedekiah's sons. They were "only" daughters.

This may not seem significant to some today but in Old Testament times this was a critical issue. The kings of the earth propagated their lineage through their sons. Their daughters were given in marriage to form strategic alliances and seal treaties. This was part of the reason why Solomon had so many "wives." He had been given kings' daughters, foreign women, in exchange for treaty relationships with other nations. However, there was one nation on earth that treated women differently. That nation was . . . Israel.

The Daughters of Zelophehad

The story of expanded rights for women among the tribes of Israel began in the days of Moses. Zelophehad, from the tribe of Manasseh, died without having any sons. His five daughters came to petition Moses and requested their share of their father's inheritance.

Numbers 27:1-9 [1]*Then came the daughters of Zelophehad, the son of Hepher, the son of Gilead, the son of Machir, the son of Manasseh, of the families of Manasseh the son of Joseph: and these are the names of his daughters; Mahlah, Noah, and Hoglah, and Milcah, and Tirzah.* [2]*And they stood before Moses, and before Eleazar the priest, and before the princes and all the congregation, by the door of the tabernacle of the congregation, saying,* [3]*Our father died in the wilderness, and he was not in the company of them that gathered themselves together against the LORD in the company of Korah; but died in his own sin, and had no sons.* [4]*Why should the name of our father be done away from among his family, because he hath no son? Give unto us therefore a possession among the brethren of our father.* [5]*And Moses brought their cause before the LORD.* [6]*And the LORD spake unto Moses, saying,* [7]*The daughters of Zelophehad speak right: thou shalt surely give them a possession of an inheritance among their father's brethren; and thou shalt cause the inheritance of their father to pass unto them.* [8]*And thou shalt speak unto the children of Israel, saying, If a man die, and have no son, then ye shall cause his inheritance to pass unto his daughter.* [9]*And if he have no daughter, then ye shall give his inheritance unto his brethren.*

When Moses took the daughter's petition before Almighty God, He responded quickly.

- The daughters were right!
- Since no sons had been born, they were entitled to receive their father's inheritance.
- If there were no sons or daughters living, the inheritance would pass to his brothers.
- But there was a catch!

Numbers 36:6-9 [5]*And Moses commanded the children of Israel according to the word of the LORD, saying, The tribe of the sons of Joseph hath said well.* [6]*This is the thing which the LORD doth command concerning the daughters of Zelophehad, saying, Let them marry to whom they think best; only to the family of the tribe of their father shall they marry.* [7]*So shall not the inheritance of the children of Israel remove from tribe to tribe: for every one of the children of Israel shall keep himself to the inheritance of the tribe of his fathers.* [8]*And every daughter, that possesseth an inheritance in any tribe of the children of Israel, shall be wife unto one of the family of the tribe of her father, that the children of Israel may enjoy every man the inheritance of his fathers.* [9]*Neither shall the inheritance remove from one tribe to another tribe; but every one of the tribes of the children of Israel shall keep himself to his own inheritance.*

In order to be a recipient of the inheritance, the daughters must marry someone as close as possible in family heritage. At the very minimum, they must marry someone within their same tribe. This would continue God's promises and prophetic blessings to each tribe, and it would also keep inheritance and property rights within the family.

Back To Zedekiah's Daughters

Because of God's Word to Moses, hundreds of years before, the daughters of Zedekiah were eligible heirs to the throne of their father. Their brothers had been killed, and were unable to ascend to the throne. Nebuchadrezzar, king of Babylon, did not regard women as viable heirs, because he did not understand the ways of the God of Israel. This ignorance on his part literally saved the lives of Zedekiah's daughters. God had ordained these girls in His plan to carry on King David's royal lineage as He had promised in 2 Samuel 7:16.

2 Samuel 7:16 [16]*And thine house and thy kingdom shall be established for ever before thee: thy throne shall be established for ever.*

God had made the prophet Jeremiah the guardian over the seed royal. When he was called to prophesy by Almighty God, he was told that he *would root out, pull down, destroy, tear down, and also build and plant* (Jeremiah 1:10). He had seen the House of Judah rooted, pulled down, and destroyed. Now it was time to take the kings daughters and build and plant. But how? Where?

Do you recall the divine prophecy that God gave to Jeremiah in Jeremiah 33:17? God promised that David would never want a man to sit upon his throne. This posed a problem. Zedekiah's daughters could never be men! Somehow, these daughters had to be married to men of their own tribe, and especially men of their own bloodline! Where could they be? Nebuchadrezzar had killed every man in the royal lineage in the House of Judah.

Apparently Jeremiah discovered God's direction in verse 17. The Scriptures fall silent at this point, but history picks up the story.

Jeremiah 33:17 [17]*For thus saith the LORD; David shall never want a man to sit upon the throne of the house of Israel.*

Jeremiah was about to take a journey, along with Baruch, his faithful scribe, and also with Zedekiah's daughters. Where would they go? They would go searching for their scattered Israelites. The House of Judah was in Babylonian captivity. They would not search there. Instead, Jeremiah recognized what God was doing. He was transferring the lineage of kings to the House of Israel. Yes, they were scattered, but God knew where they were.

History Tells The Story

According to the writings of noted historians such as Sir Thomas Gray (Scalacronica, 1355 A.D.), a small band of people came ashore in present-day Spain. Early European history notes this band continued their journey by land and sea, arriving in present-day Ireland. Who was in the group?

- There was an old man in the group called Ollam Folla.
- He had a servant and companion called Simon Brug.

- And he had a young woman with him that was a princess. She was called Tamar, or Tea Tephi.

This band also had a few items in their possession.

- They had several scrolls of ancient writings.
- They also had a harp from an ancient king.

And around this same time, Irish lore states another object appeared in the land. It was a stone!

- This stone was called the "fatal-stone," or "Lia-Fail."
- This also means "stone of destiny."
- The Archaeological Journal (September, 1856) called this stone the most ancient, respected monument in the world.
- This stone contained iron rings embedded in the ends, so it could be carried with a rod. According to historic lore, this is Jacob's pillar stone, the stone of the covenant.
- This is said to be the rock that followed Israel through their journeys.
- It is the coronation stone of Israel.

Connecting The Dots

Ollam Folla is actually a Hebrew term. It means "revealer," or "prophet." It is highly likely that Simon Brug was Jeremiah's faithful scribe, Baruch. The harp was known as the harp of David. Today, it is still part of the ancient crest of Ireland (the only nation in the world with a musical instrument on its crest).

What happened to Tea Tephi? Tea Tephi had come to a part of the House of Israel, where the 10 tribes had scattered, but her kinsmen, the House of Judah, resided there also. Do you remember the curious story of the twins born to Tamar in an earlier chapter (Genesis 38)? The twins were sons of Judah, which later became the royal lineage. Pharez had been born first, but Zarah had breached the womb with his hand. The midwife had tied a scarlet cord around his wrist. Something special was reserved for his seed.

When Jeremiah reached the shores of Ireland, he encountered a unique band of people. They were the children of the red hand. Their emblem was (and is to this day) a scarlet cord bound around the wrist, which honored their ancient ancestor. God had led Jeremiah to a family that was a direct descendent of Judah, one that would carry on the lineage and inheritance of the seed of David. Through that marriage came the dynasty that has now reigned over Western Europe for hundreds of years. The royal families of Europe, including Britain, Ireland, Scotland, Spain, Sweden, Norway and many others, descend from this royal union. What qualifies them to be royalty? They are of the house and lineage of King David. This author has verified these statements personally with those associated with the British royal family. His first correspondence was in 1981, when he obtained a copy of the genealogical chart from The Covenant Publishing Company, Ltd. In 2011, he contacted the facebook site of the Queen of England, and received verification from an assistant that the British royal family does indeed believe this information to be true.

The Coronation Stone

The Lia-Fail, the stone of destiny, was used by the kings and queens of Ireland for centuries. Every one was crowned while seated upon that stone, until 850 A.D. Saint Patrick of Ireland blessed the stone, claiming it was God's will that the Kings of Israel be crowned upon it. King Kenneth I took the coronation stone with him back to Scotland, where it resided in a monastery in Scone, Scotland for generations. However, when Edward I of England fought against William Wallace in 1296 A.D., one of the things he took back to England as booty was Lia-Fail. He took the stone!

King Edward commissioned a hand-carved coronation throne to be built to hold the stone in 1301 A.D. The throne is seated upon lions, the symbol of the tribe of Judah and house of David.

The crowning ceremony is administered by the church, just as the coronations were led by the priests in the Old Testament. The king or queen is given the royal crown and the vestments or robes, along with the scepter. This is known as the testimony. When the king is crowned, the people cry out, "God save the king!"

In 1779, Edward Perronet was commissioned to write a hymn and penned a standard still used today. The original title was, "The Coronation Hymn." Below are the original words, in their complete and unedited form.

The Coronation Hymn

Edward Perronet, 1779

All hail the power of Jesus Name! Let angels prostrate fall
Bring forth the royal diadem, and crown Him Lord of all
Bring forth the royal diadem, and crown Him Lord of all.

Ye seed of Israel's chosen race, ye ransomed from the fall
Hail Him, who saves you by His grace, and crown Him Lord of all.
Hail Him, who saves you by His grace, and crown Him Lord of all.

Hail Him, ye heirs of David's line, whom David Lord did call
The Lord incarnate, Man divine, and crown Him Lord of all
The Lord incarnate, Man divine, and crown Him Lord of all.

Sinners, whose love can ne'er forget, the wormwood and the gall
Go, spread your trophies at His feet, and crown Him Lord of all
Go, spread your trophies at His feet, and crown Him Lord of all.

Let every kindred, every tribe, on this terrestrial ball
To Him all majesty ascribe, and crown Him Lord of all
To Him all majesty ascribe, and crown Him Lord of all.

O that with yonder sacred throng we at His feet may fall
We'll join the everlasting song, and crown Him Lord of all
We'll join the everlasting song, and crown Him Lord of all.

Jacob's pillar stone has been a source of contention among the tribes for many years. It remained in the hands of England, closely guarded in the castle of the king, or at Westminster Abbey in London, until 1996. On November 15, 1996, the stone of destiny was returned to Scotland as a gesture of goodwill, with the provision that it be returned and used for the coronation of monarchs as the need arose. Today, it resides in Edinburough Castle, Scotland, on well-guarded display. The future of this incredible stone is in the hands of the Lord.

Why Did God Use A Stone?

Why would the Almighty God, the Lord of Abraham, Isaac and Israel, choose to use a stone as a testimony? Many nations used rocks, trees and other articles as items of worship. Doesn't this seem like idolatry? No.

First, God never attached significance for worship to Jacob's pillar stone. It was a symbol of His literal covenant. Stones do not erode or decay easily over time. This one article could be carried by the tribes, and could be recognized as a testimony to God's eternal goodness. The scattered House of Israel needed a common connecting point during their season of dispersion. It was the stone. In the last days, God is reuniting the House of Israel, to fulfill His eternal Word. The stone speaks of His steadfastness, but there is more that God has to say and do. One of His prophecies is greatly significant. It will shake the entire world. Could this prophecy be soon fulfilled? Yes, it could. There is yet another amazing turn in the road ahead.

CHAPTER 9

The Battle For The Birthright

The year was 587 B.C., and the prophet Ezekiel had a problem. He was with living with some of the Israelite refugees in Babylon, along the Chebar (or Khaber) river, when God gave him a series of visions. Ezekiel had been known for his visions, but these were truly unique. They involved people that were divided and scattered when God gave the vision. The House of Israel had been partially scattered around 740 B.C., when the tribes of Reuben, Gad and part of Manasseh were conquered. They had lived across the Jordan and were more vulnerable to enemy attack. Then in 722 B.C., Assyria had completely scattered the remainder of the 10 tribed Kingdom. The House of Israel would never return to the land of Abraham's promise.

The House of Judah was also taken captive. Babylon had conquered them in 597 B.C., but had grown tired of their rebellious ways. As Ezekiel was living among the tribes, Babylon had struck again. It was only a matter of a few years before the House of Judah would swell the ranks of the captives along the river, as they were forcibly removed from Jerusalem and the surrounding countryside. They would live in Babylonian captivity for 70 years before their children would be allowed to return to restore and rebuild Jerusalem.

Despite their captivity, God had plans for these nations. The House of Judah would return and become the sole possessors of the land. The House of Israel would scatter throughout portions of Europe and Asia before gathering together again, in the last days. This latest vision given to Ezekiel dealt with one of these two nations, as well as with a curious person that would become a force to be reckoned with. The problem was this: a coalition of nations would arise in later years and would unite under a mighty leader. This coalition would attack and nearly destroy either the reassembled House of Israel or Judah. But God's hand was against this mighty coalition. They would be repelled, and his name would forever live in infamy. Who was this hated adversary? His name was . . . Gog.

Ezekiel 38:1-7 [1]*And the word of the LORD came unto me, saying,* [2]*Son of man, set thy face against Gog, the land of Magog, the chief prince of Meshech and Tubal, and prophesy against him,* [3]*And say, Thus saith the Lord GOD; Behold, I am against thee, O Gog, the chief prince of Meshech and Tubal:* [4]*And I will turn thee back, and put hooks into thy jaws, and I will bring thee forth, and all thine army, horses and horsemen, all of them clothed with all sorts of armour, even a great company with bucklers and shields, all of them handling swords:* [5]*Persia, Ethiopia, and Libya with them; all of them with shield and helmet:* [6]*Gomer, and all his bands; the house of Togarmah of the north quarters, and all his bands: and many people with thee.* [7]*Be thou prepared, and prepare for thyself, thou, and all thy company that are assembled unto thee, and be thou a guard unto them.*

God had given Ezekiel many prophecies, chiefly for the Houses of Israel and Judah. Now God directed Ezekiel to prophesy against a nation, and rebuke it for its activities in future days. But Gog was a relative unknown at the time of this prophecy. He had to be associated with other nations in order to be identified clearly. He would be well-known at the time the prophecy was fulfilled, but when Ezekiel prophesied, he was mixed with other people.

- Who is he?
- Where did he come from?
- Where does he live?
- Why does God judge him?
- How does He intersect with Israel?

These are questions we can answer because of the revelations given to us in God's Word. Let's dig out the clues.

Where Does Gog Reside?

<u>Verse 2</u> tells us that Gog lives in the region of Magog. Who is Magog, and where did he come from? To answer this we must dig back

further, in fact clear back to the time of Noah! Noah had 3 sons: Shem, Ham, and Japheth.

- The name Shem means "*honor, authority, character, famous and renown.*" Out of this man descended the Chaldeans and the Shem-ites. This became known as the Semite or Semitic culture. The Houses of Israel and Judah are direct descendents of Shem.
- The name Ham means "*hot, warm.*" Ham moved south to warmer climates, and Canaan the cursed was his firstborn son. Various cultures ranging from Egypt to Sheba and farther south trace their heritage to Ham.
- The name Japheth means "*expansion.*" Japheth's seed grew and multiplied! Their single-most notable trait was large populations.

Genesis 10:2 lists Magog as a descendent of Japheth. Japheth's sons multiplied and spread throughout Asia, but they also moved northward into the area between the Caspian and the Black Seas. In *"The Antiquities Of The Jews"* the Jewish Historian Josephus tells us that the Greeks called the "Magogians" by a different name. They called them Scythians. Herodutus, the "Father of History," agrees, and also states that they were a bloodthirsty people! The word "Magog" in Hebrew literally means, "*a barbarous northern region.*" In fact, there was a wall built to keep some of the Magog invaders away from some of Japheth's other seed that had migrated into China. This is why in Arabic the Great Wall is called "*the wall of Al Magog.*"

Magog's Brothers

1 Chronicles 1:5 [5]*The sons of Japheth; Gomer, and Magog, and Madai, and Javan, and Tubal, and Meshech, and Tiras.*

Japheth had other sons and they were plentiful. They continued to grow in the region of Magog, but were known by different names. Two of these sons were Meshech and Tubal. Gog lived in the land, or region, of Magog and had risen in authority. He was the chief prince of Meshech and Tubal, according to Ezekiel 38:2-3.

- The term "chief prince" in Hebrew is the word "rosh." Gog is "rosh," the principal ruler of the territory.
- "Meshech" is a non-Hebrew word, from a foreign root. In Hebrew, it can also be translated "Mosoch." Assyrian writings call the people the "Mushki."
- "Tubal" is also a non-Hebrew word, and less is known about it. Writers have speculated that this tribe was connected to some of the residents of present-day Syria. Still others have linked Tubal with the residents of Turkey or present-day Tiblisi. Some Georgians claim to be descendents of Tubal to this present day. Regardless, these nations are all aligned under the same mindset and thought process when it comes to Israel. This author believes Tubal to be Georgia and the region of Turkey.

Based on these simple clues, let's assume for a moment that Gog is Russia. In order for this to be accurate, he must be the chief prince of the Mushki, or Moscow, and also influence or control Tubal. Today Russia does just that! He is the chief prince that leads every one of the nations discussed thus far. He lives in the land originally inhabited by a barbaric people. But just who is he?

1 Chronicles 5:4 lists the descendents of the tribe of Reuben. They were the first to go into captivity, 150 years before the House of Judah fell. One of the sons of Reuben is listed as Gog! This son of Reuben, the eldest son of Israel, has abandoned his heritage completely. He now lives among the heathen and leads them in their region.

God Judges Gog

Through Ezekiel, God foretold of a time when He would oppose Gog in a strange way. God would bring this nation into war against other people. But first, he would do a few things to Gog, that would precede the war itself.

- Verse 4 states that God will: turn Gog back; put hooks in his jaws; and bring him (Gog) forth with all sorts of armies and military equipment.

Russia has been turned back. During the 20th century, Russia embraced communism, forsaking the God of Israel and amalgamated other nation-states together into the USSR. God lifted His hand of blessing, and the USSR ultimately failed. The grand experiment of living without Almighty God as the Ultimate King of the nation failed. In short, Russia was turned back.

The hook is in Russia's jaw. Despite the fact that Russia failed in their endeavor to control Eastern Europe, Russia has continued to maintain alliances with these nations. Russia is the main trading partner and exporter, and has profited handsomely from the commerce. Two of the major exports have been military supplies and nuclear assistance.

In January, 2006, *U.S. News and World Report* editor Mortimer Zuckerman wrote an article titled *"Moscow's Mad Gamble."* Alluding to the lucrative nuclear sales to Iran, he stated the following:

> *It sold the nuclear power plant at Bushehr to Iran and contracted to sell even more to bring cash into its nuclear industry. As one American diplomat put it, this business is a "giant hook in Russia's jaw." Russia provided critical assistance in the development of Iran's Shihab missile, which has an ever expanding delivery range and can carry a warhead designed for a nuclear charge.*

Russia will engage in war. God definitely stated that Gog would come forth for war after he had been turned back, and the hook had been set into his jaw. Both of these prophecies have now been fulfilled. When will Russia attack?

Gog's Allies

Several nations are mentioned in verses 5 and 6 that will align themselves with Russia in their invasion. They are:

- Persia;
- Ethiopia;
- Libya;
- Gomer;
- Togarmah and all his bands; and many people (or other nations).

Are these the nations that are presently known by some of these names, or are they different? After all, there is no nation of "Gog" on the map today, but he definitely exists. What about the others?

Persia is mentioned as Russia's ally. Ancient Persia was a great kingdom. It encompassed present day Iran, Afghanistan, Iraq, and even parts of Pakistan. Today, the Islamic Republic of Iran is the most notable nation aligned with this ancient prophecy, but the others also matter. They are aligned together in common religion, heritage and ideology. Most important, they are all connected in some way or another to Russia.

Ethiopia is also listed as an ally to Russia. This nation descended from Cush, who was one of Ham's sons (the son of Noah). Ancient Ethiopia occupied a great deal of Northern Africa, together with Libya. Somalia was once within its borders as well as a great number of smaller African tribes. Ethiopia fell under communist influence, largely due to the influence of the USSR. Although this has been removed to a degree, they are still connected to Russia.

Libya is another ally of Russia. Their ancient kingdom was northward along the Mediterranean, whereas Ethiopia was further east. Libya also occupied parts of Chad, Morocco, Niger and Sudan during their reign. Today, most of these nations are Muslim, and are also closely aligned with Russia in their trading and ideology.

Who is **Gomer**? Listed as an ally of Russia, this nation is alive and well, but under another name. According to 1 Chronicles1:5, Gomer was another son of Japheth along with Magog. There has been much discussion about his actual boundaries, and more is revealed when you factor in the name of one of his sons. He is Togarmah. Before we delve into his locations, we can state that there is a solid likelihood that Gomer and all his bands are a coalition of the slavic nations and others formerly under the realm of the USSR.

Gomer's son was **Togarmah,** as listed in 1 Chronicles 1:6. The Hebrew/Chaldee Lexicon defines his nation as "a northern nation and country sprung from Gomer, the Cimmerians; abounding in horses and mules." Today, the Armenians proudly refer to themselves as being "of the house of Togarm." Other tribes in the south of Turkey also claim Togarmah as their heritage. His rulership encompassed this entire region.

Who are **the many people** listed in Ezekiel 38:6? They are the allies of Gog. Currently, Russia's allies are spread throughout the world. They include nations of many people, including China, that has the largest standing army in the world. (Russia has the arms; China has the manpower.) Others could include Venezuela, Cuba, and other Arab-bloc nations that align with Persia, Ethiopia and Libya in ideology. While they are not ideal allies, they all share a common hatred for their enemy.

The Nations That Russia Guards

There are several telltale signs that show when this prophetic passage will be fulfilled. One of those signs is found in verse 7. It says, *"Be thou prepared, and prepare for thyself, thou, and all thy company that are assembled unto thee, and be thou a guard unto them."*

In other words, Russia will do several things.

- First, Russia will adopt a mindset of war. He will prepare militarily for war and invasion and not just for self-defense.
- Russia will also prepare for the company of allies. It will be an arms dealer and distributor, especially for the coalition of nations around the region. Russia will equip the armies of other nations, in preparation for future events.

But the most notable event will be the third.

- Russia will be a guardian. Russia will be the overarching protector over several nations of the earth, especially those listed in this chapter. This is being fulfilled. Russia has protected other nations with its vote on the United Nations security council. It has also threatened retaliation against the United States and the Jewish State of Israel, when Iran or Eastern European nations are threatened. Russia has emphatically declared that any attack against their coalition will be taken as an attack against themselves, and they are prepared to defend their interests. Russia is the guardian over their coalition.

Ezekiel foresaw this coaltion forming in the last days only by the power of the Holy Spirit. It did not exist in his day, but God directed him to prophesy this event. The coalition of attacking nations would assemble, and would lay aside their differences to launch an attack. This battle-ready group could easily annihilate most of the nations of the world, singlehandedly. (Russia alone presently has approximately 7 million troops.) They are an overwhelming force. But who would be the nation that they came against?

Thirteen Criteria

Ezekiel 38:8-12 [8]*After many days thou shalt be visited: in the latter years thou shalt come into the land that is brought back from the sword, and is gathered out of many people, against the mountains of Israel, which have been always waste: but it is brought forth out of the nations, and they shall dwell safely all of them.* [9]*Thou shalt ascend and come like a storm, thou shalt be like a cloud to cover the land, thou, and all thy bands, and many people with thee.* [10]*Thus saith the Lord GOD; It shall also come to pass, that at the same time shall things come into thy mind, and thou shalt think an evil thought:* [11]*And thou shalt say, I will go up to the land of unwalled villages; I will go to them that are at rest, that dwell safely, all of them dwelling without walls, and having neither bars nor gates,* [12]*To take a spoil, and to take a prey; to turn thine hand upon the desolate places that are now inhabited, and upon the people that are gathered out of the nations, which have gotten cattle and goods, that dwell in the midst of the land.*

After God showed Ezekiel the coalition of nations led by Gog (or Russia), He also revealed the nation that would be attacked. It was Israel! But there was a problem. Would they attack the 2-tribe House of Judah, or the 10-tribe House of Israel? Both nations were in captivity and scattered at the time of this prophecy. Which nation was God speaking about? Apparently it was a unique nation Ezekiel had never seen, because God provided thirteen criteria that would be fulfilled. He did not recognize the land as one he had known. Therefore, every one of these criteria must be met in order for this nation to be considered as the Israelite nation that Russia and the coalition would seek to destroy.

The physical land would include these thirteen characteristics:

1. It was brought back from the sword.
2. It was gathered out of many people.
3. The land had mountains and had been known as wasteland.
4. It was brought forth out of the nations.
5. It was dwelling safely.
6. The land had unwalled villages.
7. It was at rest.
8. The cities and houses had no bars nor gates.
9. The land had desolate places that were now inhabited.
10. Again, it was gathered out of the nations.
11. It was noted again that the cities were without walls.
12. The people have much cattle and material goods.
13. The people also dwell in the midst of the land (it's a land between seas or boundaries of water).

Is It The House of Judah?

Many teachers have told us that this passage is a prophecy of Russia attacking the Jewish State of Israel (as the House of Judah is called today). In order for this to be the case, the Jewish State must fulfill all thirteen criteria. How does it match up?

Category	**Jews**
1. Brought back from the sword	Yes
2. Gathered out of many people	Yes
3. Mountains/wasteland	Yes
4. Brought forth out of the nations	Yes
5. Dwelling safely	No
6. Unwalled villages	No
7. At rest	No
8. No bars nor gates	No
9. Desolate places now inhabited	Yes
10. Gathered out of the nations	Yes
11. Without walls	No

12. Have much cattle/goods	No
13. Dwell in the midst of the land	Yes

The Jewish State of Israel fulfills several of the criteria Ezekiel listed. They have been been victorious in war and are gathered from many people and nations. However, they are not dwelling safely, nor have they been since their reestablishment as a nation in 1948. Their villages are walled, and they have many bars and gates around their kibbutzes. Although they are a highly innovative nation, they have nowhere near the cattle and food resources of other nations around the world. Some of these criteria could be adjusted over time, but others will never be satisfied. This passage does not talk about Russia versus the Jews.

Is It The House Of Israel?

Let's lay the thirteen criteria against the United States of America (as the House of Israel is called today). Please keep in mind that in order for this to satisfy the Biblical view, all thirteen criteria must be met.

Category	Jews	USA
1. Brought back from the sword	Yes	Yes
2. Gathered out of many people	Yes	Yes
3. Mountains/wasteland	Yes	Yes
4. Brought forth out of the nations	Yes	Yes
5. Dwelling safely	No	Yes
6. Unwalled villages	No	Yes
7. At rest	No	Yes
8. No bars Nor gates	No	Yes
9. Desolate places Now inhabited	Yes	Yes
10. Gathered out of the nations	Yes	Yes
11. Without walls	No	Yes
12. Have much cattle/goods	No	Yes
13. Dwell in the midst of the land	Yes	Yes

Do you see what I see? Russia will attack the United States of America! It will assemble a coalition of nations that hates the influence and dominance of Western thought and culture, led by America. They will attack the United States and attempt to destroy her! Ezekiel had never seen this land before, and he had to describe her characteristics as the land where the House of Israel lived in later years. This is why he never referred to the land of Israel specifically.

What Other Clues Do We Have?

These issues are also explained further when we deal with prophetic timing. Do you remember the timeline we studied earlier in the book? There was a time we dealt with known as the last days. These days began after the ascension of Jesus Christ into heaven, and continue until His return. Ezekiel 38:8 tells us the time of these events. They happen in the "latter years." In Hebrew, this translates to *"last days, extreme end."* Therefore, this chapter is a prophecy for the last days!

Verse 9 tells us that Russia and her allies will come like a storm and shall cover the land. The word "*storm*" is defined in Hebrew as: *"to rush over (as a storm hits suddenly), a tempest."* This denotes surprise, or a surprise attack. The word "*cover*" means *"to engulf or overwhelm."* America will be stunned by a surprise attack when they least expect it.

Verses 10 and 11 tell us the nature of Russia's mindset. He is a nation that thinks an evil thought. He thinks about attacking those that are at rest and are prospering. He is envious and jealous of America's success. He wants more than he has and he is willing to attack the United States to get what he wants.

This mindset was displayed by Russia's leader Mikhail Gorbachev, when he addressed the Supreme Soviet (their parliament) in 1989. He told his leaders that "*Peristroika*," their economic reforms, and "*Glasnost*," their openness and friendship, were ploys used to eliminate the United States development of advanced military technology. He further stated that his desire was to *"deplete the U.S.' military arsenal, and prepare them for eventual acknowledgement of a Supreme Soviet government."* Russia has not changed her mind.

The Reason For War

Not only was Ezekiel given the time and the details of this last day war, he was also given the reason.

Ezekiel 38:12-13 [12]*To take a spoil, and to take a prey; to turn thine hand upon the desolate places that are now inhabited, and upon the people that are gathered out of the nations, which have gotten cattle and goods, that dwell in the midst of the land.*

[13]*Sheba, and Dedan, and the merchants of Tarshish, with all the young lions thereof, shall say unto thee, Art thou come to take a spoil? hast thou gathered thy company to take a prey? to carry away silver and gold, to take away cattle and goods, to take a great spoil?*

The reason Russia would attack the United States of America would be to take spoil. Several items are mentioned including silver, gold, cattle and goods. Reuben was a tribe that loved their cattle (Numbers 32:1-5). Russia still loves their cattle and the United States has many of them. The United States has more material wealth than any nation on earth and Russia wants that. However, there is a deeper reason for this war, a reason that is rooted in Biblical history.

God reaffirmed His covenant with Jacob in Genesis 35, and changed his name to Israel. Prince with God! His sons would be blessed by this covenant, but one son would sin against his father. It was Reuben. In Genesis 35:22, Reuben slept with his father's concubine, Bilhah. Israel withheld his personal judgment until the end of his life, allowing God to prophetically judge his son.

In Genesis 49, Jacob gathered his sons together, to prophesy over them before he died. Reuben was his firsborn, the one who was entitled by birthright to receive the greatest blessing of material wealth. He should have had a double portion of property and inheritance. Instead, Israel spoke a curse over him (Genesis 49:3-4). The birthright blessing of material wealth was given to Joseph instead (Genesis 49:22-26). This was passed on to Joseph's two sons, with the greatest part of it going to his youngest son, Ephraim (Genesis 48:13-22). Ephraim had the blessing of the right hand. This is reiterated in the ancient genealogies of 1 Chronicles, in a curious passage found in chapter 5.

1 Chronicles 5:1-4 [1]*Now the sons of Reuben the firstborn of Israel, (for he was the firstborn; but, forasmuch as he defiled his father's bed, his birthright was given unto the sons of Joseph the son of Israel: and the genealogy is not to be reckoned after the birthright.* [2]*For Judah prevailed above his brethren, and of him came the chief ruler; but the birthright was Joseph's:)* [3]*The sons, I say, of Reuben the firstborn of Israel were, Hanoch,* *and Pallu, Hezron, and Carmi.* [4]*The sons of Joel; Shemaiah his son, Gog his son, Shimei his son,*

Reuben should have been a tribe that had great blessing and material wealth. However, just as Adam's sin brought sin to all of mankind, so Reuben's sin and rebellion cost his future generations their blessing as a nationality. Instead, Joseph and his sons thrived perpetually, wherever they went, because God was with them.

1 Chronicles shows that the birthright was removed from Reuben's family. Instead, it was given to the sons of Joseph. Reuben had several sons and grandsons in his family line, and one of them was a man named . . . *Gog*! Gog would grow through the years and migrate into the land of Magog, where he would become a chief prince. He should be blessed. He would have natural resources, intelligence, and he would be a proud and ancient nation. But he would have to watch in anger and jealousy as the young, upstart tribe of Ephraim would build *the* nation that would be blessed more than any other. The United States of America! Gog would covet the birthright blessing, and he would come to take it away by force in the last days!

The United States Is Stunned!

Ezekiel 38:13-16 [13]*Sheba, and Dedan, and the merchants of Tarshish, with all the young lions thereof, shall say unto thee, Art thou come to take a spoil? hast thou gathered thy company to take a prey? to carry away silver and gold, to take away cattle and goods, to take a great spoil?* [14]*Therefore, son of man, prophesy and say unto Gog, Thus saith the Lord GOD; In that day when my people of Israel dwelleth safely, shalt thou not know it?* [15]*And thou shalt come from thy place out of the north parts, thou, and many people with thee, all of them riding upon horses, a great company, and a mighty army:* [16]*And thou shalt come up against my people of Israel, as a cloud to cover the land; it shall be in the latter days, and I will bring thee against my land, that the heathen may know me, when I shall be sanctified in thee, O Gog, before their eyes.*

One of the characteristics of the House of Israel in the last days (The USA) would be her multi-ethnic population. This people was gathered out of the nations, and all of them would be stunned when Russia invaded. Among them are Sheba, Dedan, and merchants of Tarshish.

- **Sheba** is defined in Hebrew as "*springing from Ethiopia.*" Sheba is a descendent of Noah's son, Ham (Genesis 10:7). These are probably Africans. Sheba was known for their trafficking in *spices, gold and precious stones* (I Kings 10:1-10, II Chronicles 9:1-12). The Queen of Sheba visited Solomon, presenting him with gifts representative of her nation's wealth. She was thought to have come from central or south-central Africa. The wealth of Africa is in South Africa. This region is particularly noted for their vast stores of gold, diamonds (precious stones) and spices (e.g., curry, ginger, garlic, etc.). Thus, it could be concluded that a number of Central and/or South Africans will reside in the United States when it is attacked.
- **Dedan** also descended from Ham, and is related to Sheba (Genesis 10:7). They traded in *ebony, ivory and semi-precious stones* (Ezekiel 27:15-16). It is interesting to note that most of the United States' slaves and black heritage have their origins in Africa's famed "Ivory Coast." Sheba and Dedan most likely represent the black heritage within the United States.
- **The Merchants of Tarshish** are an interesting group. Tarshish was a descendent of Noah's son, Japheth (Genesis 10:2-4). The Hebrew definition of "Tarshish" means "*delightsome.*" We also know, based on history, that Tarshish had many dealings with the Israelites, and that they were deeply involved in *shipping and exporting* (II Chronicles 9:21, Psalms 48:7, Isaiah 2:16). They were ruled by a monarchy, or *royal family* (Psalms 72:10), and they dwelt in the *Isles* or islands (Isaiah 23:2,6, Isaiah 60:7). Ezekiel 27:12 states that they were the merchants of *all kinds of riches*. Since they descend from Japheth (who spawned many of the Asian nations), it is thought that the Merchants mentioned here could well be Asians living in the United States.
- **The Young Lions** are also mentioned. Who are they? The Hebrew translation of this phrase brings out the thought of "*towns*" or "*new villages.*" The Hebrew/Chaldee lexicon further amplifies this by stating that it represents "*the heads of state.*" The young lions could be elected officials from various levels of government. When the attack comes, nobody in state and local government will be prepared. It will catch them all off guard.

Everyone involved, the entire United States population, will be shocked when Russia attacks. Verse 13 says America will be surprised by their evil intent, to plunder, steal and destroy the goods of the land.

Russia will sense the time when the United States does not feel threatened, and dwells safely (or carelessly). They will know it, perhaps because of spies, and perhaps because of their understanding of the culture after studying their enemy for decades. This mindset has grown through the years, to the point that Russia, China, and many other nations are no longer considered a threat to the United States. We live "safely," and they know it!

The Russian coalition will attack out of the north. According to U.S. military sources, the most vulnerable penetration point into the mainland U.S. is to come through Alaska, and over the North Pole. They will come with masses of troops and will cover the land as a cloud. They will literally be everywhere at once. (They learned this tactic by observing the military invasions mounted by the United States in Panama, Grenada, Iraq and other nations during the past decades.) The nation of America will be in desperate straits.

God Has Spoken About This Before

Ezekiel 38:17 *[17]Thus saith the Lord GOD; Art thou he of whom I have spoken in old time by my servants the prophets of Israel, which prophesied in those days many years that I would bring thee against them?*

When God does something, He is entirely fair. This prophecy is one that He uses to judge Gog in the last days. He also uses it to judge and purify the House of Israel, as we will understand later. But God has spoken of this before. In fact, He has spoken of it several times.

As we have learned in previous chapters, God always speaks in the mouths of two or three witnesses. Since this is the case, Ezekiel was not the only prophet that described this last days event. There were others that foretold it too. Why haven't we understood this more clearly? It's simple. Many have relegated all last days prophecy to the House of Judah, the Jews. They believe that most of what the Scriptures prophesy will happen "over there," and we will just sit back and watch it unfold. Nothing could be further from the truth!

The Apostle Paul told Timothy to *"study to show thyself approved unto God, a workman that needeth not to be ashamed, rightly dividing the word of truth"* (2 Timothy 2:15). A right division of the Word of God, with surgical precision, reveals that the House of Israel is alive and well in the last days. They will undergo a ferocious attack. Other prophets have also foretold this event and we must study earnestly to undertand. Prophets such as Hosea, Amos, Daniel and others must be studied to understand their interpretation of this same, last day event.

God Judges Gog For His Sins

Ezekiel 38:18-23 *[18]And it shall come to pass at the same time when Gog shall come against the land of Israel, saith the Lord GOD, that my fury shall come up in my face. [19]For in my jealousy and in the fire of my wrath have I spoken, Surely in that day there shall be a great shaking in the land of Israel; [20]So that the fishes of the sea, and the fowls of the heaven, and the beasts of the field, and all creeping things that creep upon the earth, and all the men that are upon the face of the earth, shall shake at my presence, and the mountains shall be thrown down, and the steep places shall fall, and every wall shall fall to the ground. [21]And I will call for a sword against him throughout all my mountains, saith the Lord GOD: every man's sword shall be against his brother. [22]And I will plead against him with pestilence and with blood; and I will rain upon him, and upon his bands, and upon the many people that are with him, an overflowing rain, and great hailstones, fire, and brimstone. [23]Thus will I magnify myself, and sanctify myself; and I will be known in the eyes of many nations, and they shall know that I am the LORD.*

As the Russian-led coalition attacks the United States of America, there will be a tremendous outcry from the people of the land. America has forsaken Almighty God, and she must be judged. As she cries out, God will hear, and will judge her attackers.

Many will argue that the land of Israel is the land where the Jewish State of Israel dwells. However, this cannot be the case, because that land will never fulfill the criteria God specified earlier in this prophecy. God counts the United States, the House of Israel, as the land of Israel, too. He is guarding it for His glory, but they must return to serve Him completely.

How will God help America?

There will be **a great shaking** in the land (verse 19-20). Massive earthquakes will shake the nation. These could be due to after-effects of a limited nuclear strike on the nation, most likely over the cities. (A complete nuclear event would destroy the cattle and goods, so much of this invasion will use non-nuclear strategy.) Other natural disasters could also come into play, including the eruption of volcanoes in some mountain ranges (e.g., the Cascades), and the eruption of the Yellowstone caldara.

There will be **battle and bloodshed** (verse 21). God will help America as they do battle in the mountains and hills of the nation. It will be a bloody, urgent time for the United States, and they will be forced to call on Almighty God. The enemy may also turn on itself as the battle continues.

God will use **natural disasters** against them (verse 22). There will be bloodshed, but God will also use overflowing rain, hailstones, fire and brimstone (perhaps due to volcanic eruptions), and pestilence against the enemy. **Job 38:22-23** says, *"[22]Hast thou entered into the treasures of the snow? or hast thou seen the treasures of the hail, [23]Which I have reserved against the time of trouble, against the day of battle and war?"*

God has literally stored up natural disasters to be used in America against her enemies, to show the world that this truly is the House of Israel in these last days! He helped Israel under Joshua's command in the Old Testament (Joshua 10:11), when He used hailstones to destroy the enemy. God's people were shielded from the disaster during the battle, but the enemy was destroyed. He will help Israel again.

Every Nation Shall Know And Understand

When God judges Gog, and preserves the House of Israel, the nations of the world will know and understand the fact that God has His sovereign hand on the nations (verse 23). He guards His covenant with Abraham, Isaac and Israel to this day, when His people cry out to Him for help. But the battle will be so fierce, and the coalition will be so powerful, that there will be a critical question that must be answered. Will America survive?

CHAPTER 10

Will America Survive?

God didn't give the prophet Ezekiel visions in neat and tidy chapters. Those were inserted into God's Word later, to make it more readable for you and me. But God did stop periodically, to summarize what had been seen, so that the truth could be unveiled line upon line and precept upon precept.

Ezekiel 39 continues God's prophecy to Russia, or Gog, and speaks of his judgment as he attacks the United States, or Israel, with a coalition of nations. It begins with a summary of some of the items found in chapter 38.

Ezekiel 39:1-2 [1]*Therefore, thou son of man, prophesy against Gog, and say, Thus saith the Lord GOD; Behold, I am against thee, O Gog, the chief prince of Meshech and Tubal:* [2]*And I will turn thee back, and leave but the sixth part of thee, and will cause thee to come up from the north parts, and will bring thee upon the mountains of Israel:*

God has several things to say.

- **First**, He is against Gog. Russia has turned its back on God and prefers to live in a self-sufficient way, going the way of the world without embracing the covenant of Almighty God as its source of strength and blessing.
- **Second**, Gog is the chief prince of Meshech and Tubal. He is the leader of this coalition of nations. They are not godly. In fact they are anti-Christian in their heritage and their ideology. They attack the House of Israel, the United States of America, because they want the blessing God brings without embracing God as the giver of that blessing.

- **Third**, Gog has been turned back. He possesses only 1/6th of his strength. This was accomplished in Russia when the USSR broke up. Russia still controls many of the nations around her, but she has no direct authority or supervisory control. Perhaps a threat to her strength is one of the reasons she decides to attack.
- **Fourth**, Gog comes against Israel, specifically the House of Israel, in the last days. This is the United States of America, not the Jewish State of Israel. He attacks from the north and completely surprises America.

God Judges Gog

Ezekiel 39:3-6 [3]*And I will smite thy bow out of thy left hand, and will cause thine arrows to fall out of thy right hand.* [4]*Thou shalt fall upon the mountains of Israel, thou, and all thy bands, and the people that is with thee: I will give thee unto the ravenous birds of every sort, and to the beasts of the field to be devoured.* [5]*Thou shalt fall upon the open field: for I have spoken it, saith the Lord GOD.* [6]*And I will send a fire on Magog, and among them that dwell carelessly in the isles: and they shall know that I am the LORD.*

When God judges Gog, He does a complete work. Russia's strength will be her surprise attack and her military might. But she will not be as effective as she might be. The birthright blessing still belongs to Ephraim, not Gog. God will help the United States come through the fight.

God will smite the bow and arrow from Gog's hands. His military arms will fail. Russia and the coalition will fall in the mountains and on the plains. There will be a fire upon Magog. This may be a retaliatory strike of some kind by America against the land of Magog. God also judges the coasts or isles of nations that helped in the attack. They will be burned as well. The nations shall know that God is the Lord God Almighty.

Russia and her coalition will be forced to fall back in disarray. They may continue to have military power, but they will not dominate as before unless they join with other forces such as Islam and globalism for future events.

What Happens To America?

The damage done to the United States of America will be tremendous. Millions will die. The cities will be destroyed. Those that escape will be faced with rebuilding a nation totally consumed by war. Is this a nation worth reclaiming? The answer is an emphatic . . . yes!

Ezekiel 39:7 [7]*So will I make my holy name known in the midst of my people Israel; and I will not let them pollute my holy name any more: and the heathen shall know that I am the LORD, the Holy One in Israel.*

The reason America is ripe for judgment has now been made clear. The House of Israel forsook God. They were once founded upon the promise of Jesus Christ and a covenant with Almighty God, but they forsook their foundations. They chose instead to worship the golden bull and the works of their hands, just as their forefathers in the ancient land of Israel. God must judge them, for greed, abortion, and a host of other sins. But God is not done with His land.

After the invasion, God has promised to reclaim His people, Israel. Verse 7 makes this clear.

- God's holy Name will be known in America. There will no longer be a multi-cultural melting pot of idols and mixed religions. America will be a Christian nation. One nation under one God!
- America will be a morally pure nation. God's Name and character will not be polluted any more. The United States will return to the intent of the Founding Fathers, as they framed the nation. She will not tolerate any behavior, law, or mindset that opposes Almighty God and His Word.
- America will be known as a nation protected by Almighty God. The rest of the world will know and understand that God alone preserved America. This will be a cause for amazement and an understanding that God establishes His covenant with His people forever.

Is this a nation worth standing for? Yes it is! She may not be a global superpower, but she will be strong in the power of the Lord. Armed with this knowledge, the people of the land will begin to reclaim their nation for the glory of God.

The Nation Rebuilds

Ezekiel 39:8-22 [8]*Behold, it is come, and it is done, saith the Lord GOD; this is the day whereof I have spoken.* [9]*And they that dwell in the cities of Israel shall go forth, and shall set on fire and burn the weapons, both the shields and the bucklers, the bows and the arrows, and the handstaves, and the spears, and they shall burn them with fire seven years:* [10]*So that they shall take no wood out of the field, neither cut down any out of the forests; for they shall burn the weapons with fire: and they shall spoil those that spoiled them, and rob those that robbed them, saith the Lord GOD.* [11]*And it shall come to pass in that day, that I will give unto Gog a place there of graves in Israel, the valley of the passengers on the east of the sea: and it shall stop the noses of the passengers: and there shall they bury Gog and all his multitude: and they shall call it The valley of Hamongog.* [12]*And seven months shall the house of Israel be burying of them, that they may cleanse the land.* [13]*Yea, all the people of the land shall bury them; and it shall be to them a renown the day that I shall be glorified, saith the Lord GOD.* [14]*And they shall sever out men of continual employment, passing through the land to bury with the passengers those that remain upon the face of the earth, to cleanse it: after the end of seven months shall they search.* [15]*And the passengers that pass through the land, when any seeth a man's bone, then shall he set up a sign by it, till the buriers have buried it in the valley of Hamongog.* [16]*And also the name of the city shall be Hamonah. Thus shall they cleanse the land.* [17]*And, thou son of man, thus saith the Lord GOD; Speak unto every feathered fowl, and to every beast of the field, Assemble yourselves, and come; gather yourselves on every side to my sacrifice that I do sacrifice for you, even a great sacrifice upon the mountains of Israel, that ye may eat flesh, and drink blood.* [18]*Ye shall eat the flesh of the mighty, and drink the blood of the princes of the earth, of rams, of lambs, and of goats, of bullocks, all of them fatlings of Bashan.* [19]*And ye shall eat fat till ye be full, and drink blood till ye be drunken, of my sacrifice which I have sacrificed for you.* [20]*Thus ye shall be filled at my table with horses and chariots, with mighty men, and with all men of war, saith the Lord GOD.* [21]*And I will set my glory among the heathen, and all the heathen shall see my judgment that I have executed, and my hand that I have laid upon them.* [22]*So the house of Israel shall know that I am the LORD their God from that day and forward.*

Several notable things occur while America rebuilds as God's covenant people.

- The weapons that are left behind are burned and used to heat the homes of the nation for seven years. This military technology is converted to civilian use and is a great blessing to America. Some have speculated that the weapons themselves will be burned, while others have thought that Ezekiel saw elements of the military armament being converted over to civilian use, especially for utility purposes.
- The dead bodies of the enemy forces will be so numerous that Israel will section off an entire valley for their burial. It will take seven months to gather the majority of them and transport them for burial. After that period, people will be employed to locate and transport the remains of the dead that are found as the nation returns to productivity.
- The beasts of the field and fowls of the air will also help to locate dead bodies as they feast upon the carcases of the dead. It will be a part of God's "clean-up plan," as He helps His people to return to a state of normalcy.
- The Lord reiterates once again (verse 21) that His glory over America will be known and recognized by the heathen. They shall understand that this victory was due to God's hand over the nation and not because of the might, technology, wealth or intellect of the people. God will receive the glory.
- The Lord also emphasizes His glory over the nation itself (verse 22). From this point forward, the House of Israel (e.g., the United States of America) will be a Christian nation. They will recognize only God Almighty within their land.

How Significant Is this Battle?

God has a reason for judging Gog, or Russia. He also has a reason for using Gog to attack the United States of America. Both nations have opposing ideologies at their cores and God must use one to judge the other. In ancient times, God used heathen and ungodly nations to judge His people repeatedly. This time He would use Russia to judge America, because America has sinned greatly! The heathen must understand the righteousness of Almighty God.

By the time this battle occurs, the world has come to the place where they think globalism is acceptable. They do not understand that God sets up nations and kings (Daniel 2:21). God determined the boundaries of every nation by establishing beforehand the land He would give to the sons of Israel (Deuteronomy 32:8-10). God hates globalism, and intends to make a statement in the last days as He returns the United States of America and finally the Jewish State of Israel, to embrace Jesus Christ as their Redeemer and King.

Ezekiel 39:23-24 [23]*And the heathen shall know that the house of Israel went into captivity for their iniquity: because they trespassed against me, therefore hid I my face from them, and gave them into the hand of their enemies: so fell they all by the sword.* [24]*According to their uncleanness and according to their transgressions have I done unto them, and hid my face from them.*

The House of Israel will finally understand God's hand in the world. The heathen will know the reasons behind the battle, too.

The Restoration And Revival

Ezekiel 39:25-29 [25]*Therefore thus saith the Lord GOD; Now will I bring again the captivity of Jacob, and have mercy upon the whole house of Israel, and will be jealous for my holy name;* [26]*After that they have borne their shame, and all their trespasses whereby they have trespassed against me, when they dwelt safely in their land, and none made them afraid.* [27]*When I have brought them again from the people, and gathered them out of their enemies' lands, and am sanctified in them in the sight of many nations;* [28]*Then shall they know that I am the LORD their God, which caused them to be led into captivity among the heathen: but I have gathered them unto their own land, and have left none of them any more there.* [29]*Neither will I hide my face any more from them: for I have poured out my spirit upon the house of Israel, saith the Lord GOD.*

For years, many in America have pled with God to send a revival of His Holy Spirit to the nation. They have watched as many came to salvation in the other nations of the world. Has God passed by America, never to return? Absolutely not!

This passage in Ezekiel 39 demonstrates the fact that God will reclaim the United States of America with a revival of epic proportions!

- God will return those that have been scattered, perhaps as prisoners of war. He will undoubtedly also bring Christians from around the world to rebuild this nation as one that lives in God's glory. The enemy will still live in foreign lands and not be receptive to the hope and change God brings. Their pride will be too great. Consequently, there may be a flood of Christian migration that pours into America.
- The shame of sin and idolatry will leave a permanent mark upon the people of America. They will understand that their departure from God in every area of society is the reason for their judgment. They will begin to destroy every vestige of secular, global government. Every home, school, business, and governmental entity will be impacted. Laws will be repealed. The Word of God will be inserted into every area of society. The nation will be sanctified.
- As a result, the glory of the Holy Spirit will fill America as never before! The revival will be far more significant than a "good church service." It will be a revival of every area of society. This revival will be known in the houses of worship, and it will reach to every corner of America. Business, homes, the economy, laws, schools, every facet of society will change. The world will witness a nation that is saved and lives under the hand of Almighty God.

Others Have Foreseen This Event

God has revealed this battle and subsequent victory to many others in the body of Christ. The names are too numerous to list, but those below are a few.

- Rick Joyner, a respected minister and missionary, prophesied of a limited nuclear strike in 1989, while appearing on a nationally televised broadcast of the Trinity Broadcasting Network.
- John Paul Jackson, a Missouri minister, foretold war coming to the United States in a 1990 prophecy.

- Zelma Kirkpatrick received a vision of Russia and China attacking the United States, traveling on roads which were not yet built. Mrs. Kirkpatrick was given this vision in the early 1960's, while living in Oregon, and since that time all of the roads have now been constructed!
- Demos Shakarian, Founder of the Full Gospel Business Men's Fellowship International, wrote of a future event in his book "the Happiest People On Earth." According to Mr. Shakarian, there will come a time that they will have to flee Southern California, just as his family fled from Armenia before it fell to the Turks.
- Romanian minister Dimitru Duduman, Founder of Hand of Help, was directed by God and miraculously expelled from Communist Romania in the 1980s to warn America that war and judgement was coming to her soil.
- Respected pastor, seminarian, and teacher, Leonard Ravenhill, wrote several books. One of them is titled "America Is Too Young To Die." In this book, he talks of God's judgement of the U.S.A.
- David Wilkerson, pastor of Times Square Church, and founder of Teen Challenge ministry, warned repeatedly during his ministry about the impending judgment of God through war in the United States of America.
- Dr. Charles Stanley, Pastor, First Baptist Church of Atlanta, prophesied in July, 1989 that America would be judged by war.

George Washington's Vision

In the era before the War Between the States (e.g., the Civil War), a document appeared that was attributed to General George Washington. Since that time, it has been attributed to another writer from that era, but the accuracy of the prophetic message is still astounding. In this document, three wars are presented. All three occur on the soil of the United States of America.

This document has been reprinted several times in many publications As you read this, consider the era in which it was published, and the prophetic words that were spoken. I give the account here as it was reprinted in the U.S. war veterans' paper, *The National Tribune*, in

December, 1880. *The National Tribune* is now *The Stars and Stripes*. This article was reprinted in the *Stars and Stripes* December 21, 1950.

George Washington's Vision: America In Prophecy

Our Future Revealed

The father of our country, George Washington, was a man of prayer. We have all read of how he went to the thicket many times to pray during the winter his army was at Valley Forge. However, little publicity has been given to the vision and prophecy he received at that time.

The account of this vision was given in 1859 by an old soldier. He gave it to a writer, Wesley Bradshaw, who published it. In the vision God revealed to George Washington that three great perils would come upon the Republic. He was given to know that America was going through the first peril at that time. The old soldier who told the story of the vision said that the nation would soon see the account verified by the second peril descending upon the land.

Wesley Bradshaw wrote:

The last time I ever saw Anthony Sherman was on the fourth of July, 1859, in Independence Square (Philadelphia, Pennsylvania). He was then ninety-nine years old, and becoming very feeble. But though so old, his dimming eyes rekindled as he gazed upon Independence Hall, which he came to visit once more.

Withheld Message Disclosed

"Let us go into the hall," he said. "I want to tell you of an incident of Washington's life—one which no one alive knows of except myself; and if you live, you will before long see it verified. Mark the prediction, you will see it verified."

"From the opening of the Revolution we experienced all phases of fortune, now good and now ill, one time victorious and another conquered. The darkest period we had, I think, was when Washington after several reverses, retreated to Valley Forge (Pennsylvania), where he resolved to pass the winter of 1777. Ah! I have often seen the tears coursing down our dear commander's care-worn cheeks, as he would be conversing with

a confidential officer about the condition of his poor soldiers. You have doubtless heard the story of Washington's going to the thicket to pray. Well, it was not only true, but he used often to pray in secret for aid and comfort. And God brought us safely through the darkest days of tribulation."

"One day, I remember it well, the chilly winds whistled through the leafless trees, though the sky was cloudless and the sun shone brightly. He remained in his quarters nearly all the afternoon, alone. When he came out I noticed that his face was a shade paler than usual, and there seemed to be something on his mind of more than ordinary importance. Returning just after dusk, he dispatched an orderly to the quarters of an officer, who was presently in attendance. After a preliminary conversation of about a half an hour, Washington, gazing upon his companion with that strange look of dignity which he alone could command, said to the latter:"

An Uninvited Guest

"'I do not know whether it is owing to the anxiety of my mind, or what, but this afternoon, as I was sitting at this table engaged in preparing a dispatch, something in the apartment seemed to disturb me. Looking up, I beheld standing opposite me a singularly beautiful being. So astonished was I, for I had given strict orders not to be disturbed that it was some moments before I found language to inquire the cause of the visit. A second, a third, and even a fourth time did I repeat my question, but received no answer from my mysterious visitor except a slight raising of the eyes.'"

"'By this time I felt strange sensations spreading through me. I would have risen but the riveted gaze of the being before me rendered volition impossible. I assayed once more to speak, but my tongue had become useless, as if paralyzed. A new influence, mysterious, potent, irresistible, took possession of me. All I could do was to gaze steadily, vacantly at my unknown visitor.'"

"'Gradually the surrounding atmosphere seemed to fill with sensations, and grew luminous. Everything about me seemed to rarefy, the mysterious visitor also becoming more airy and yet more distinct to my sight than before. I began to feel as one dying, or rather to experience the sensations which I have sometimes imagined accompany death. I did not think, I did not reason, I did not move. All were alike impossible. I was only conscious of gazing fixedly, vacantly at my companion.'"

The Revelation

"'Presently I heard a voice saying, 'Son of the Republic, look and learn,' while at the same time my visitor extended an arm eastward. I now beheld a heavy white vapor at some distance rising fold upon fold. This gradually dissipated, and I looked upon a strange scene. Before me lay, spread out in one vast plain, all the countries of the world—Europe, Asia, Africa and America. I saw rolling and tossing between Europe and America the billows of the Atlantic, and between Asia and America lay the Pacific. 'Son of the Republic,' said the same mysterious voice as before, 'look and learn.'"'

"'At that moment I beheld a dark, shadowy being, like an angel, standing, or rather floating in mid-air, between Europe and America. Dipping water out of the ocean in the hollow of each hand, he sprinkled some upon America with his right hand, and with his left he cast some over Europe. Immediately a cloud arose from these countries, and joined in mid-ocean. For awhile it remained stationery, and then it moved slowly westward, until it enveloped America in its murky folds. Sharp flashes of lightning gleamed through it at intervals, and I heard the smothered groans and cries of the American people. (This may be interpreted to have been the Revolutionary War, then in progress.)'"

A Great Victory

"'A second time the angel dipped water from the ocean and sprinkled it out as before. The dark cloud was then drawn back to the ocean, in whose heaving billows it sank from view.'"

"'A third time I heard the mysterious voice saying, 'Son of the Republic, look and learn.' I cast my eyes upon America and beheld villages and towns and cities springing up one after another until the whole land from the Atlantic to the Pacific was dotted with them. Again, I heard the mysterious voice say, 'Son of the Republic, the end of the century cometh, look and learn.'"'

"'And this time the dark shadowy angel turned his face southward. From Africa I saw an ill-omen spectre approach our land. It flitted slowly and heavily over every town and city of the latter. The inhabitants presently set themselves in battle array against each other. As I continued looking I saw a bright angel on whose brow rested a crown of light, on

which was traced the word "Union." He was bearing the American flag. He placed the flag between the divided nation and said, 'Remember, ye are brethren.'"

"'Instantly the inhabitants, casting down their weapons, became friends once more and united around the National Standard.'"

"'Again I heard the mysterious voice saying, 'Son of the Republic, look and learn.' At this the dark, shadowy angel placed a trumpet to his mouth, and blew three distinct blasts; and taking water from the ocean, he sprinkled it upon Europe, Asia and Africa.'"

Frightful—Incredible

"'Then my eyes beheld a fearful scene. From each of these continents arose thick black clouds that were soon joined into one. And throughout this mass there gleamed a dark red light by which I saw hordes of armed men. These men, moving with the cloud, marched by land and sailed by sea to America, which country was enveloped in the volume of cloud. And I dimly saw these vast armies devastate the whole country and burn the villages, towns and cities which I had seen springing up.'"

"'As my ears listened to the thundering of the cannon, clashing of swords, and the shouts and cries of millions in mortal combat, I again heard the mysterious voice saying, 'Son of the Republic, look and learn.' When the voice had ceased, the dark shadowy angel placed his trumpet once more to his mouth, and blew a long and fearful blast.'"

Heaven Intervenes

"'Instantly a light as of a thousand suns shone down from above me, and pierced and broke into fragments the dark cloud which enveloped America. At the same moment the angel upon whose head still shone the word "Union," and who bore our national flag in one hand and a sword in the other, descended from the heavens attended by legions of white spirits. These immediately joined the inhabitants of America, who I perceived were well-nigh overcome, but who immediately taking courage again, closed up their broken ranks and renewed the battle.'"

"'Again, amid the fearful noise of the conflict I heard the mysterious voice saying, 'Son of the Republic, look and learn.' As the voice ceased, the shadowy angel for the last time dipped water from the ocean and sprinkled

it upon America. Instantly the dark cloud rolled back, together with the armies it had brought, leaving the inhabitants of the land victorious.'"

"'Then once more, I beheld the villages, towns and cities springing up where I had seen them before, while the bright angel, planting the azure standard he had brought in the midst of them, cried with a loud voice: 'while the stars remain, and the heaven send down dew upon the earth, so long shall the Union last.' And taking from his brow the crown on which blazoned the word 'Union,' he placed it upon the Standard while the people, kneeling down said, 'Amen.'"

The Future

"'The scene instantly began to fade and dissolve, and I, at last saw nothing but the rising, curling vapor I at first beheld. This also disappeared, and I found myself once more gazing upon the mysterious visitor, who, in the same voice I had heard before, said, 'Son of the Republic, what you have seen is thus interpreted: Three great perils will come upon the Republic. The most fearful for her is the third. But the whole world united shall not prevail against her. Let every child of the Republic learn to live for his God, his land and Union.' With these words the vision vanished, and I started from my seat and felt that I had seen a vision wherein had been shown me the birth, the progress, and destiny of the United States.'"

"Such, my friends," the venerable narrator concluded, "were the words I heard from Washington's own lips, and America will do well to profit by them."

September 11, 2001

Although some dreams and visions may be given to speculation and dismissal, this author knows of one supernatural occurrence that happened. It is nothing less than remarkable. This authors' parents, Pastors David and Nona Grant, pastored Faith Fellowship Church in Lakewood, Colorado, in 2001. This material was gleaned firsthand from their experiences in Washington, D.C., around the time of September 11, 2001.

Pastors David and Nona Grant had long understood the correlation between the United States of America and its origins as the House of Israel. In 2001, they felt led by the Holy Spirit to join a group of pastors traveling from various parts of the U.S. to Washington, D.C., for a tour and briefing. They prepared a proclamation, to be read on the steps of the U.S. Capitol Building, as directed by God and they made their reservations.

The Grants flew to Washington, D.C., on Monday, September 10, 2001, and stayed at the Capitol Holiday Inn downtown. However, during the night, Pastor David Grant could not sleep. Arising at 3:00 a.m. Eastern Daylight Time, early on September 11th, Pastor Grant began to pray. Then, taking a pen and a hotel notepad, he hastily wrote these words:

> *"Because America has not repented of her sins, I prophesy judgment of God to come upon our nation, and thru that judgment, there will be repentance and a turning back to God. After our nation has been purged and dealt with by Almighty God, I prophesy and call forth a mighty move of the Holy Spirit to come upon the people remaining in this land. And this people will be strong in the Lord and do exploits."*

After resting, the Grants rose early on September 11, 2001, and toured the White House. As they were leaving the White House, the burning wreckage of the World Trade Center was displayed on a security television. Shortly thereafter, the second plane slammed into the Twin Towers, and a third hit the Pentagon, just a short distance from the White House. The Grants retreated to the Washington Mall in the ensuing chaos, not knowing what to do or where to go. They prayed.

At length, they decided to return to their hotel room. They were caught in town. Airline travel was shut down nation-wide, and there were no rental vehicles available. (Even U-Hauls and trucks had been rented by those escaping Washington.) As they rested and prayed, Pastor Grant's mind remembered what he had written on the hotel notepad. (He has it to this day and this author has an exact copy.) Almighty God was speaking to the nation.

The Grants were able to witness the joint gathering of Congress on the evening of September 11th but their business in Washington, D.C. was cancelled. Why did God have them in the city? Everything was closed, and the national sites were completely locked down. They could not leave town. What should they do?

September 13, 2001

Two days later, early on Thursday, September 13, 2001, the Grants rose early and felt led to walk to the U.S. Capitol building. It had been closed, and placed under heavy security. But this morning, something was different. The security tape had been moved! They could get to the Capitol building! Pastors David and Nona Grant climbed the stairs of the U.S. Capitol. Facing west, toward the heartland, they began to read a heavenly proclamation over the land.

> *"Whereas we understand, according to the Holy Scriptures, that the United States of America is Ephraim of the House of Israel, and,*
>
> *Whereas our country has had a Godly foundation, Godly roots from our fathers, Abraham, Isaac and Jacob, and our Lord Jesus Christ, and,*
>
> *Whereas we understand the material blessing upon our country that is desired by peoples all over the world is because of the double portion birthright blessing given to Joseph and his son Ephraim, and,*
>
> *Whereas we see how far the people in our country and churches have strayed from the God of our Fathers, and our Godly heritage, and,*
>
> *Whereas we know to whom much is given, much is required, and,*
>
> *Whereas we know our holy God will not tolerate or leave sin unpunished, and according to Scripture, this nation will be judged,*
>
> *We hereby decree that this nation will return unto Jehovah God and will repent of their deeds and sins that we have allowed into this land, and that they will turn from their wicked ways and idolatries, and that the fear of God will once again be upon the people of this nation, and that this nation will be known as a nation whose God is THE LORD;*
>
> *We further decree that from judgment and repentance will emerge the United States of America as a country that will once again bring glory and honor to God Almighty and His Word;*

We decree that out of the judgment on our land will come the Glorious Church, a part of the Bride of Christ, without spot, wrinkle, blemish or any such thing, and that the power of the Lord through the Holy Spirit will bring forth a mighty revival greater than what has ever been seen in the United States of America, and upon the churches/people who call themselves Christians;

We decree that we stand firm, believing the words the Lord has given to us written or personally, knowing THE BEST IS YET TO COME;

We call for fulfillment of the plan God predestined for this nation to be completed in the spiritual and natural, in God's timing.

This document is presented to the Lord God Almighty, WHO WAS, and IS and IS TO COME, this Thursday, September 13, 2001, in our nation's capitol, Washington, D.C.

Amen!

Signed,
Pastor D.W. Grant, Faith Fellowship Church, Lakewood, Colorado
Nona C. Grant, Faith Fellowship Church, Lakewood, Colorado

After snapping a few photographs, Pastors David and Nona Grant walked down the Capitol steps, returning to their room. They discovered a rental car was available, and they departed Washington, D.C. Within an hour of the divine proclamation another threat came into Washington, D.C. The Capitol was sealed off again, and would remain off-limits to the public for weeks. It didn't matter. The mission God had ordained was done in the city. God had spoken. America was His.

CHAPTER 11

What Do You Believe?

As I write the words of this closing chapter, my eyes drift toward the calendar. March 13th. *Thirteen.* The number of Ephraim and of the United States of America. I pause for a moment and rejoice, knowing that the feeble affairs of men are still sovereignly guided by the divine hand of Almighty God. It is a moment that cannot be put into words.

America's story does not end with Ezekiel 39. God gave another vision to the prophet Ezekiel, one that begins in chapter 40. There are riches in the following chapters' that are revelations from God about the House of Israel, the United States of America. But it all depends on how you think and what you believe.

What do you believe?

Is America in the Bible? If you agree with the pastor whose quote started this book, then you do ***not*** believe America is mentioned in Scripture. The voices of history and the words of the prophets, priests and kings are silenced. The ancient Scottish Declaration of Independence from 1320 that claims their heritage to be Israelite in origin is ignored. So too are the ancient prophecies given by Jacob and Moses over the tribes of Israel. Contemporary theology is embraced over the wisdom of the elders. America is either lucky, or a Babylonian pawn in a globalist game. She became the greatest nation in the last days without the blessing of Almighty God, while somewhere His chosen people languished in poverty, living only under the spiritual blessing of Abraham while the heathen received the rest. Is this what you believe?

If you believe America is ***not*** in the Bible, then somehow God messed up. She was wealthier than every other nation, she fed the world, she sent out missionaries by the thousands to preach the gospel of Jesus Christ, and she was mighty. But somehow she was not under Abraham's covenant with Almighty God. Ultimately then, she will decline, fail and meld into the nations of the heathen that succumb to the mark of the beast's system. Her people will either endure torment or be spirited away and that is the only hope remaining. Is this what you believe?

If, however, you believe that America **is** in the Bible, then your instruction is about to deepen. This may be humbling for some, who realize they have missed this truth for much of their Christian life. It will take study. Charles Totten made the statement that 7/8ths of the Scripture is hidden until one understands the difference between the Houses of Israel and Judah. Now you can read the Bible with fresh understanding and your heart will come alive as God reveals Himself to you. You will understand why every heathen enterprise in the world hates America, from Islam to communism. They all understand the true nature of the land is spiritual and they hate everything that pertains to Israel, whether it is in the Jewish State of Israel, or the United States of America.

If you believe America **is** in the Bible, you will know that America must be punished for her sins. God does not revoke His covenant, but He punishes His covenant people. America will be judged. You may heed God's warning and take personal steps to relocate, prepare, and tell others about the impending judgment upon the United States. Or, you may ignore the voice of the prophet and reap destruction.

If you believe America **is** in the Bible, you will be in the minority . . . for a while. Most Christians in the nation are patriotic and have a love for the land, but they are ignorant and have failed to connect the dots. Like many of us, they have not yet understood why America has been blessed. Some of them will hear, but others will scorn. You may be misunderstood because you have discovered the truth. Will you embrace the truth anyway?

Is This Elitist?

Perhaps you consider the viewpoint that America is in the Bible to be elitist. You may want to think that everyone on earth is a part of "God's children" and that we are all equal as nations in the sight of God. However, from Genesis to Revelation, we find this theology is not the case. All may be saved, but God has made covenant with Israel that is everlasting in nature. In Revelation 21, God gives us a revelation of a spectacular city that we call "New Jerusalem." It has 12 foundations that have the names of the 12 apostles. It also has 12 gates that are the names of the 12 tribes of Israel. The kings of the earth are on the outside and bring their glory to this people, Israel. God clearly loves the tribes of Israel.

Many hate the Jews today and call them elitist because they claim they are "God's chosen people." They have a right to that claim as the House of Judah. Christians honor them, even though at this point many have not embraced Jesus Christ as Messiah and King. Think of it. They are a secular nation, and yet we can call them the blessed of the Lord because of their heritage.

Who Did God Choose?

As the House of Israel, the United States of America is also God's chosen, His people. Psalm 33:12 says *"Blessed is the nation whose God is the Lord, and the people He has chosen for His own inheritance."* God did the choosing and America must give Him honor as a nation. Racial heritage will never save us eternally, nor will good works. But this does not nullify the fact that God has established the nations and has chosen Israel as His beloved.

The facts have been presented to you in this book. The founders believed America was established by Almighty God. Tyndale and other Bible translators believed it as well. This author believes it, and presents the case to you.

America. Heaven's kingdom. Now, what do you believe?

About Steven Grant

Steven Grant is a pastor, speaker, author and musician that has pastored churches in Colorado and Indiana. He currently pastors Destiny Christian Center in the Greeley, Colorado area. This ministry shares God's Word with every segment of society, ranging from the individual to the halls of government. The message is profound and timely for this generation, and is now available to you the reader. Steven and his wife Cheryl have two daughters, Elisabeth and Sarah who are also active in the ministry. Steven also co-hosts In Defense Of A Nation with his brother Stan, a broadcast dealing with issues pertaining to God and government.

9946322R00181

Made in the USA
San Bernardino, CA
05 April 2014